RISK MANAGEMENT
WITH SUICIDAL PATIENTS

Risk Management
with Suicidal Patients

Edited by

BRUCE BONGAR
ALAN L. BERMAN
RONALD W. MARIS
MORTON M. SILVERMAN
ERIC A. HARRIS
WENDY L. PACKMAN

THE GUILFORD PRESS
New York   London

© 1998 The Guilford Press
A Division of Guilford Publications, Inc.
72 Spring Street, New York, NY 10012
http://www.guilford.com

Printed in the United States of America

This book is printed on acid-free paper.

Last digit is print number: 9 8 7 6 5 4 3 2 1

Library of Congress cataloging-in-publication
data is available from the Publisher.

ISBN 1-57230-302-6 (hard)

Contributors

Alan L. Berman, PhD, Executive Director, American Association of Suicidology; private practice, Washington Psychological Center, Washington, DC

Bruce Bongar, PhD, Clinical Psychology Program, Pacific Graduate School of Psychology, Palo Alto, California; Department of Psychiatry and Behavioral Sciences, Stanford University School of Medicine, Stanford, California

Mark J. Goldblatt, MD, Department of Psychiatry, Harvard Medical School, Boston, Massachusetts

Eric A. Harris, EdD, JD, Massachusetts School of Professional Psychology, West Roxbury, Massachusetts

Robert E. Litman, MD, Los Angeles Suicide Prevention Center; Department of Psychiatry, University of California at Los Angeles, Los Angeles, California

Ronald W. Maris, PhD, Director, Center for Suicide and Life-Threatening Behavior, and Department of Sociology, The University of South Carolina, Columbus, South Carolina

Wendy L. Packman, JD, PhD, Department of Pediatrics, Division of Behavioral and Developmental Pediatrics, University of California, San Francisco, San Francisco, California

Alan F. Schatzberg, MD, Department of Psychiatry and Behavioral Sciences, Stanford University School of Medicine, Stanford, California

Morton M. Silverman, MD, Director, Student Counseling and Resource Service, and Department of Psychiatry, The University of Chicago, Chicago, Illinois

Andrew Edmund Slaby, MD, PhD, MPH, Department of Psychiatry, New York University and New York Medical College, New York, New York

Contents

RISK MANAGEMENT
WITH SUICIDAL PATIENTS

Introduction

BRUCE BONGAR

In this short volume, my fellow editors and I bring together some of the top national experts on working with suicidal patients. As a starting point for this project, we asked The Guilford Press and the American Association for Suicidology for permission to reprint three previously published, widely cited papers on outpatient and inpatient standards of care in working with the suicidal patient. To strengthen this volume further as a critical resource for the average clinician, we also commissioned four new chapters by some of the most distinguished authorities on the clinical and forensic risks of working with suicidal patients.

A word on the structure of the volume is in order. This volume can be conceptualized as a forum for the exploration of avoiding liability in working with the suicidal patient. As a natural course of events in bringing together top experts in the field (all with their own sets of opinions), the experts will at times disagree. Just as in the real world of courtrooms and consultation rooms, the reader will struggle (as do actual juries and judges) to sort out a consensus position among the many thoughtful and yet at times diverging views of national authorities on this highly complex subject. The reader should note, in particular, that we are not positing a *standard* of care in this volume. Rather, we are presenting principles of care giving that might be considered *optimal*, impossible to achieve in their entirety but worthy of consideration. Our overall goal has been to challenge professionals to improve upon their own standards and, consequently, to lessen the need for such a volume in future years. We have attempted to accomplish this by providing a rich and wide-ranging set of opinions and guidelines, from which the reader will need to draw his or her own conclusions as to which ones are most syntonic with his or her own actual practice situation.

As an introduction to risk management and standards of care, Chapter 1 is a reprint of a widely cited paper on general outpatient standards of care, which includes an analysis of common failure scenarios. Chapter 2 presents new material that specifically illuminates a psychiatrist/suicidologist's comprehensive approach to general outpatient psychiatric care and management issues. This is followed by two further general chapters (Chapters 3 and 4) on inpatient standards of care; these chapters also specifically review the relevant case law on inpatient suicide.

Because the most common malpractice suits in outpatient settings revolve around the prescription of drugs (especially antidepressants or tranquilizers), Chapters 5 examines specific medical and legal issues in the pharmacotherapy of the suicidal patient, and Chapter 6 provides an in-depth look at pharmacological interventions with the hospitalized suicidal patient from a forensic perspective. In Chapter 7, two lawyer/psychologists provide the clinician with their perspective as attorneys on the legal complexities and risks in working with suicidal patients.

Finally, in two "postscripts," we include an exchange of correspondence between two forensic authorities to underscore and illustrate the complexities in the role that expert witnesses assume when they provide testimony to guide the court (audience) concerning accepted standards of professional practice and any departures therefrom.

We hope that the diverse selection of opinions and suggested approaches to practice contained in this book will provide the reader with a chance to see how some of the top psychiatric and psychological authorities on suicide in the United States formulate their approaches to standards of care and risk management. The guiding and unifying principle in all our efforts toward the care of suicidal patients should always be to keep the benefit to the patients foremost in our minds. Accordingly, our efforts toward the detection of elevated risk and the taking of affirmative precautions (based on detected risk) must in the end rest on a foundation of highly individualized, yet systematic and integrative, care within the context of a sound therapeutic alliance (Bongar, Peterson, Harris, & Aissis, 1989; Bongar, 1991).

As noted in Chapter 1, it has been said that suicide is the most feared outcome in mental health care, signaling a calamitous, irrevocable failure in treatment (Gill, 1982). Kahn (1982) has observed that nowhere in the range of professional activities of the clinician is he or she under more intense and significant stress than when treating a potentially suicidal patient. The stress and anxiety that this clinical situation provokes in the therapist is a two-edged sword, however: It can mobilize the clinician to greater clinical alertness and therapeutic vigilance. Thus, lives can be saved.

REFERENCES

Bongar, B. (1991). *The suicidal patient: Clinical and legal standards of care.* Washington, DC: American Psychological Association.

Bongar, B., Peterson, L. G., Harris, E. A., & Aissis, J. (1989). Clinical and legal considerations in the management of suicidal patients: An integrative overview. *Journal of Integrative and Eclectic Psychotherapy, 8*(1), 53–67.

Gill, A. D. (1982). Outpatient therapies for suicidal patients. In E. L. Bassuk, S. C. Schoonover, & A. D. Gill (Eds.), *Lifelines: Clinical perspectives on suicide* (pp. 71–82). New York: Plenum Press.

Kahn, A. (1982). The moment of truth: Psychotherapy with the suicidal patient. In E. L. Bassuk, S. C. Schoonover, & A. D. Gill (Eds.), *Lifelines: Clinical perspectives on suicide* (pp. 83–92). New York: Plenum Press.

1

Outpatient Standards of Care and the Suicidal Patient

BRUCE BONGAR
RONALD W. MARIS
ALAN L. BERMAN
ROBERT E. LITMAN

Until the 1970s, the incidence of lawsuits against mental health professionals was quite low, especially when compared to suits against members of what the courts regard as other medical specialties (Robertson, 1988). Generally speaking, when there was a lawsuit, the defendant practitioner almost always prevailed (Robertson, 1988). While in recent years there has been a steady rise in malpractice actions against mental health professionals, the incidence of claims against psychiatrists and psychologists still remains comparatively low. Indeed, of the "relatively small number of cases that actually get to trial (some estimates place this as low as 6%), the majority—80% in some estimates—continue to be won by clinicians" (Gutheil, 1992, p. 156, see also Robertson, 1988). Nevertheless, the fact remains that logic and reasonableness do not always hold sway when it comes to litigation and patient suicide, and that, as Gutheil has commented:

> Either plaintiff's attorneys (or appellate court judges, when cases are appealed) may be consciously or unconsciously inclined to treat the

physician's actuarially determined insurance policy as a sort of victim compensation superfund, whereby this money, seen as somehow separate from the physician, is used to compensate victims of loss. . . . Medical malpractice juries, not just psychiatric ones, may be swayed to the "just give the money" position as an alternative to doing direct mental battle with the thorny causal issues at stake in a case. Against such a position, there is no defense under the control of the physician, but, fortunately, this is not the most common outcome. (p. 156)

Gutheil further noted that the primacy of suicide in mental health litigation should not lead to practitioners' responding with "fear, defensive practice, or other adversarializing reactions" (p. 166). The model proposed by the authors of the present paper is in accord with Gutheil (1992) that the best solution to the specter of liability following a patient's suicide is for the clinician to have provided good clinical care that followed acceptable standards of practice; also, that appropriate risk management is the core of a preventive approach to the unfortunate possibility of liability after the suicide of a patient.

WHAT PRACTITIONERS CAN LEARN
FROM THE MALPRACTICE CLAIMS DATA

If a claim of malpractice is filed against a mental health practitioner, it is often the case that the practitioner's insurance carrier (often a specific mental health discipline's insurance trust) has a responsibility to defend its policy holder. Therefore, one way of examining the incidence and prevalence of outpatient suicide claims is to examine data from each of the major mental health disciplines insurance databases (i.e., the number and type of claims, whether the case went to trial or was settled, and for what dollar amount).

However, these records are often difficult to study (and, as noted below, at times difficult to acquire). Further complicating the picture is that claims made in any one year may not close (be decided/settle) for several years and other claims may not be lodged until some years after the alleged malpractice occurred ("occurrence-based claims"). Thus in 1991, the American Psychiatric Association had closed "almost all" claims for the "1984 experience year," while practically none had closed for 1990 (Slawson, personal communication, October 30, 1991).

In addition, for each of the mental health disciplines, suicide represents a class of complaint which can be examined relative to other classes of complaints with regard to frequency (proportion of all complaints) and severity (average dollar settlement or award).[1] Also, each of the disciplines' insurance trusts carefully control access to information about claims made. For example, The National Association of Social Workers (NASW) refused to provide even summary information on closed claims (NASW personal communication, November 21, 1991). In one analysis of claims against psychiatrists for the years 1980 to 1985, lawsuits following a patient's suicide resulted in the largest number of suits and the largest dollar amounts in settlements. Suits for suicide accounted for 21% of the claims filed and 42% of the dollars paid in settlement or verdict (Robertson, 1988).[2]

The American Psychological Association's Insurance Trust (APAIT) has provided summary data that indicate that the suicide of a patient was the sixth most common category for a claim, but ranked second in the percentage of total costs (5.4% of the claims and 10% of the costs) (personal communication with APAIT Claims Frequency, May 1990). Out of a total of 1,892 open and closed claims, there were 102 specifically in the category of suicide.

A further complication in understanding the data is that a very small proportion of claims proceeds to trial. Litman (1982) has argued that perhaps only 1 in 10 cases goes to trial. Slawson (personal communication, October 30, 1991) suggested that the proportion may be closer to 5%, with the vast majority of these cases being won by the defendant practitioner, while Gutheil (1992) estimates the level to be approximately 6%. If these estimates are correct, it becomes clear that while lawsuits against mental health professionals that go to trial are traumatic experiences, they remain relatively rare occurrences. Thus the fear of being sued probably has more widespread and deleterious effects on clinicians than do actual lawsuits (Bongar, 1991; Hoge & Appelbaum, 1989).

In addition, these estimates of frequency of trial decisions suggest that case law (based on trial decisions) may be a seriously biased framework within which to learn of, and to educate the practitioner regarding, risk management issues. The overwhelming majority of cases that go to a trial

---

[1]The average dollar awards will almost certainly increase once the data set is complete, because trivial claims settle early and cases brought to jury trials are the last to be completed.

[2]As noted previously, the American Psychiatric Association did provide some summary information via Dr. Paul Slawson (see above), who is in the process of analyzing overall closed cases.

deal with issues of inpatient management and treatment (Bongar, 1991; Litman, 1982).

While an examination of case law (cases that go to trial and to appeal) may give the impression that it is rare for an outpatient clinician to be sued (and sued successfully), we believe that outpatient therapists today are as likely as inpatient practitioners to be the targets of a suit. Pragmatically, attorneys understand that most of these cases settle before trial, often out of fear that a jury will side with the bereaved plaintiff versus the unfeeling, and insurance-rich, practitioner. Plaintiffs' attorneys typically work on contingent fees, and thus cases which possess settlement possibilities represent potential income. Attorneys are also aware—as any clinician who has been sued for malpractice can attest—that for the defendant there is a roller coaster of emotional turmoil in the years before settlement (the most frequent outcome). This emotional turmoil and the stress of defending oneself often increases the likelihood that the defendant will settle.

NEGLIGENCE AND MALPRACTICE[3]

While there is no specific set of clinical practices that can absolutely guarantee a practitioner that she or he will be immune either from losing a patient to suicide or from being sued (or even from a judgment for the plaintiff), there are some sources of reassurance, as well as ways to reduce overall risk when assessing or treating a suicidal patient (Hoge & Appelbaum, 1989).

The standard of care is "that degree of care which a reasonably prudent person or professional should exercise in same or similar circumstances" (Black, 1979, p. 1260). Deviations from the standard of care are usually referred to as "negligence" or "gross negligence." Suicide or suicide attempts obviously represent damages to the patient and perhaps to others. Damages can be compensatory or punitive. Usually the courts require gross negligence to award punitive damages (Amchin et al., 1990). However, a suicide attempt or completion is unusual in that the specific damages were intentionally caused by the patient himself or herself—yet he or she, or the family, may benefit from the tragedy. The damages may be physical or emotional, and may include potential lost income, loss of companionship,

---

[3]Portions of this section are adapted from Bongar (1991). Copyright 1991 by the American Psychological Association. Adapted by permission.

expenses occurred through resulting death or disability, loss of quality of life, and so forth. A key issue is whether or not, and with what degree of reasonable medical certainty, the suicide or suicide attempts could have been foreseen or predicted (Maris, Berman, Maltsberger, & Yufit, 1992).

A further complication is that since suicide is a rare event, the accurate prediction of suicide is extremely difficult and results most often in false, not true, positives (Pokorny, 1983). At issue is the relative benefit of a standard of care that necessitates great health care expense and yet provides a large number of false positives. Since suicide is a multifaceted, multicausal product (Shneidman, 1985), it is extremely difficult to determine if a therapist's actions or failures to act, decisions, and so forth, actually caused a suicide. The law tends to utilize the concept of "proximate cause." This concept is like a billiard ball theory of causation—one predictor effecting one outcome in very close proximity. Suicide does not fit a model of causation well, even though the law allows for more than one proximate cause. Prior to the 1940s, "the patient's suicidal action was considered to break the causal chain between clinician's negligence and the patient's death. . . . For reasons too complex to be of interest to any but legal scholars, this model changed after that point, and clinicians began to be held liable for negligence that actually led to suicide" (Gutheil, 1992, pp. 150–151).

Both Perr (1979) and Meyer, Landis, and Hays (1988) noted that mental health clinicians carry a tremendous legal burden when it comes to a patient's suicide, for simply stated, the clinician is asked to be responsible for someone else's behavior. Although typically the law does not hold any person responsible for acts of another, suicidal and other self-destructive acts present a clear exception:

> The duty of therapists to exercise adequate care and skill in diagnosing suicidality is well established (see *Meier v. Ross General Hospital,* 1968). When the risk of self-injurious behavior is identified an additional duty to take adequate precautions arises (*Abille v. United States,* 1980; *Pisel v. Stamford Hospital,* 1980). When psychotherapists fail to meet these responsibilities, they may be held liable for injuries that result. (Meyer, Landis, & Hays, 1988, p. 38)

Further confusing the issue is a contradiction in clinical and legal philosophies: Psychotherapists "on the one hand are told . . . not to hospitalize unless the need is blatantly clear; on the other, they are threatened with legal liability if they do not do so and thus minimize a patient's ability to kill himself" (Perr, 1979, p. 91). Also, paradoxically, there are times when good care actually can *increase* the possibility of a suicide. For example, it is well known that many antidepressant medications reduce so-called "vegetative symptoms" (sleep, libido, appetite, etc.) of affective disorder before elevating mood (Mann & Kapur, 1991). Although most suicides are mentally disordered at the time of their suicides (Blumenthal & Kupfer, 1990), we must not rule out the possibility that proper care may help individuals see clearly and rationally that their future is relatively hopeless and devoid of sufficient quality of life to be reasonably continued.

Thus many practitioners are reluctant to work with suicidal patients for fear of being sued if a patient takes his or her own life, though decisions by courts have usually maintained that clinicians are not liable if they have maintained adequate care for their patients (Kermani, 1982). The attorneys for the family of a deceased patient often argue that the patient's suicide, perhaps the most unfortunate result possible within the context of treatment (as frequently stated by plaintiff lawyers), was the result of the defendant clinician's failure to act reasonably to protect his or her patient from harm (Harris, 1988). More specifically, it is argued that the mental health professional did not correctly diagnose the patient, thus preventing him or her from foreseeing the potential for suicide, and that the subsequent lack of proper treatment led directly to the patient's death (Harris, 1988; Simon, 1988). It is hardly surprising that for the clinician, suicide is one of the most emotionally dreaded outcomes in clinical work.

The threat of litigation compounds the burden that a patient's death creates for the clinician (Rachlin, 1984). In a general clinical practice setting, the threat of patient suicide is always a possibility. A recent review of risk assessment and treatment procedures for suicidal patients estimates that 10 to 15% of patients with major psychiatric disorders (i.e., affective disorder, substance use disorders, and schizophrenia) will die by suicide. This review states unequivocally that the assessment and diminution of suicide potential among psychiatric patients should be a task of the highest priority for mental health professionals (Brent et al., 1988).

VandeCreek, Knapp, and Herzog (1987) have determined that lawsuits over suicide usually fall into one of three legal fact patterns: Psychotherapists or institutions may be sued when (1) an inpatient commits suicide, with survivors claiming that the facility failed to provide adequate care and supervision; (2) a recently released patient commits suicide; or (3) an outpatient commits suicide. The fundamental concept that underlies malpractice actions against mental health professionals is the concept of negligence (Robertson, 1988; Simon, 1988). Simon (1988) pointed out that negligence on the part of a mental health professional can be "described as doing something which he or she should not have done [commission] or omitting to do something which he or she should have done [omission]" (p. 3). The fact that a mental health professional's act that injures a patient is not willful, but is rather a consequence of carelessness or ignorance, does not excuse the clinician from liability (Robertson, 1988; Simon, 1988). The law "presumes and holds all practitioners and psychotherapists to a stand- ard of reasonable care when dealing with patients" (Robertson, 1988, p. 7).

Sadoff (cited in Rachlin, 1984) noted that there are four essential legal elements in establishing negligence. Each of these must be demonstrated by the plaintiff by a preponderance of evidence and "may be remembered by the **4D** mnemonic: **D**ereliction of–**D**uty–**D**irectly causing–**D**amages" (Rachlin, 1984, p. 303). Rachlin further noted that in the case of suicide, where damages are readily apparent, there is an "obvious appeal to the sympathies of a jury when the bereaved family claims that the patient was being treated because of suicidal behavior and professional intervention failed to prevent a fatal outcome" (Rachlin, 1984, p. 303). The simple fact that the patient was receiving any psychological treatment makes the relationship between the two parties such that a legal duty of care is created.

Furthermore, the most common legal action involving psychiatric care is the failure to "reasonably" protect patients from harming themselves (Simon, 1987, 1988). Harris (1988) has cautioned that as non psychiatric clinicians (e.g., professional psychology) seek parity with psychiatry in the area of professional privileges (such as voting membership on hospital staffs and full admitting privileges), the profession will expose itself to many of the same clinical risks and liabilities to which psychiatry is exposed. Gutheil and Appelbaum (1982) stated that "to the extent that psychologists, social workers, and nurses assume primary responsibility for patient care, they can be said to establish the same duty of care, within the context of a fiduciary relationship, that exists for psychiatrists" (p. 175).

At the present time, much of the case law on suicide is based on claims that allege liability for a misdiagnosis or lack of prediction of the risk of suicide (Swenson, 1986; VandeCreek, Knapp, & Herzog, 1987). Most suits brought on this basis are directed against hospitals and institutions for clinical care, and involve either inpatients or recently discharged patients (Rachlin, 1984). However, the potential certainly exists for an increase in suits involving outpatient care. One authority, Perr (1985), in his review of suicide litigation and risk management, pointed to a study of completed suicide in Veterans Administration patients. This study found that 65% of the suicides occurred outside the hospital (Farberow, 1981). It is important to underscore that suicide prevention is an ideal, and that the responsibility of the clinician or institution is to follow acceptable standards of care. Also, that these standards of care are dynamic and ever-changing. Clinicians must understand that there is no magical "right" way to act in every clinical situation, and that for every decision in clinical practice there are always potential risks and benefits.

THE CASE OF OUTPATIENT SUICIDE

Fremouw, de Perczel, and Ellis (1990) stated that because outpatient therapists have much less control over their patients' behavior, outpatient therapists have not been held as responsible for their patients' actions as have the therapists of inpatients. They cited the case of *Speer v. United States* (1981), in which the court held that a psychiatrist's duty to outpatients is less than his or her responsibilities to inpatients.

The case of *Bellah v. Greenson* (1978) is of particular interest in this regard, because unlike so many cases where a lawsuit followed an inpatient's suicide, the *Bellah* case involved the suicide of an outpatient. Specifically, the parents of Tammy Bellah, who died by an overdose of pills, brought a malpractice action for wrongful death against Tammy's psychiatrist, Daniel Greenson. Dr. Greenson, who was treating Tammy as an outpatient at the time of her death, appears to have determined that Tammy was

> disposed to suicide, and he recorded his conclusion in his written notes. ... The plaintiffs instituted the present action for wrongful death alleging that defendant had failed to take measures to prevent Tammy's suicide; that he failed to warn plaintiffs of the seriousness of Tammy's condition and of the circumstances which might cause her to commit suicide; and that he failed to inform plaintiffs that Tammy was consorting with heroin addicts in the plaintiffs home. Plaintiffs complaint purported to state two causes of action, one based upon simple negligence, and one based upon the defendant's negligent performance of his contract with plaintiffs to care for their daughter, which contract allegedly contained the implied term that defendant would use reasonable care to prevent Tammy from harming herself. (*Bellah v. Greenson*, 1978, p. 537)

The court in this case refused to mandate a *Tarasoff*-like "duty to warn" (*Tarasoff v. Board of Regents of the University of California*, 1976), though the outpatient was a "danger to self." The court held that "a requisite special relationship does exist in the case of a patient under the care of a psychiatrist and that a psychiatrist who knows that his patient is likely to attempt suicide has a duty to take protective measures" (Bellah v. Greenson, 1978, p. 538). In its decision, the court clarified the differences between the duty of care for an outpatient and that for inpatients. The court specifically cited the cases of Vistica v. Presbyterian Hospital (1967) and Meier v. Ross General Hospital (1968). In Vistica, the cause of action was found to exist against the hospital; in Meier, it was found to exist both against the hospital and against the decedent's attending physician.

In Meier, the court determined that the facts of the case supported a theory of liability based on a duty to protect the decedent from his own actions, voluntary or involuntary. The doctor and hospital breached their duty of care when they placed a patient, following an attempted suicide, in a second-floor room with a fully openable window. Fremouw, de Perczel, and Ellis (1990) cited a more recent case, Texarkana Memorial Hospital v. Firth (1988), with a similar outcome. In this case, the family of a 33-year-old woman

> who was admitted for suicidal risk and psychosis was awarded over $950,000 for gross negligence by the hospital. When she was admitted the locked ward had no empty beds. To lower her risk of suicide, she was sedated but placed in an open ward with no special suicide precautions. Upon awakening, she jumped to her death. (Fremouw, de Perczel, & Ellis, 1990, p. 8).

However, the Bellah court stated that Tammy Bellah's case is readily distinguishable from both Vistica and Meier: "Obviously the duty imposed upon those responsible for the care of a patient in an institutional setting differs from that which may be involved in the case of a psychiatrist treating patients on an out-patient basis" (Bellah v. Greenson, 1978, p. 538).

The court did hold that the facts of this outpatient suicide were sufficient to bring a cause of action for breach of a psychiatrist's duty of care towards his patient. Moreover, the court held that the nature of the precautionary steps that Dr. Greenson could or should have taken presents "purely a factual question to be resolved at trial on the merits, at which time both sides would be afforded an opportunity to produce expert medical testimony on the subject" (Bellah v. Greenson, 1978, p. 538). That is to say resolution of the case would require the testimony of expert witnesses, analyzing Dr. Greenson's performance after the fact, to determine if negligence had occurred.

However, in refusing to impose a *Tarasoff* duty upon Dr. Greenson, the court stated:

> The imposition of a duty upon the psychiatrist to disclose to others vague or even specific manifestations of suicidal tendencies on the part of the patient who is being treated in an out-patient setting could well inhibit psychiatric treatment . . . the dynamics of interaction between the psychotherapist and the patient seen in office visits are highly complex and subtle. Intimate privacy is a virtual necessity for successful treatment. Were it not for the assurance of confidentiality in psycho-therapist–patient relationship, many in need of treatment would be reluctant to seek help. Even those who do seek help under such circumstances may be deterred from fully disclosing their problems. An element usually assumed essential is the patient's trust that matters disclosed in therapy will be held in strict confidence. (*Bellah v. Greenson,* 1978, p. 539)

The *Bellah* court held that *Tarasoff* requires that a therapist disclose the contents of a confidential communication only "where the risk to be prevented thereby is danger of violent assault, and not where the risk of harm is self-inflicted harm or mere property damage. We decline to further extend the holding of *Tarasoff*" (*Bellah v. Greenson,* 1978, p. 540). Fremouw, de Perczel, and Ellis (1990) stated that with outpatients, although a Tarasoff-type of duty to warn relatives of potential suicide risk is not the current case law, it remains one of the options for action clinicians should consider seriously when a patient presents as at risk.

Lastly, VandeCreek and Knapp (1983) summarized and noted that when the suicide attempt is foreseeable, the treatment provided must be consistent with professional standards. They also cited the case of *Speer v. United States* (1981), in which a psychiatric outpatient hoarded pills and then took a lethal overdose of the medication. VandeCreek and Knapp pointed out that the psychiatrist was exonerated because he had followed accepted medical standards in prescribing for the patient. They further noted that "although non-medical psychotherapists would not be treating patients through medication, they would have to follow acceptable procedures in their treatment of suicidal outpatients" (p. 278).

Honest errors of judgment are inevitable in clinical practice, and the courts have recognized that "the accurate prediction of dangerous behavior, and particularly suicide and homicide, are almost never possible. Thus, an error of prediction, or even of judgment does not necessarily establish negligence" (Stromberg et al., 1988, p. 468).

In the case of an outpatient suicide, the courts typically struggle with two central issues—namely, foreseeability and causation (Simon, 1988). Specifically, their examination turns on whether the outpatient psychotherapist should have predicted the suicide and, whether there was sufficient evidence for an identifiable risk of harm, and whether the psychotherapist did enough to protect the patient (VandeCreek, Knapp, & Herzog, 1987).

Berman (1989) presents one example of this, an outpatient malpractice case reviewed by two consultants (Motto and Sanders), *both* of whom exonerated the defendant therapist in spite of one consultant's (Motto) being asked to view the case from the perspective of the plaintiff. Even so, this case ended in a large jury award to the plaintiff.

Based on our own clinical and forensic experience, there are some common themes in complaints lodged against outpatient therapists, reflecting possible breaches in the duty of care and the practitioner's failure to act in a reasonable and prudent manner. Attention to these "failures" may therefore represent a clarion call to develop appropriate risk management strategies.

COMMON FAILURE SCENARIOS
IN OUTPATIENT PRACTICE

Table 1.1 lists some of the most common "failure" situations involving the outpatient practitioner (i.e., from the perspective of the plaintiff and his/her attorneys, outpatient suicide cases in which a lawsuit was filed). Following is a discussion of these situations.

Failure to Evaluate Properly the Need for
Psychopharmacological Intervention
or Unsuitable Pharmacotherapy

The most common malpractice suits in outpatient settings revolve around the prescription of drugs, especially antidepressants or tranquilizers. Gutheil (1992) noted that one of the "psychopharmacological ironies peculiar to psychiatric treatment, the most lethal medications in the pharmacopeia—antidepressants—are normally prescribed for those conditions

TABLE 1.1. Outpatient Suicide: Common Failure Scenarios

1. Failure to properly evaluate the need for psychopharmacological intervention, or unsuitable pharmacotherapy.
2. Failure to specify criteria for and to implement hospitalization.
3. Failure to maintain appropriate clinician–patient relationships (e.g., dual relationships, sexual improprieties and dual relationships with patients, etc.).
4. Failures in supervision and consultation.
5. Failure to evaluate for suicide risk: At intake.
6. Failure to evaluate for suicide risk: At management transitions.
7. Failure to secure records of prior treatment/inadequate history taking.
8. Failure to conduct a mental status exam.
9. Failure to diagnose.
10. Failure to establish a formal treatment plan.
11. Failure to safeguard the outpatient environment.
12. Failure to adequately document clinical judgments, rationales, and observations.

most likely to evoke their lethal misuse—depressions" (p. 155). Gutheil also pointed out that many psychiatric treatment centers are reluctant to initiate a course of electroconvulsive treatment as the initial therapy of choice for a severe depression, and instead tend to try psychotropic medications first. A result was that patients became just enough better (under the antidepressants) to "mobilize sufficient energy to destroy themselves" before the full antidepressant benefit was realized (Gutheil, 1992, p. 155).

Litman (personal communication, December 1991) also noted an increase in lawsuits over the drug Prozac and almost every other antidepressant. Here, the claim is that the drug aggravated or provoked suicidal ideation and consequent suicidal action. Litman's position is that none of these lawsuits will prevail, provided the prescribing doctor followed the procedures of ordinary prudence and competence by completing a mental status examination, making a diagnosis, prescribing the drug under the manufacturer's guidelines, and appropriately following up for action and side effects.

Physicians who practice in large clinics or hospitals are especially exposed when they fail to obtain the history of the patient. For example, it becomes difficult to defend the behavior of a physician who prescribed a large quantity of Tofranil to a patient who had nearly died not long before of an overdose of Tofranil. Physicians are reminded to take a history of previous drugs prescribed in treatment and the course of action of these drugs. In a similar vein, physicians can be sued when they give the wrong medication or too little of the right one. In one case a schizophrenic had been taking 40 milligrams a day of Stelazine, and the physician, through an oversight, allowed the board and care case manager to gradually reduce the dose of Stelazine to 5 milligrams a day, an insufficient dose. When the patient committed suicide, the case manager (who was a resident physician) said that he thought he was doing what the prescribing physician wanted, but the prescribing physician stated that he had no knowledge of what was going on. In the subsequent lawsuit, the prescribing physician's ignorance of the error did not help in the defense.

If pharmacotherapy is deemed not to benefit a particular patient, a documented rationale for not trying this intervention should be entered in the patient's chart. A standard of care for the reasonable and prudent physician requires that there be adequate follow-up after a prescription. However, although the experienced practitioner is not bound to follow slavishly the recommendations of the manufacturers in prescribing drugs, specifically antidepressants, there is one recommendation that should be emphasized. Depressed persons who are candidates for antidepressant drugs are often suicidal and remain suicidal for considerable periods of time after the initial consultation. Thus, there should be follow-up within a day or two, and again within a week. Also there should be a discussion with the patient, and ideally with the family, about possible side effects, and about the need to stay in touch with the doctor.

The important guideline is that people who are receiving antidepressant drugs are at increased risk for suicide, and reasonable efforts must be made to maintain contact with patients. Also, certain drugs and combinations of drugs can be depressing and may be associated with suicide if they fail to ameliorate the symptom for which they are prescribed (e.g., analgesics of various kinds that are prescribed for back trouble and for other painful syndromes). Gutheil (1992) also noted that to cope with the overdose potential inherent in the prescribing of tricyclics, a number of clinicians use the technique of short-term prescribing, and while this approach has a common-sense validity, there are a number of pitfalls in its use. Specifically, if short-term prescribing is used, it should always be conducted within the context of the therapeutic alliance with the "healthy side" of the patient. Gutheil pointed out that an additional mechanism that may be useful is to

> conceptualize the medications themselves as representing temptations to action that need to be controlled. . . . These models make it clear that the physician is working with the healthy side of the patient against impulsivity, rather than the physician, in a more oppositional manner, sees the patient as an adversary to be outfoxed. (p. 156)

Last, Gutheil noted that an additional danger in short-term prescribing is that it may lull the clinician and the patient into a false sense of certainty that the situation is now under control: "a patient may scrupulously adhere to the precise medication regimen suggested by the physician and still use a gun from home to commit suicide" (p. 157).

Failure to Specify Criteria for and to Implement Hospitalization

Clinicians mindful of maintaining a coherent treatment philosophy with their suicidal patients are protected to the extent that they demonstrate the best professional judgment in assessing the therapeutic risks of freedom. They also must carefully assess decisions (their own and those of others), to reduce the level of supervision of suicidal patients, whether those decisions involve discharge, transfer, decision to commit, or other actions. (Knapp & VandeCreek, 1983). However, it is critical to remember that when a "patient is dangerously suicidal, hospitalization and close supervision are clearly indicated—an 'open door' policy does not mean an open window policy for highly suicidal patients" (p. 277).

Appelbaum and Gutheil (1991) pointed out that a central clinical and legal concern involves negligence in evaluating a patient for hospitalization. Simon (1988) has demonstrated how the use of a decision chart for assessment and risk estimation can easily be integrated into treatment planning—for example, defining risk categories as follows: high risk, immediate hospitalization; medium risk, hospitalization or frequent outpatient visits, reevaluate the treatment plan frequently, remain available to the patient; low risk, continue with current treatment plan.

The decision to hospitalize or not hospitalize is based always on a judgment call. As such, it is the correctness of that judgment which is called into question should a patient suicide. Hospitalization, however, like medication, does not *prevent* suicide. Suicides occur in hospitals and during periods of hospitalization through elopements, weekend passes, and so forth. At the same time, the hospital is an essential component of a treatment plan and should be considered with other criteria demanding sanctuary and stabilization (i.e., when greater control over a patient's life and environment are needed than would be allowed by outpatient psychotherapy). The treatment plan and judgments made during treatment by an outpatient psychotherapist should reflect consideration of these criteria in order to support the therapist's rationale for maintaining outpatient treatment under conditions of increased risk. Especially when this decision reflects a therapeutic gamble (i.e., least restrictive care in order to foster respect for a patient's self-control), consideration of how symptoms and behaviors are to be controlled out of the hospital should be well documented in the clinical record.

Failure to Maintain Appropriate Clinician–Patient Relationships

Litman (personal communication, December 1991) maintained that the third most common source of lawsuits in outpatient practice are boundary violations or sexual intimacies in the treatment situation, which are then followed by a suicide attempt or completed suicide on the part of the patient. Litman has had at least six case consultations where there are allegations (usually justified) of undue intimacy on the part of the therapist, and where the patient attempted suicide.

Extreme therapies, as well as innovative or regressive therapies, in addition to sexual seduction by therapists and malignant countertransferences can be taken as evidence of treatment gone awry. The presence of such factors may increase the risk of suicide significantly (Pope, 1986, 1989; · Simon, 1987). It is also critical to note that boundary violations that harm patients can be non-sexual (Pope & Vasquez, 1991).

Failures in Supervision and Consultation

Many practitioners serve as supervisors of trainees, interns, employees and other colleagues. By one estimate, 64% of psychologists spend at least part of their professional time in supervision (VandeCreek & Harrar, 1988). Although to date very few court cases in the mental health field are based solely on supervisor negligence, "Slovenko (1988) has warned that supervisor liability may be the 'lawsuit of the future.' . . . the principles under which supervisor liability can be claimed have been established in other fields such as medicine and could be applied to professional psychology" (VandeCreek & Harrar, 1988, p. 13).

Simon (1987, 1988) and VandeCreek and Harrar (1988) both observed that under the doctrine of *respondeat superior* (let the master respond), psychiatrists, psychologists, and other mental health professionals may be held monetarily responsible for the negligent acts of others working under their supervision, control, or direction. Under a doctrine of vicarious liability, the one who controls the conduct of the treatment may be required to pay damages to the plaintiff. Simon (1987), however, cautioned that there is very little case law on the specific subject of clinical supervision in the field of mental health and negligence.

Bongar (1991) noted that clinicians should be particularly on guard when assigning what might be construed as high-risk activities to trainees or interns, for a supervisor is expected to exercise very close supervision and control. They should carefully note the training and competence of supervisees, and make certain that they do not assign to a trainee a patient whose problems may be beyond the trainee's level of training, education, and experience.

Additional factors come into play when the alleged substandard treatment was not directly provided by the supervising practitioner. Vande-Creek and Harrar (1988) have stated directly that patients and their families have a right to an informed consent as to the trainee status of the psychotherapist. That is, there is an ethical and legal obligation to tell patients of the therapist's trainee status and level of experience. The failure to provide patients with this information may expose both trainee and supervisor to "possible lawsuits alleging fraud, deceit, misrepresentation, invasion of privacy, breach of confidentiality, and lack of informed consent" (VandeCreek & Harrar, 1988, p. 14).

Also, quality supervision mandates that the supervisors themselves be well trained and knowledgeable in working with suicidal patients. It is essential to note that even when a patient gives informed consent to care by a trainee, the patient has not thereby consented to receive substandard care. VandeCreek and Harrar point out the conclusion of some courts that trainees should have the "same standards of care as professionals who provide the same service" (p. 14) (e.g., *Emory University v. Porubiansky*, 1981). For note well: When a patient is harmed, the student, supervisor, employing hospital/agency/clinic, and possibly the sponsoring educational institution may all be made defendants, and liability alleged as either direct or vicarious.

Failure to Evaluate for Suicide Risk: At Intake

A fundamental expectation in any reasonable standard of outpatient care is attention to the issue of "foreseeability" of a potential suicide (often defined retrospectively with the accuracy of hindsight following a patient's death). The common complaint will often allege: "failure to recognize the patient's suicidal tendencies" which, in turn and in consequence, led to a "failure to take precautionary measures to protect the patient."

Gutheil (1992) noted that one of the most problematic situations in the outpatient context is the single evaluation in the clinic, private office, or emergency room setting. Here, the clinician will have neither an "extensive knowledge of the patient over time nor a lasting therapeutic alliance" to be drawn on as sustaining resources. These "one-shot" evaluations necessitate great care on the part of the clinician and require special sensitivity and diligence. Unfortunately, it is more typical that because this type of evaluation often takes place in a high turnover setting—for example, the emergency room of a general hospital—there is often very little time allotted for a thorough and careful evaluation.

Failure to Evaluate for Suicide Risk: At Management Transitions

Suicide risk is not static. It ebbs and flows with the dynamic interaction between inner states, historical conflicts, and external stressors. The clinician needs to be aware of when to formally assess risk during the course of treatment, particularly when signs or symptoms convey potential shifts in the patient's equilibrium or ability to self-regulate.

The issues of changes of therapist and therapist absences are worthy of a further cautionary note. Motto (1979) commented that the period of time surrounding a loss or change of a therapist is an especially vulnerable time for the suicidal patient. He cited an example where at one institution, an examination of four recent suicides revealed that three had occurred in the context of vacation interruptions. This problem is common in training institutions, because trainees, interns, and residents often move in and out of clinical assignments and leave the area after completion of training.

Failure to Secure Records of Prior Treatment/Inadequate History Taking

Patients always come to us with a history, often with a history of prior evaluations and treatment. For example, a family history of a mental disorder, prior treatment, and previous suicidal behavior can teach us about possible genetic and psychosocial predispositions; an early developmental history provides clues to appropriate diagnostic formulations; prior treatments can establish a baseline for assessing the current presenting problem(s), the course of interventions tried successfully or unsuccessfully, expectation for compliance, and so forth.

Few mental health practitioners would underestimate the value of taking an adequate history of the patient. Yet it is surprising how lax therapists may appear in the eyes of the law if they fail to consider the observations and judgments other professionals have made in past contacts with their patient. Here, it is not uncommon to find that there may be an overreliance on patient or family self-report and no evident imperative to secure records from past caregivers. Records from, or at a minimum verbal consultation with, prior caregivers are seen by some authorities as essential for understanding patients and establishing an effective therapeutic plan. However, some authorities believe that obtaining records from previous treatment is more an ideal standard than usual and customary behavior for clinicians (Litman, personal communication, January, 1992). Other authorities (Bongar, 1991) believe that a reasonable standard would dictate that some effort always be made to receive these inputs into the current case formulation (where and when they exist), particularly information that summarizes the distal past and data that adequately communicate a picture of the years more proximal to the presenting problem.

Failure to Conduct a Mental Status Exam

The mental status exam is a hallmark of inpatient evaluations. Often, however, it is curiously absent in the records of outpatient practitioners. Perhaps it is the nature of the 50-minute (or now 45-minute) hour to essentially describe the outpatient's presenting problems and overview his/her history within the context of family background, existential realities, and so forth, and not to describe observations of the current mental status. Perhaps where outpatients are involved, there may be an erroneous presumption that since the patient is a voluntary outpatient and is functional enough to be maintained as an outpatient, the questions of appearance, judgment, orientation, and so forth are not deemed necessary to document. However, such observations are essential to any reasonable evaluation of risk and to a quality diagnostic formulation, particularly where there may be subtle hints of a thought disorder.

Failure to Diagnose

An outpatient psychotherapist's business is often to provide treatment. Usually, such treatment occurs within the context of individual psychotherapy based on a particular theoretical orientation (e.g., psychodynamic, cognitive-behavioral, family systems, etc.), with the additional possibility of pharmacotherapy. Group psychotherapy and family therapy also may be provided. Treatments are chosen and offered because they are what therapists do; that is, patients are most likely to receive the type and format of psychotherapy in which the therapist is most experienced, has been trained, or is devoted to (Beutler, 1989). Unfortunately, it is not uncommon to find that outpatient care can be independent of a careful formal diagnosis of the patient's condition.

An effective outpatient standard of care requires that the practitioner provide treatment appropriate to the presenting problem. For example, whereas one may not be able to argue convincingly that cognitive-behavioral treatment is, or is not, superior to an object relations approach to the treatment of an acutely anxious patient, the correct diagnosis of an anxiety disorder is essential to establish a reasonable treatment plan (see next section), to assess the patient's ability for self-control, and the patient's potential to lose control. Furthermore, as many suicidal patients have comorbidity with a variety of DSM Axis I, II, and III disorders, and as these patients may be more at risk for suicidal behavior, a thorough diagnostic picture is essential in order to grasp fully the complexity of the particular case. If there is no appropriate and formal diagnostic formulation, attorneys who examine the case retrospectively will press forward with hard questions about the adequacy of the practitioner's understanding of the patient's problems and the clinician's decision to employ a specific course of treatment and management.

Failure to Establish a Formal Treatment Plan

If a formal diagnosis is necessary, then it follows that a formal treatment plan also is required under any effective standard of outpatient care. Such a treatment plan needs to specify therapeutic methods and to operationalize strategies or interventions to be employed as part of effective treatment (based on specific treatment goals that clearly emerge from a formal diagnostic process).

Furthermore, it is worth mentioning that the clinician must not hesitate to contact others in the life of the patient and enlist their support in the treatment plan (Slaby et al., 1986). Litman (1982) recommended that if a psychotherapist treats a high risk outpatient who thinks he or she can function as an outpatient, it is the psychotherapist's responsibility to ensure that the risk is made known to all concerned parties (i.e., the family and significant others).

Failure to Safeguard the Outpatient Environment

Realistically, the clinician should ensure that any weapons in the patient's possession are placed in the hands of a third party (Mintz, 1961; Schutz, 1982; Slaby et al., 1986). Bongar (1991) pointed out that because the availability of firearms and especially handguns plays such a prominent role as the "method of choice" for many completed suicides, the clinician should assiduously assess the presence, access to, and knowledge of the patient with respect to this highly lethal means. This also necessitates a careful thinking through of the patient's entire life environment and of the way in which the patient spends each day, so as to determine proactively the presence of any potentially lethal means (e.g., hoarding of pills; access to poisons; whether the patient has a means in mind—hanging, jumping from a particular building, driving the car off the road, etc.).

It makes little sense to work with an outpatient at risk for suicide without consideration of safeguarding the environment of that patient from the more obvious and available lethal means. Although it is evident that knives, ropes, heights, and so forth are still available to any outpatient, choice of method is often governed by issues of knowledge and familiarity, personal meaning, and simple immediacy of accessibility (Berman & Jobes, 1991). If a patient is thwarted by a lack of access to a preferred method, time and intervention are possible antidotes to impulsive action. The patient confronted with the unavailability of a preferred agent of harm is immediately confronted with a new problem requiring problem-solving skills which momentarily may not be in evidence due to the patient's cognitive constriction, and so forth. Thus, it is essential that outpatient therapists personally or through available significant others remove available lethal means from the patient's access, or, at a minimum, arrange for significant delay in their ready accessibility.

Failure to Document Adequately Clinical Judgments, Rationales, and Observations

Asked to defend any of the above aspects of good care in a malpractice suit, the outpatient psychotherapist has but one source of information to present, the clinical record. In outpatient practices, this record typically includes an intake form completed by the patient, bills reflecting patient contacts, and the therapist's clinical notes of observations, treatment decisions, judgments, progress, and so forth. The clinical record should also include information regarding collateral contacts, consultations with colleagues, relevant telephone calls, and the like. These provide a contemporaneous record of what happened or did not happen in the course of treatment now alleged to have been below the standard of care. Consequently, such records need to be decipherable to an independent observer, allowing that observer (expert witness) to testify to the appropriateness of what was attempted and planned, even though the suicidal death reflects *ipso facto* the failure of the treatment plan.

If a psychotherapist elects outpatient care for a suicidal patient, a number of strict management rules should be followed. However, the courts have tended to be less stringent in evaluating outpatient suicide in the absence of clear signs of foreseeability, because of the obvious increased difficulty in controlling the patient's behavior (Simon, 1988). The case law seems to put forward a basic rule that the psychotherapist should correctly recognize the risk of suicide and appropriately balance this risk with the benefits of greater control through hospitalization (Simon, 1987, 1988).

SUMMARY: PRACTICAL CONSIDERATIONS IN FORMULATING AN OUTPATIENT STANDARD OF CARE

It has been said that suicide is the most feared outcome in psychotherapy, signaling a calamitous, irrevocable failure in treatment (Gill, 1982). Kahn (1982) noted that nowhere in the range of professional activities of the clinician is he or she under more intense and significant stress than when treating the potentially suicidal patient. The stress and anxiety that this clinical situation provokes in the therapist is a two-edged sword. It can mobilize the clinician to greater clinical alertness and therapeutic vigilance. However, if the clinician becomes preoccupied with the issue and threat of a patient's suicide, it can divert the clinician from the primary task of attending to more disposition-based treatment (Beutler, 1989)—therapeutics that are solidly grounded in an understanding of the power of a sound therapeutic alliance and on a well-formulated treatment plan based on the detection of known elevated risk factors (Bongar, 1991; Bongar et al., 1989; Gill, 1982; Simon, 1988).

Motto (1979) noted that the first management decision in treating a suicidal patient is to determine treatment setting, which includes consideration of characteristics of both the patient and therapist, and a careful evaluation (including a clear definition of the risks and the rationale for the decisions that one is making). The central reason for not using outpatient management is the clinician's firm judgment that "the patient is not likely to survive as an outpatient" (Motto, 1979, p. 3). Typically, the outpatient management of suicide will involve patients in the category of low to medium (moderate) risk (Bongar, 1991; Bongar et al., 1989; Peterson & Bongar, 1989; Peterson & Bongar, 1990; Simon, 1987, 1988). Thus, hospitalization in such cases is the setting of choice, because the opportunities to control and anticipate suicide are greater in the inpatient setting.

However, the clinician must never forget that each management decision is a result of both the unique characteristics of the patient and his or her social matrix, and the therapist's equally unique capabilities and tolerances for stress and uncertainty. For example:

> At times, high-risks persons with near-psychotic levels of disorganization have been treated as outpatients because in work settings they seemed able to use their defenses—especially obsessive patterns—effectively; suicidal impulses were diminished remarkably as long as they were at work. Others can manage at home when home is experienced as a protective environment. When no readily available setting affords relief, a hospital becomes the preferred setting. (Motto, 1979, p. 3)

One of the first tasks in determining appropriate patient populations for outpatient management is to distinguish between acute clinical states related to DSM Axis I clinical syndromes and chronic suicidal behavior that is part of an Axis II personality disorder (Goldsmith, Fyer, & Frances, 1990; Simon, 1988). Simon (1987, 1988) pointed out that the clinician may be held liable who makes the gross error of deciding not to seek commitment for an outpatient meeting the legal criteria for commitment (Simon, 1988).

Also, it is important to note Litman's cautionary dictum that most chronically suicidal patients have a history of contacts with mental health professionals; 20% of the suicides in this patient group were in treatment at the time of their death, and 50% were in treatment with psychiatrists (Litman, 1988). Litman pointed out that the actual ongoing treatment of these difficult patients calls for flexibility and the use of a variety of therapeutic modalities. The major complication to treatment is therapist burnout.

Fremouw, de Perczel, and Ellis (1990) believe that the clinician must then move immediately to determine the imminence of the risk. The assessment of imminence is based on the evaluation of a combination of demographic factors, the clinical interview, and any other sources of infor-

mation (e.g., self-report measures, psychological tests, suicide risk estimators, information from significant others, consultations, etc.). They pointed
out that in the presence of an imminent danger, the clinician's first decision
point is to determine whether outpatient management continues to be a
viable option. That is, can the clinician and other caretakers reasonably
ensure the protection of the patient? If the probability of the suicidal
behavior "is judged as low enough to warrant continued outpatient treatment, then treatment could continue on an intensified basis. . . . If, for a
variety of reasons, outpatient treatment is not appropriate, then hospitalization is warranted" (Fremouw, de Perczel, & Ellis, 1990, p. 93).

In determining imminence and dangerousness, it also may be helpful
to conceptualize more generally the patient's "danger-to-self" thoughts,
feelings, and behaviors along a thought–impulse–action continuum.
Shneidman found that a communication of intent is present in 80% of
completed suicides (Shneidman, 1989). Although placing such communication by patients at the 50% to 70% level, Fawcett (1988) noted that
high-risk suicidal patients tend to communicate their intent to their significant other only, while those in the moderate- to mild-risk group more
frequently threaten suicide to doctors, other family members, and so forth.
It is clear that except where contraindicated by toxic interpersonal matrices,
comprehensive information gathering and collaboration with the family
and significant others are vital elements in any successful management
plan.

Although a number of psychological assessment instruments have
shown some promise in clinical research environments, there are currently
no established standards of care that require specific psychometric or risk
estimator evaluation techniques as part of the usual and customary determination of elevated risk for suicide. (A complete discussion of this particular topic would require an entire chapter by itself; the reader is directed
to Bongar, 1991, and to Eyman & Eyman, 1992, for a comprehensive review
of psychological assessment and risk estimators in the evaluation of elevated risk of suicide.)

When more time is available (e.g., outside of emergency situations), it
behooves clinicians to use data from the specific risk factors for suicide,
knowledge of the general formulation of clinical judgment, and their own
clinical experience and training, combined with common sense, to make
an estimate of risk. For example, Motto (1989) points out that if the patient
has exhibited any previous suicidal behavior, this behavior demonstrates a
breach of resistance to pain, as a suicide attempt must be considered an

indication of increased vulnerability. Also, Clark, Gibbons, Fawcett, and Scheftner (1989) suggested that when considering patients with moderate to severe affective disorders, the clinician "should not interpret the absence of any recent suicide attempts to mean that the patient is at relatively low risk for attempting suicide in the future. . . . Suicide attempts made many years ago may have equal value to recent attempts when estimating an individual's predisposition to non-lethal attempts in the future" (p. 42). In addition, Shneidman (1987, 1989) stressed the evaluation of perturbation, lethality, and environmental "press" as critical factors in the estimation of risk.

It also needs to be mentioned that, as Shneidman (1981) has suggested, the number of high-risk suicidal patients a clinician should treat at any given time should not exceed one or two (Mintz, 1968; Shneidman, 1981), and certainly no more than two or three, moderate- to high-risk patients (Bongar, 1991; Peterson & Bongar, 1990; Wekstein, 1979).

However, the clinician must realize that therapeutic concern cannot extend to an assumption of total responsibility for the patient's life. In short, the practitioner must avoid the trap of the omnipotent rescuer, and instead convey to the patient a sense of enlightened caring and concern (Bongar, 1991; Bongar et al., 1989; Gill, 1982; Peterson & Bongar, 1990).

Clinicians in outpatient settings should be prepared to increase their treatment options for suicidal patients—for example, providing 24-hour coverage and adequate evening, weekend, and vacation backup arrangements (Harris, 1988; VandeCreek, Knapp, & Herzog, 1987). The frequency of therapy appointments also may have to be increased (Farberow, 1957; Mintz, 1968), with the diagnosing clinician meeting much more frequently with the patient for increasingly greater amounts of time (Wekstein, 1979). And in general, the clinician should maintain contact with "life forces" by talking to the part of the patient that wants to keep living, and by enlisting the cooperation of family members and friends (Farberow, 1957). By increasing the number of visits and contacts, clinicians diminish their reliance on long-term estimates of the likelihood of suicide (Bongar et al., 1989; Schutz, 1982; Simon, 1988). The telephone can also be an invaluable instrument in the outpatient management of the suicidal patient.

Clinicians who treat suicidal patients on an outpatient basis need to consider seriously routine consultation with a professional who has expertise in dealing with suicidal patients (Bongar, 1991; Peterson & Bongar, 1990; VandeCreek, Knapp, & Herzog, 1987).

It is critical for the clinician who assesses and/or treats suicidal outpatients to know the resources that are available for emergencies and outpatient crises. For whether the clinician works in a college counseling center, a community mental health agency, an inpatient setting, or an outpatient private practice, he or she is likely to see patients who present with an elevated risk for suicide. The clinician must have readily at hand the crisis intervention and emergency management tools necessary to deal with the problem of patient suicidality. There is a consensus that crisis management principally entails therapeutic activism, the delaying of the patient's suicidal impulses, the restoring of hope, environmental intervention, and consideration of hospitalization (Fremouw, de Perczel, & Ellis, 1990). Regarding this last point, it is imperative that the clinician not become interested in a readiness to confront outpatient suicidality, to the extent of regarding hospitalization as a permanent interruption to ongoing therapy. Here, the danger is that, in an attempt to avoid this interruption, some psychotherapists may inadvertently expose their patients to even greater danger by avoiding hospitalization (Farberow, 1957).

As stated previously, suits against mental health professionals are traumatic experiences, yet relatively rare occurrences. The fear of being sued probably has more widespread and deleterious effects on clinicians than do actual lawsuits. There is no specific set of clinical practices that can guarantee a clinician immunity either from losing a patient to suicide or from being sued, or from a judgment for the plaintiff in a suit. However, there are some sources of reassurance, as well as ways to reduce overall risk when assessing or treating a suicidal patient (Hoge & Appelbaum, 1989). Pope (1986) stated that in assessing and treating the suicidal patient, "perhaps most importantly communicate that you care" (p. 20).

Clinicians must resist the temptation to use inappropriate defensive clinical practices that, while limiting their liability exposure, may not be to the patient's benefit. Such temptations—for example ordering excessive precautions or treatments to prevent or limit liability, or avoiding procedures or treatments out of fear of a suit, even though such treatments may be to the patient's benefit—are both "unconscionable and potentially legally catastrophic" (Simon, 1988, p. 7). The clinician who conducts her/his practice so inappropriately is not automatically shielded from charges of negligence.

The guiding principle in all our efforts toward the care of the suicidal patient is to keep the benefit to the patient foremost in our mind. Hoge and Appelbaum (1989) observed that when a clinician is uncertain of what to do in a particular situation, the best course is "that which is consonant with the patient's therapeutic interests" (p. 619). They further noted that even if this "leads to a poor result . . . acting in the patient's interests will almost always be taken as evidence of good faith on the therapist's part" (p. 619). They concluded that too many psychotherapists become needlessly paralyzed in the face of difficult decisions with potential legal ramifications "when a return to first clinical principles is really all that is necessary" (p. 619).

Clinicians, in seeking to understand clinical and legal requirements, also should "emphasize principles that can be generalized to new situations, rather than blind rules." (Hoge & Appelbaum, 1989, p. 620). That above all, legal regulation must be seen in the context of clinician–patient relationships (Hoge & Appelbaum, 1989; Simon, 1988). The presence or absence of a good working therapeutic alliance can be utilized as an ongoing and robust measure of the treatment's effect on the patient's vulnerability to suicide (Bongar et al., 1989). It is critical to understand that our best efforts toward the detection of elevated risk and the taking of affirmative precautions (based on detected risk) must, in the end, rest on a foundation of highly- individualized, systematic, and integrative care within the context of a sound therapeutic alliance (Bongar, 1991; Bongar et al., 1989).

It seems suitable to close this chapter with Rachlin's (1984) wise counsel:

> We cannot afford to be so afraid of litigation as to deny our patients their right to learn to live. Clinical decisions are to be made on a case by case basis, and should represent the most thorough knowledge available. In this way, manageable standards of care will be set by us as mental health professionals and presumably, courts will follow our reasonableness. (p. 306)

ACKNOWLEDGMENT

This chapter is reprinted from *Suicide and Life-Threatening Behavior, 22*(4), 453–478, Winter 1992. Copyright 1992 by the American Association of Suicidology. Reprinted by permission.

REFERENCES

Abille v. United States, 482 F. Supp. 703 (N.D. Cal., 1980).

Amchin, J., Wettstein, R. M., & Roth, L. H. (1990). Suicide, ethics, and the law. In S. J. Blumenthal & D. J. Kupfer (Eds.), *Suicide over the life cycle* (pp. 637–664). Washington, DC: American Psychiatric Press.

Appelbaum, P. S., & Gutheil, T. G. (1991). *Clinical handbook of psychiatry and the law* (2nd ed.). Baltimore: Williams & Wilkins.

Bellah v. Greenson, 146 Cal.Rptr. 535 (1978).

Berman, A. L. (Ed.). (1989). Case consultation: Malpractice. *Suicide and Life-Threatening Behavior, 19,* 395–402.

Berman, A. L., & Jobes, D. A. (1991). *Adolescent suicide: Assessment and intervention.* Washington, DC: American Psychological Association.

Beutler, L. E. (1989). Differential treatment selection: The role of diagnosis in psychotherapy. *Psychotherapy, 26,* 271–281.

Black, H. C. (1979). *Black's law dictionary.* St Paul, MN: West.

Blumenthal, S. J., & Kupfer, D. J. (Eds.). (1990). *Suicide over the life-cycle.* Washington, DC: American Psychiatric Press.

Bongar, B. (1991). *The suicidal patient: Clinical and legal standards of care.* Washington, DC: American Psychological Association.

Bongar, B., Peterson, L. G., Harris, E. A., & Aissis, J. (1989). Clinical and legal considerations in the management of suicidal patients: An integrative overview. *Journal of Integrative and Eclectic Psychotherapy, 8*(1), 53–67.

Brent, D. A., Kupfer, D. J., Bromet, E. J., & Dew, M. A. (1988). The assessment and treatment of patients at risk for suicide. In A. J. Frances & R. E. Hales (Eds.), *American Psychiatric Press review of psychiatry* (Vol. 7, pp. 353–385). Washington, DC: American Psychiatric Press.

Clark, D. C., Gibbons, R. D., Fawcett, J., & Scheftner, W. A. (1989). What is the mechanism by which suicide attempts predispose to later suicide attempts? A mathematical model. *Journal of Abnormal Psychology, 98*(1), 42–49.

Emory University v. Porubiansky, 282 S.E.2nd 903 (1981).

Eyman, J. R., & Eyman, S. K. (1992). Assessment of suicide risks using psychological tests. In B. Bongar (Ed.), *Suicide: Guidelines for assessment, management, and treatment.* New York: Oxford University Press.

Farberow, N. L. (1957). The suicidal crisis in psychotherapy. In E. S. Shneidman & N. L. Farberow (Eds.), *Clues to suicide* (pp. 119–130). New York: McGraw-Hill.

Farberow, N. L. (1981). Suicide prevention in the hospital. *Hospital and Community Psychiatry, 32,* 99–104.

Fawcett, J. (1988, May 7). Interventions against suicide. In D. G. Jacobs & J. Fawcett (Chairs), *Suicide and the psychiatrist: Clinical challenges.* Symposium conducted at the American Psychiatric Association Annual Meeting, Montreal, Quebec, Canada.

Fremouw, W. J., de Perczel, M., & Ellis, T. E. (1990). *Suicide risk: Assessment and response guidelines.* New York: Pergamon Press.

Gill, A. D. (1982). Outpatient therapies for suicidal patients. In E. L. Bassuk, S. C. Schoonover, & A. D. Gill (Eds.), *Lifelines: Clinical perspectives on suicide* (pp. 71–82). New York: Plenum Press.

Goldsmith, S. J., Fyer, M., & Frances, A. (1990). Personality and suicide. In S. J. Blumenthal & D. J. Kupfer (Eds.), *Suicide over the life cycle* (pp. 155–176). Washington, DC: American Psychiatric Press.

Gutheil, T. G. (1992). Suicide and suit: Liability after self-destruction. In D. Jacobs

(Ed.), *Suicide and clinical practice* (pp. 147-167). Washington, DC: American Psychiatric Press.

Gutheil, T. G., & Appelbaum, P. S. (1982). *Clinical handbook of psychiatry and the law.* New York: McGraw-Hill.

Harris, E. A. (1988, October). *Legal issues in professional practice.* Workshop materials for the Massachusetts Psychological Association, Northampton, MA.

Hoge, S. K., & Appelbaum, P. S. (1989). Legal issues in outpatient psychiatry. In A. Lazare (Ed.), *Outpatient psychiatry: Diagnosis and treatment* (2nd ed., pp. 605-621). Baltimore: Williams & Wilkins.

Kahn, A. (1982). The stress of therapy. In E. L. Bassuk, S. C. Schoonover, & A. D. Gill (Eds.), *Lifelines: Clinical perspectives on suicide* (pp. 93-100). New York: Plenum Press.

Kermani, E. J. (1982). Court rulings on psychotherapists. *American Journal of Psychotherapy, 36*(2), 248-254.

Litman, R. E. (1982). Hospital suicides: Lawsuits and standards. *Suicide and Life-Threatening Behavior, 12,* 212-220.

Litman, R. E. (1988, May 7). Treating high-risk chronically suicidal patients. In D. G. Jacobs & J. Fawcett (Chairs), *Suicide and the psychiatrist: Clinical challenges.* Symposium conducted at the American Psychiatric Association Annual Meeting, Montreal, Quebec, Canada.

Mann, J. J., & Kapur, S. (1991). The emergence of suicidal ideation and behavior during antidepressant pharmacotherapy. *Archives of General Psychiatry, 115,* 1027-1033.

Maris, R. W., Berman, A. L., Maltsberger, J. T., & Yufit, R. I. (Eds.). (1992). *Assessment and prediction of suicide.* New York: Guilford Press.

Meier v. Ross General Hospital, 69 Cal 2d 420, 71 Cal. Rptr 903, 445 P.2d 519 (1968).

Meyer, R. G., Landis, E. R., & Hays, J. R. (1988). *Law for the psychotherapist.* New York: Norton.

Mintz, R. S. (1968). The psychotherapy of the suicidal patient. In H. L. P. Resnick (Ed.), *Suicidal behaviors: Diagnosis and management* (pp. 111-124). Boston: Little, Brown.

Motto, J. A. (1979). Guidelines for the management of the suicidal patient. *Weekly Psychiatry Update Series Lesson, 3,* 3-7.

Motto, J. A. (1989). Problems in suicide risk assessment. In D. G. Jacobs & H. N. Brown (Eds.), *Suicide: Understanding and responding. Harvard Medical School perspectives on suicide* (pp. 129-142). Madison, CT: International Universities Press.

Perr, I. N. (1979). Legal aspects of suicide. In L. D. Hankoff & B. Einsidler (Eds.), *Suicide: Theory and clinical aspects* (pp. 91-100). Littleton, MA: PSG.

Perr, I. N. (1985). Suicide litigation and risk management: A review of 32 cases. *Bulletin of American Academy of Psychiatry and the Law, 13,* 209-219.

Peterson, L. G., & Bongar, B. (1989). The suicidal patient. In A. Lazare (Ed.), *Outpatient psychiatry: Diagnosis and treatment* (2nd ed., pp. 569-584). Baltimore: Williams & Wilkins.

Peterson, L. G., & Bongar, B. (1990). Training physicians in the clinical evaluation of the suicidal patient. In M. Hale (Ed.), *Teaching methods in consultation-Liaison psychiatry* (pp. 89–108). Basel, Switzerland: Karger.

Pisel v. Stamford Hospital, 180 Conn. 314, 430 A.2d 1 (1980).

Pokorny, A. D. (1983). Prediction of suicide in psychiatric patients. *Archives of General Psychiatry, 40,* 249–257.

Pope, K. (1986, January). Assessment and management of suicidal risks: Clinical and legal standards of care. *Independent Practitioner,* pp. 17–23.

Pope, K. (1989, January). Malpractice suits, licensing disciplinary actions, and ethics cases. *Independent Practitioner,* pp. 22–26.

Pope, K. S., & Vasquez, M. J. T. (1991). *Ethics in psychotherapy and counseling.* San Francisco: Jossey-Bass.

Rachlin, S. (1984). Double jeopardy: Suicide and malpractice. *General Hospital Psychiatry, 6,* 302–307.

Robertson, J. D. (1988). *Psychiatric malpractice: Liability of mental health professionals.* New York: Wiley.

Schutz, B. M. (1982). *Legal liability in psychotherapy.* San Francisco: Jossey-Bass.

Shneidman, E. S. (1981). Psychotherapy with suicidal patients. *Suicide and Life-Threatening Behavior, 11,* 341–348.

Shneidman, E. S. (1985). *Definition of suicide.* New York: Wiley-Interscience.

Shneidman, E. S. (1987). A psychological approach to suicide. In G. R. Vanden-Bos & B. K. Bryant (Eds.), *Cataclysms, crises, and catastrophes: Psychology in action* (pp. 147–183). Washington, DC: American Psychological Association.

Shneidman, E. S. (1989). Overview: A multidimensional approach to suicide. In D. G. Jacobs & H. N. Brown (Eds.), *Suicide: Understanding and responding. Harvard Medical School perspectives on suicide* (pp. 1–30). Madison, CT: International Universities Press.

Simon, R. I. (1987). *Clinical psychiatry and the law.* Washington, DC: American Psychiatric Press.

Simon, R. J. (1988). *Concise guide to clinical psychiatry and the law.* Washington, DC: American Psychiatric Press.

Slaby, A. E., Lieb, J., & Tancredi, L. R. (1986) *Handbook of psychiatric emergencies* (3rd ed.). New York: Medical Examination.

Slovenko, R. (1980). On the need for record keeping in the practice of psychiatry. *Journal of Psychiatry and Law, 7,* 399–440.

Speer v. United States, 512 F.Supp. 670 (1981).

Stromberg, C. D., Haggarty, D. J., Leibenluft, R. F., McMillan, M. H., Mishkin, B., Rubin, B. L., & Trilling, H. R. (1988). *The psychologist's legal handbook.* Washington, DC: Council for the National Register of Health Service Providers in Psychology.

Swenson, E. V. (1986). Legal liability for a patient's suicide. *Journal of Psychiatry and Law, 14,* 409–434.

Tarasoff v. Regents of the University of California et al., 551 P.2d.334, 131 Cal. Rptr. 14, Cal. Sup. Ct. (1976).

Texarkana Memorial Hospital, Inc. v. Firth, 746 S.W.2d. 494 (1988).

VandeCreek, L., & Harrar, W. (1988). The legal liability of supervisors. *Psychotherapy Bulletin, 23*(3), 13–17.

VandeCreek, L., & Knapp, S. (1983). Malpractice risks with suicidal patients. *Psychotherapy: Theory, Research, and Practice, 20,* 274–280.

VandeCreek, L., Knapp, S., & Herzog, C. (1987). Malpractice risks in the treatment of dangerous patients. *Psychotherapy: Theory, Research, and Practice, 24,* 145–153.

Vistica v. Presbyterian Hospital, 67 Cal.2d 465, 62 Cal. Rptr. 577, 432 P.2d 193 (1967).

Wekstein, L. (1979). *Handbook of suicidology: Principles, problems and practice.* New York: Brunner/Mazel.

2

Outpatient Management of Suicidal Patients

ANDREW EDMUND SLABY

The need to develop a plan of management for suicidal patient may occur at the moment of evaluation or may arise in the course of treatment. In the former instance, either a patient states that he or she is suicidal, or the fact that the patient considering suicide emerges from direct questioning. If a patient is actively suicidal, the clinician is left no option other than to provide protective custody. If a patient is thinking of suicide, the patient is evaluated to ascertain the degree of risk of harm to self if he or she is not hospitalized. If the risk is evaluated as only mild to moderate and the patient has appropriate social supports, the patient must convince the clinician that he or she will inform the clinician, the clinicians backup, a friend or family member, or another caregiver of the need to be hospitalized if his or her desire to die increases. A clinician is not always able to prevent a patient from committing suicide, but the clinician is always able to provide what is humanly possible to minimize the occurrence of self-inflicted death even in an outpatient setting.

In some instances, patients who have not been self-destructive become so during the course of therapy. There are a number of situations in which this may occur. Such patients may be suffering from an evolving depression.

If appropriate medication is not instituted in a timely manner in doses sufficient to ameliorate the depression, or if the patients are treatment-resistant, they may become suicidal. At other times, failure of symptoms to remit or the continuing absence of change for the better in patients' lives leads to hopelessness. It is hopelessness more than depression that enhances suicide risk (Beck, Steer, Beck, & Newman, 1993). We all get depressed at times, but when we feel nothing will ever improve our dismal state, suicide risk increases. People who die by suicide do not want to die; they simply want to end their pain. If something short of self-inflicted death will provide the sought relief, it is not necessary to die. When ending pain by any means other than suicide is seen as impossible, risk is greatest (Slaby, 1994, 1995).

Suicidal thoughts may also emerge as a result of physical illness or pharmacological intervention. Not all patients who suffer from AIDS or Huntington's chorea wish to kill themselves. Some, however, independent of any psychosocial factors, sustain changes in cerebral metabolism that lead to depression and impulsivity. These people, like those who take a medication such as prednisone or an antihypertensive drug with depression as a side effect, may kill themselves. Recreational drugs can lead to suicide as well. A patient on a hallucinogen may jump out of a window because he or she is terrified of the changes in perception. Patients may also crash after use of speed (amphetamines) or a cocaine binge and in the ensuant depression sometimes kill themselves.

Borderline patients are particularly difficult to manage (Fyer et al., 1988; Shearer, Peters, Quaytman, & Woodman, 1988). They may be non-suicidal for years, with no need to restrict medications prescribed for them or need to hospitalize them, and then may respond to what appears to most to be a trivial insult with suicide or a suicide attempt. There is no easy way to prevent such occurrences. Clinicians are not gods and are not able to predict or prevent all deaths by suicide. This is most true when they are dealing with Axis II personality disorders, impulse control disorders, treatment-resistant bipolar disorders, schizophrenia, and schizoaffective disorder.

TREATMENT PLAN

The essential elements of the outpatient care of the suicidal or potentially suicidal patient are as follows:

1. Conducting both initial and concurrent evaluations for suicidal ideation and plans.
2. Estimating risk, given what is known about factors that enhance or diminish self-destructive behavior.
3. Determining need for hospitalization.
4. Evaluating and instigating psychopharmacotherapy to treat the disorder that is putting the patient at risk for suicide, as well as to diminish impulsivity.
5. Enhancing social support indirectly through work with the patient, and directly through work with family and friends.
6. Providing individual and family therapy.
7. Providing concurrent substance use when needed.
8. Providing medical consultation if required.
9. Providing outpatient electroconvulsive therapy (ECT) if needed.
10. Educating the patient and significant others about evolving signs of a need for more intensive treatment, and for a plan to provide what is needed.
11. Arranging access to the therapist and other caregivers if acute need for intervention arises.
12. Helping the patient, family members, and friends to understand that goals must be realistic and that there are limits to what is possible.
13. Keeping careful records.

I now discuss each of these elements in turn.

Initial and Concurrent Evaluations

The evaluation of risk of deliberate self-harm is one of the most anxiety-provoking tasks confronting psychiatric clinicians. This is especially true today when certification for reimbursement for inpatient care requires in most instances an immediate danger of suicide and not just recurrent suicidal ideation. Studies indicate (Diekstra & Van Egmond, 1989) that 32% to 69% of those who attempt suicide see their primary physicians within a week of the act. In most instances clinicians are unaware of the increased risk, because they do not ask about it and it is not readily apparent.

From 0.5% to 1% of the population dies by suicide annually (Farmer, 1988). Suicide is among the top 10 killers from adolescence through late adulthood. Rates of suicide among adolescents have increased two- to threefold in the past three decades (Garfinkel et al., 1982; Slaby, 1986; Rudd, 1989; Slaby & Garfinkel, 1994) making suicide currently the third most common cause of death among 15- to 24-year-olds in the United States (after accidents and homicides), accounting for 18.8% of deaths in this age group (Pfeffer, 1986). It is the third leading cause of death in the U.S. military (Rothberg, Ursano, & Holloway, 1987) and a frequent cause of death in jails. The rates have decreased somewhat among older age groups in the past several decades, but one study found that men over 65 are still at greatest risk in England and Wales (Murphy, Lindesay, & Grundy, 1986). Suicides may be obfuscated in victims of car and pedestrian vehicular accidents; in older people, who may require little more than therapeutic doses of medication to cause cardiac arrhythmia or respiratory depression; in victims of provoked homicides; and in victims of what appear to be firearm "accidents." The fact that suicidal ideation is common—with up to 60% of adolescents reporting it in some surveys (Friedman et al., 1983; Smith & Crawford, 1986), and suicide attempts and gestures occurring in as many as 9% of adolescents (Friedman et al., 1983; Smith & Crawford, 1986)—highlights the need for clinicians to discern which patients are most likely to die by suicide if not placed in a protective environment.

All patients upon initial evaluation should be asked whether they have ever seriously thought of killing themselves, whether they have ever attempted suicide, and whether they are currently suicidal. Many people will report a history of "parasuicide" (viz., mildly self-destructive acts that will not result in death), more frequently referred to as "gestures." Those at greatest immediate risk are those who have made attempts on their lives that would have resulted in death, and/or those with immediate plans that would result in their death. If an attempt is recent, risk is greater, especially if there is current ideation. (Risk factors are discussed below in greater detail.)

Individuals who have suicidal ideation at the time of evaluation, but no imminent plans to kill themselves, must be recurrently assessed until these thoughts diminish. Patients in high-risk groups, such as those who feel hopeless or fail to respond to a number of therapeutic interventions when severely depressed, must be evaluated until they are stabilized. It is obviously not necessary for clinicians to ask all patients who have been at one time seriously suicidal whether they have any immediate plans to kill themselves every time the clinicians see them, but this must be done during periods of greatest symptom intensity to minimize risk of death. Some people will kill themselves because of abrupt changes in clinical status.

Others may lie to their therapists to avoid interference with their plan. Most who may die, however, will show signs of a deteriorating condition and will confirm in words that they require more intensive treatment.

Estimation of Risk

The majority of reported suicides have suffered from psychiatric illness. It is unusual to find a person without a psychiatric history (treated or untreated) who commits suicide. When such suicides do occur, there is often a secret: The patient was homosexual and knew his or her spouse or parents would not accept it; the patient had AIDS; the patient was conducting an extramarital liaison that created stress; or the patient had suffered a political or business reverse. Even in these instances, most suicides have also suffered from clinical depression, disabling anxiety, and/or substance use disorders prior to their death. When individuals with a terminal illness elect to take pain or sedating medication to the extent that it terminates their lives with dignity, death is often ascribed to the primary illness (e.g., cancer, chronic obstructive lung disease) unless there is a blatant overdose. Technically, these may be called suicides, but in many instances the lethal dose and the dose required for comfort differ little toward the end of a terminal illness.

Depression in one form or another is the most common psychiatric disorder found among suicides (see Table 2.1). Outpatients who are depressed are at greatest risk for suicide, and therefore require both repeated assessment of risk and diagnosis-specific interventions to ameliorate this risk factor. Risk is enhanced in depressed patients and the other diagnostically vulnerable groups listed in Table 2.1 when certain psychosocial and clinical variables that further increase risk (see Table 2.2) are present.

TABLE 2.1. Psychiatric and Medical Disorders Associated with Increased Suicide Risk

AIDS	Major depression
Bipolar disorders	Narcissistic personality disorder
Borderline personality disorder	Obsessive–compulsive disorder (OCD)
Cyclothymic disorder	Other anxiety disorders
Dementia	Panic disorder
Dysthymic disorder	Posttraumatic stress disorder (PTSD)
Eating disorders	Schizoaffective disorder
Impulse control disorders	Schizophrenia
Learning disabilities	Substance use disorders

TABLE 2.2. Variables Enhancing Risk of Suicide among Vulnerable Groups

Adolescence and late life	Living alone
Bisexual or homosexual gender identity	Lethality of previous attempt
Criminal behavior	Low self-esteem
Cultural sanctions for suicide	Male gender
Delusions	Physical illness or impairment
Disposition of personal property	Previous attempts that could have resulted in
Divorced, separated, or single marital	death
status	Protestant or nonreligious status
Early loss of or separation from parents	Recent childbirth
Family history of suicide	Recent loss
Hallucinations	Repression as a defense
Homicide	Secondary gain
Hopelessness	Severe family pathology
Hypochondriasis	Severe psychiatric illness
Impulsivity	Sexual abuse
Increasing agitation	Signals of intent to die
Increasing stress	Suicide epidemics
Insomnia	Unemployment
Lack of sleep	White race
Lack of future plans	

Approximately 60% to 70% of all suicides suffer from either major depression or bipolar illness (Bulik et al., 1990; Slaby, 1992). The majority of these usually suffer from a comorbid mental disorder, usually alcoholism and/or an Axis II disorder (Henriksson et al., 1993). Affective illness also increases the risk of suicide when it is comorbid with panic disorder and other anxiety disorders (Rudd, Cahm, & Rajab, 1993).

The risk of suicide for an untreated or treatment-resistant person with major depression is 10% to 15% (Valzell, 1981; Murphy, 1983; Bulik et al., 1990; Slaby, 1992), or 30 times that of the population without the disorder. Bipolar patients are at the greatest risk of all, with 20% to 25% dying by their own hands; 10 to 20 times as many attempt suicide (Asnis et al., 1990). Sadly, affectively ill patients tend to be more creative, indicating that creative, sensitive people as a group are at greater risk (Slaby, 1992). The majority of suicides of patients with bipolar illness occur during a major depressive episode (Isometsa, Henriksson, Aro, & Lonnquist, 1994). When bipolar patients who are manic commit suicide, they usually do so in a mixed state (Dilsaver, Chen, Swan, Schoaib, & Krajewski, 1994), although suicide may also occur immediately after or even during pure mania (Isometsa et al., 1994). Men with bipolar disorders who commit suicide have a higher incidence of comorbid alcoholism, and are a group younger than and have briefer treatment histories than bipolar women who commit suicide. Patients with affective illness who commit suicide also have an increased frequency of suicide in their family histories (Papadimitriou, Linkowski, Delarbre, & Mendlewicz, 1991).

Rates of suicide among the depressed are greatest in the presence of neurovegetative signs (especially worsening insomnia and agitation) (Murphy, 1988), suicide ideation, and substance abuse, and in the absence of social supports; they are also higher among males. Furthermore, risk increases among the depressed early in the course of treatment, as energy returns before hopelessness and depressed affect abate (Robbins & Alessi, 1985; Achte, 1986; Modestin & Kopp, 1988; Roy-Byrne et al., 1988; van Praag & Plutchik, 1988; Roy et al., 1989; Bulik et al., 1990).

Another 20% of those who die by suicide have experienced illnesses with a strong depressive component, so that 80% or more of all suicides have suffered depressive disturbance to a greater or lesser degree. This group includes those with dysthymic disorder, cyclothymic disorder, narcissistic and borderline personality disorders, posttraumatic stress disorder (PTSD), schizoaffective disorder, and schizophrenia. Suicidal ideation and attempts occur more frequently than in the general population among individuals with a history of PTSD (Hendin & Haas, 1991). Those with PTSD who report suicidal behavior and thinking are more likely to suffer also from depression or dysthymia (Kramer, Lindy, Green, Grace, & Leonard, 1994). Borderline personality disorder patients with suicidal behavior tend to be older and to have histories of a previous attempt, impulsive actions, depressive moods, and/or antisocial behavior (Casey, 1989; Soloff, Lis, Kelly, Cornelius, & Ulrich, 1994).

Many who attempt or die from suicide suffer from "double depression"—episodes of major depression superimposed on more sustained depression, such as that seen with dysthymic disorder. Adolescents who do not receive diagnosis-specific treatment for a major depressive episode in their teenage years often develop enduring low self-esteem and depression, due to the fact that they felt this way at a time when their identity was solidifying. The sustained dysphoric state became an integral part of their adult sense of self. Their career and romantic aspirations are low, and they have no sense of self-worth. How could they do better for themselves? Often drug abuse begins in such cases during adolescence; further psychological development is compromised or arrested until the substance abuse ceases, and this impedes the mastery of critical adult tasks, such as the achievement of intimacy and a consistent identity. When another depressive episode occurs later in life, with disturbances in energy, appetite, sleep, and sexual interest, it is possible to treat the acute episode psychopharmacologically and psychotherapeutically to ameliorate the neurovegetative signs and attenuate the desire to die. However, the dysthymia often remains: The person has a depressive cast to his or her personality and is always somewhat mad or irritable, because the untreated major depressive episode was experienced at the time of identity formation.

The incidence of suicide in schizophrenia is about the same as that in major depression (viz., 10% to 15%), but far fewer people suffer from schizophrenia (only approximately 0.9% to 1.1% of the population). The suicide rate for schizophrenics is 20 times greater (Brier & Astrachan, 1984) than that of the general population, with two-thirds of the 10% to 15% who commit suicide dying within the first 10 years of the illness (Cohen, Test, & Brown, 1990). The incidence of suicide among young schizophrenics is so great that it is now the leading cause of death in this group (Caldwell & Gottessman, 1990). Risk is particularly high among schizophrenics when a thought disorder is combined with depression and impulsivity. Schizophrenic patients who commit suicide generally tend to do so in a planned or organized manner, to escape an intolerable life situation (Tanney, 1992) they feel hopeless about changing. Risk nevertheless is difficult to predict in this group (Roy, 1983; Reich, 1989; Dassori, Mezzich, & Keshavan, 1990; Weiden & Roy, 1990). The incidence of self-mutilation is also increased among schizophrenics. Thought-disordered patients who suicide tend to be male, younger, never married, and depressed, and to fail to communicate their desire to die after a stressful life event (Brier & Astrachan, 1984; Prasod & Kumar, 1988; Cohen et al., 1990). Command, mandatory, or imperative hallucinations increase risk when combined with other factors (Hellerstein, Frosch, & Kownigsberg, 1987).

The remaining 20% or so of people who die by suicide includes individuals with anxiety disorders (other than PTSD, such as obsessive-compulsive disorder) individuals who have felt depressed and hopeless because of learning disabilities or physical illness, and individuals (often adolescents) who are gay and are depressed or anxious over what their sexual orientation means to them and to those around them, particularly parents and peers (Slaby, 1992).

More than 1.5% of the population suffers from panic disorder, and two to three times more experience panic attacks that do not meet the full criteria for a diagnosis of panic disorder (Weissman et al., 1989). Twenty percent of individuals with panic disorder, and 12% of those with panic attacks not meeting DSM-III-R criteria for panic disorder, attempt suicide

(Reich, 1989; Weissman et al., 1989). Moreover, fewer than a third of people with medication-responsive panic disorder suffer from this disorder only. Although lifetime risk of a suicide attempt with uncomplicated panic disorder alone is great (viz., 7%), it is greatest when complicated by other factors, such as depression, substance abuse for self-medication of the panic disorder (Johnson, Weissman, & Klerman, 1990), and borderline personality disorder (Friedman, Jones, Chernen, & Barlow, 1992; Cox, Direnfeld, Swinson, & Norton, 1994).

Physical illness may lead to suicide, independent of the associated pain, stigma, disability, and deterioration. For example, lack of social supports, wasting, and anergy all contribute to suicide among AIDS patients (Schneider et al., 1991), but HIV dementia itself is associated with disinhibition, mood lability, impaired judgment, and impulsivity (Alfonso & Cohen, 1994), which also contribute.

The outpatient therapist must consider all patients in all of the groups described here as at risk. Obviously, for the majority it is most essential to monitor degrees of suicide potential when symptoms are severe or the patients are as yet untreated or treatment-resistant. Once symptoms abate and the patients are successfully treated, risk is diminished. Subpopulations of all these groups, however, are especially at risk. Hopelessness places a person at risk more than depression does (Weishaar & Beck, 1992; Beck et al., 1993). Hopelessness plus depression is a lethal combination in a person genetically predisposed to impulsivity. People who are impulsive in other spheres of life are more likely to be impulsively suicidal. The best prediction of future behavior is past behavior.

Social isolation is dangerous, particularly for men. People who are without social supports may lack such supports because the nature of their illness (e.g., paranoid schizophrenia with depression) alienates others from them. In addition, the absence of others may allow the worsening of a depression and the emergence of suicidal ideation or an attempt go undetected. In an extreme case, if an attempt is made where rescue may be possible if the person is found early (as in an overdose), but there is no one around to find the person, death may occur. Men as a group provide less support for other men emotionally, fail to ask critical questions, and are unaware of the meaning of changes in behavior and emotion. When they hurt, some do not even recognize psychic pain, or what Shneidman (1993) calls "psychache." They are alexithymic: that is, they fail to know the words for emotions.

It cannot be emphasized too often that hopelessness always increases risk (Beck, Steer, Kovacs, & Garrison, 1985; Hendin, 1986; Prezant &

Neimeyer, 1988; Schlebusch & Wessels, 1988; Beck et al., 1990). Again, people who commit suicide do not want to die; they want to end their pain. If there was a more effective way to do so, they would select it, but no option seems apparent, and all selected have failed.

Previous suicide attempts also increase risk. To be seen as at lower risk, attempters who have overdosed, must be aware that a drug they are taking now is not lethal (Rich et al., 1990). If an attempt has been made, certain characteristics increase the risk of another, successful attempt (Goldacre & Hawton, 1985; Shafi, Carrigan, Whittenghill, & Derrick, 1985; Steer, Beck, Garrison, & Lester, 1988). If the earlier attempt was violent or painful, could have resulted in a patient's death, was impulsive, or occurred in a setting where a patient would not be found, subsequent risk is greatest.

Risk is increased if there has been a suicide attempt or completion in the family, especially in the same-sex parent. Nearly one-half of patients in one study had a family history of attempts (Roy, 1983). Of these, more than half had affective illness of some sort; still, a family history of attempts increased risk, regardless of diagnosis (Roy, 1983; Egeland & Sussex, 1985; Hutchinson & Draguns, 1987; Scheftner et al., 1988).

Cessation of medication in an outpatient is a signal of possible increased risk, particularly if the patient has a history of recurrent depressive episodes or bipolar illness (Schou & Weeke, 1988). Giving away property, especially if cherished, is another sign of increased risk. Lack of future plans is always portentous, particularly if patients fantasize how they will look at their funerals and how others will respond to their deaths.

Women on the whole attempt suicide more often than men, but succeed less often. Professional women are an exception, in that rates of suicide are increasing in this group. Women tend to overdose, whereas men tend to use more lethal means (McIntosh & Jewell, 1986; Rich, Fowler, Fogerty, & Young, 1988; Stafford & Weisheit, 1988; Hassam & Tan, 1989). With the exception of married adolescent females, marriage appears to be protective; suicide rates are highest among the divorced, widowed, and separated (Roy, 1983).

Rates tend to increase with age for men after midlife, with rates highest over 65, especially if dementia is present (Margo & Finkel, 1990). Rates for women increase until 65 and then drop off. The high rates among adolescents are not attained again until the fifth decade (Rich et al., 1986; Achte, 1988; Asarnow & Carlson, 1988; Brent et al., 1988; Husain, 1990; Pfeffer, 1990; Spurlock, 1990). Whereas adolescence on the whole increases risk of death, those who attempt (rather than succeed) are more likely to be younger and female; to experience alcohol-related problems at an early age; and to have lifetime diagnoses of major depression, antisocial personality disorder, panic disorder, phobias, generalized anxiety disorder, or substance abuse (Berglund, 1984; Roy et al., 1989).

The increased risk among lesbian, gay, and bisexual individuals relates both to the stigma associated with being homosexual and the lack of social support offered those who are gay. Risk is greatest for gay adolescents, and for those who are aging, substance-abusing, suffering from AIDS, or (as noted earlier) depressed (Garfinkel et al., 1982; Rich, Fowler, Young, & Blenkush, 1986; Schneider, Farberow, & Kruks, 1989; Slaby & Garfinkel, 1994).

Finally, rising tensions during the course of inpatient treatment, or failures to reduce tension during outpatient evaluation for suicide potential, are causes of concern. If a patient does not feel comforted by a therapeutic intervention, a clinician should continually reassess a patient for the need for hospitalization until it appears that the person is no longer at risk.

Risk of other-directed violence should also be assessed in all patients for whom there is a danger of suicide. Decreased cerebral serotonin production has been found not only in patients who have made impulsive, violent suicide attempts, but in patients who have committed heinous murders (e.g., murder of a spouse, lover, parent, or offspring). In some instances, a depressed person may persuade a love one to die with him or her in a "suicide pact." In these instances, the pact is probably more accurately spoken of as a "suicide and homicide pact" (Rosenbaum, 1983). Patients with a history of violence may die impulsively without an obvious affective component, suggesting that a different approach is required for psychopharmacological management of more violent patients (Apter et al., 1991).

In some circumstances, risk factors are present (e.g., a patient with AIDS or terminal cancer is suicidal), but they do not include mental illness. Most state laws provide only for involuntary hospitalization of those whose self- or other-directed violent impulses are produced by a mental illness. In these instances, it is especially advisable to work together with patients and their friends and families to enhance the quality of what life may be left, and to ameliorate the impact on survivors if such a patient commits suicide despite all attempts to help (Karlinsky et al., 1988). However, clinicians must be alert to the fact that not everyone who says he or she is terminally ill is really so. Some such patients have delusional depressions; the belief that they have AIDS or cancer is a somatic delusion.

The use of standardized scales to ascertain suicidality has been found to be limited (Pokorny, 1983; Clark et al., 1987; Levine, Ancill, & Roberts, 1989). Clinical parameters reflecting histories of hopelessness, previous self-destructive behavior, and impulsive behavior are better. Children who are suicidal or assaultive tend to exhibit intense aggression and to have parents with histories of assaults and suicidal behavior (Pfeffer, 1986, 1988). Individuals who make repeated attempts have attempt histories beginning early in life, feel more externally directed hostility, and feel more powerless and normless (Sakinofsky & Roberts, 1990).

Need for Hospitalization

The majority of patients with suicidal ideation do not require hospitalization and respond to outpatient treatment. Even if suicidal ideation is present, inpatient care is not required unless the patient states that he or she will not be able to inform the clinician, the clinician's backup, family members or friends, or an emergency care clinician of an increasingly powerful drive to die. Only when desire to die or impulsivity is great is this necessary (Yu-Chin & Arcuni, 1990). Risk is greatest with patients with a recent past history of attempts that would result in loss of life and with plans to do so again if relief is not forthcoming. Hopelessness, psychosis, absence of social supports, substance use, and impulsivity further increase the need for observation and sometimes restraint in a protected environment. Even in a hospital, extremely suicidal patients may require arm's-length observation to prevent self-harm.

When it becomes apparent at the time of evaluation or in the course of therapy that a patient is imminently suicidal and. requires immediate hospitalization, he or she may attempt to flee to commit suicide (Goldberg, 1987). In such instances, relatives or friends must be advised of the patient's condition and, if the patient presents himself or herself at one of their homes, of the need to bring him or her immediately to a hospital. The clinician should call the hospital to which the patient will be brought, to advise hospital personnel of the patient's condition and the need for restraint (even if this is resisted by the patient or family), if clinically it appears that the patient will commit suicide. This is sometimes difficult because in the absence of security guards, a patient may not be forcibly detained and may run out and kill himself or herself. Family members may resist the decision to hospitalize a patient; of the patient dies, however, they may—either out of guilt or with the hope of secondary gain—sue a physician or hospital for not having committed the patient. In such a case, the relatives may claim that they were distraught and could not make a rational decision, especially against the patient's own wishes. The clinician, of course, and not the family, will be seen as responsible for the decision to hospitalize. If the patient is to be treated outside the hospital, the patient's friends, family, and lover should be appraised of the risk and treatment plans and should be sensitized to signs of worsening depression, such as hopelessness, secretiveness, and development of a plan.

If a patient is hospitalized during the course of outpatient treatment, it is advisable that the community-based therapist remain in contact with the patient, the patient's family, and the inpatient treatment team, in order to facilitate the rapid development of an aftercare treatment plan that will minimize the risk of suicide and of rehospitalization. Distance sometimes precludes in-person sessions with a family and patient during a hospitalization. In such cases, telephone sessions are preferable to lack of continuity of care. If a patient appears resistant to medication or particularly prone to side effects, hospitalization may allow a change in medication or a more rapid increase in dose under controlled circumstances. If a patient appears medication-refractory, ECT may be indicated and initiated. When a patient is ECT-responsive, part of the course of ECT may be given on an outpatient basis. Patients with a history of suicidal ideation or attempts are at greatest risk for death during the first month following discharge (Roy, 1989); for some such patients, greater frequency of contacts and an action plan to be called into play should a crisis reemerge will be needed.

Psychopharmacotherapy

Most patients' suicide risk is remarkably reduced with appropriate psychopharmacotherapy. If immediate risk with impulsivity is exceptionally great or symptoms fail to respond to medication, ECT may be needed. The use of psychotropic drugs in the management of as suicidal patient is aimed at either specifically treating a neurochemical defect associated with a psychiatric disorder that enhances risk of suicide, or diminishing impulsivity that predisposes an individual to self-destruction.

Suicide appears at this time to be linked to decreased serotonin in the brain, as indicated by the decrease of its principal metabolite, 5-hydroxyindoleacetic acid, in the cerebrospinal fluid (Mann, 1987; Stanley & Stanley, 1988; Cox & Meltzer, 1989; Gross-Isseroff, Israeli, & Bregan, 1989). This decrease is associated with the lethality of an attempt as well as with a patient's impulsivity, regardless of diagnosis.

Evidence that the biological factors linked with increased risk of suicide relate to aberrations of catecholamine and indoleamine metabolism has been provided by a number of investigators (Asberg, 1980, 1986; Traskman et al., 1981; Stanley & Mann, 1983; van Praag, 1983; Lindberg et al., 1985; Mann et al., 1986; Asberg, Eriksson, et al., 1986; Asberg, Nordstrom, & Traskman-Bendz, 1986, 1990; Cheetham et al., 1986; Paul, 1986; Asberg et al., 1987; Braunig, Rao, & Fimmirs, 1989; Modai et al., 1989; Traskman-Bendz, Asberg, Nordstrom, & Stanley, 1989; Blier, deMontigny, & Chaput, 1990; Price et al., 1990; Stanley & Stanley, 1990; Traskman-Bendz, Asberg, & Schalling, 1990). Decreases in available biogenic amines at critical neuronal synapses result in mood changes that if sustained lead to hopelessness, and in some instances to increased risk of suicide (Nordstrom et al., 1994)—especially by violent means such as shooting, jumping, hanging, or cutting one's throat, regardless of diagnosis. This same neurochemically determined impulsivity appears also to fuel creativity and innovation in the arts and other areas, as seen, for example, with Vincent van Gogh. Creative people simply go with an idea, unfettered by social convention; they really don't care what the critics say or convention dictates. They act without regard to external pressure. The same people, however, when hopeless, may impulsively commit suicide.

The increased risk of suicide attendant upon other psychiatric disorders involving impulsivity (e.g., some of the eating disorders and anxiety disorders), and the response of these disorders to the same medications that are used to treat depression and suicidality, also suggest that a deficiency in available serotonin is responsible for the impulsivity. Patients with bulimia nervosa often binge and purge impulsively. Obsessive–compulsives cannot control the urge to wash their hands or check locks and stoves. People with panic disorder are impulsive and sometimes make rash errors in panic states. Patients with all these disorders may kill themselves. Self-medication of anxiety disorders with alcohol further decreases judgment and increases impulsivity, thus further enhancing risk (Roy et al., 1990).

Some individuals with PTSD, another anxiety disorder, may commit suicide and/or act out violently. These individuals also respond to antidepressants that reduce impulsivity. A notable finding is that 5-hydroxyindoleacetic acid is also decreased in individuals who commit homicide, especially impulsively. As noted earlier, those showing the greatest decrease are heinous murderers—those who kill a spouse, lover, child, or parent. Those who murder are also at greater risk of killing themselves (Alessi et al., 1984; Griffith & Bell, 1989; Kerhof & Bernasco, 1990), corroborating Freud's hypothesis that suicide is retroflected rage. Anger toward another may be turned inward . . . or sometimes outward.

Suicide is an isolated act and is not itself an illness. Most often, it is the result of a pharmacologically sensitive proclivity to impulsive self-harm; it may also be the manifestation of a medical disorder that alters perception and/or enhances impulsivity (e.g., Alzheimer's disease, epilepsy) or of drug intoxication. Although sometimes psychosocial or existential forces converge to impel a person to commit suicide, the drive for self-preservation is so great that even in the most adversarial of circumstances (e.g., the Holocaust, war), few choose to die rather than live unless biological factors are also involved. Again, the majority of suicides generally involve changes in catecholamine and indoleamine metabolism, a nonpsychiatric medical illness, or medication/street drug intoxication.

The initial step in the psychopharmacotherapy of suicidal behavior is early identification of when pharmacological intervention is necessary and will be efficacious (Slaby & Dumont, 1992). If a person is in psychic pain and hopeless because of an unidentified learning disorder, or has been ostracized because of his or her sexual orientation, a behavioral intervention is more appropriate unless neurovegetative signs of depression are present.

As noted earlier, if depression and suicidal thoughts during adolescence do not receive appropriate psychopharmacological treatment, the mood disorder and suicidal ideation can become an enduring part of the individual's adult personality. When stress triggers neurovegetative signs of depression and a suicide attempt in later life, the person is said to suffer from "double depression" (a major depressive episode superimposed on the more sustained dysthymia). One drug may work for the acute depression, whereas psychotherapy with or without another antidepressant may be required for the dysthymia, low self-esteem, and learned helplessness that have developed and endured over the years (Keller, 1990; Perez-Stable et al., 1990).

The selective serotonin reuptake inhibitors (SSRIs) are particularly useful in the management of suicidal behavior given the known deficit of serotonin in many impulsively suicidal individuals. Fluoxetine (Prozac), paroxetine (Paxil), sertraline (Zoloft), and fluvoxamine (Luvox) increase available serotonin at the neuronal synapse. Other antidepressants have more specific effects on dopamine and norepinephrine function; depending upon the nature of the underlying biochemical defect, these alone, the SSRIs alone, or some combination of these may be required. In other cases, drugs that stabilize mood (and thus further decrease impulsivity) or that augment antidepressant action may be required.

The ability of antidepressants to enhance serotonin function after prolonged treatment is believed to relate to a number of mechanisms, depending upon the nature of antidepressant therapy (Blier et al., 1990; Price et al., 1990). Monoamine oxidase inhibitors (MAOIs) are believed to increase available releasable serotonin. Both the SSRIs and the MAOIs are thought to desensitize somatodendrite autoreceptors that inhibit the neural firing rate. Tricyclic antidepressants (TCAs) and tetracyclic antidepressants are assumed to sensitize postsynaptic receptors, and SSRIs are thought to desensitize serotonin-release-inhibiting thermal autoreceptors. It appears that serotonin function is enhanced after long-term treatment with SSRIs, TCAs, and MAOIs (Price et al., 1990). Trazodone (Desyrel) has serotonin-uptake-blocking properties, in addition to having other effects on neuronal activity (Asberg, 1986).

Another reason why the SSRIs are particularly appealing in the psychopharmacotherapy of depression associated with self-destructive behavior is that drugs with fewer pharmacological effects (in the case of SSRIs, the selective blockade of neuronal reuptake of serotonin) are likely to cause fewer side effects, and thus to enhance long-term compliance where prophylaxis is required. They are also less toxic in overdose than the more broad- spectrum antidepressants (Asberg, Eriksson, et al., 1986; Asberg, Nordstrom, & Traskman-Bendz, 1986).

When depression is part of a cyclic bipolar disorder, mood stabilizers are required. These include lithium carbonate, valproic acid, carbamazepine, beta- blockers, and calcium channel blockers. These drugs are more effective in ameliorating mania and hypomania than in assuaging depression. Suicide risk is greatest in bipolar patients when their mood switches from mania to depression or vice versa, because the energy to act impulsively is present concomitantly with feelings of despair. These are sometimes referred to as "mixed states" and are believed to be more responsive to valproate or carbamazepine than to lithium. These same drugs decrease impulsivity independently of their mood-stabilizing effect, and they augment the action of antidepressants when thymoleptics are not enough.

Some antidepressants and benzodiazepines counter panic attacks and other episodic and chronic manifestations of anxiety disorders, reducing the risk of suicide gestures and attempts when internal fear seems too great to be surmounted by other means. Clomipramine, fluoxetine, fluvoxamine, and sertraline reduce the obsessions and compulsions of obsessive–compulsive disorder. Antidepressants alone reduce the intrusive memories and recurrent dreams linked with PTSD, in addition to countering the anxiety, depression, and impulsivity seem with this disorder. Neuroleptics alone or with benzodiazepine therapy—for example, risperidone (Risperdal), thiothixene (Navane), or lorazepam (Ativan)—serve to manage acute psychotic episodes of a nonschizophrenic nature, as well as those of schizophrenia. Eating disorders respond to psychopharmacotherapy coupled with appropriate psychotherapy.

Serious questions arise at this time regarding the quality of care provided to self-destructive patients when medical, surgical, and psychiatric causes of suicidal ideation are not considered. Anxiety disorders (including obsessive–compulsive disorder and PTSD), major depression, bipolar disorders, schizophrenia, schizoaffective disorder, eating disorders, and other causes must be identified in order to provide patients with diagnosis-specific treatment. Recognition of the cause does not always assure that a patient will accept treatment, but it does assure that patients and families will be offered the highest level of care that medicine offers.

Only about one-third of affective illness that is antidepressant-responsive is treated, despite the fact that it is the single greatest risk factor for suicide and the fact that mood disorders selectively affect the talented and creative to a greater degree (Clayton, 1985; Slaby, 1994). However, not all depression is responsive to medication. This reality has at times led to some misimpressions regarding psychopharmacotherapy. For example, it was reported (Teicher, Glod, & Cole, 1990) that fluoxetine (Prozac) precipitated obsessive suicidal thoughts. Although this may be possible, there are a number of more common reasons besides drug induction why such thoughts or other symptoms should be observed in depressed patients being treated with antidepressants. First, not every patient provided with medication for depression responds immediately to the first drug used; indeed, some do not respond immediately or later, at any dose, or to any drug. The frustration experienced by such patients is no different from that experienced by patients with hypertension that is unresponsive even to treatment provided by the most eminent hypertension specialists. The only difference (which is significant) is that the former patients are depressed. In the hopelessness that is part of depression, they may become still more depressed and decide in some cases to kill themselves. In the instance of hypertension, they may go on in some cases to have a stroke or heart attack.

Second, it has long been known that suicide risk increases early in treatment with antidepressants, as energy returns more rapidly than feelings of despair disappear. This change creates a situation in which a patient who may have suffered from lethargy and lack of energy along with depression and hopelessness regains the energy before the depression lifts; this may give him or her the ability to act on the drive to end the pain through self-inflicted death. Finally, drugs such as fluoxetine (Prozac) and imipramine (Tofranil) may make some patients feel nervous and anxious, much as a patient with an untreated anxiety disorder feels. This increased nervousness or anxiety as a side effect may enhance the feeling of despair, as the condition appears to be worsening. This situation then may lead to a desire to commit suicide. Patients and significant others should be informed of potential side effects, in order to enhance the patients' compliance with pharmacotherapy and to permit early intervention when a side effect requiring cessation of the drug arises.

When recent history indicates that a patient is at immediate risk for suicide, the amount of antidepressant prescribed should be limited. Still, it is impossible to prevent overdose: Patients have ready access to other medications at home, to over-the-counter medications such as aspirin, and to other substances (e.g., rat poison and household cleaners) that can result in rapid death. A depressed patient with no recent history of a suicide attempt and no stated or elicited plans for death may be given a prescription for 1 month or more, as long as he or she is followed by a primary care physician or psychiatrist at regular intervals, and the patient and family members feel they may call the treating physician, his or her backup, or an emergency facility should a crisis arise. People who made attempts on their lives several years before are often given prescriptions with renewals longer than a month when they have been without plans to die for some time, and when they feel comfortable with their therapists and their therapists with them.

Social Support

As noted in the discussion of risk estimation, suicide risk is greatest for the socially isolated, particularly divorced, single, or separated men in late life (Canetto, 1992; Conwell, Caine, & Olsen, 1990; McIntosh, 1992; Rich, Warsradt, Nemiroff, Fowler, & Young, 1991). Gay youth do not have support at their age for their gender identity, resulting in their overrepresentation among adolescent suicides. Support groups for HIV-positive patients (Schneider, Taylor, Kemeny, & Hammen, 1991), gay youth, and single parents can reduce some stress by reducing isolation and allowing sharing of coping skills. Family work is important with all patients at risk, to help both the patients and their families. Seeing a patient with one or both parents, a sibling, a friend, or a lover allows the development of bonding to lessen the pain of depression; it also opens lines of communication between patients, support systems, and therapists. Mutually acceptable options and resources are explored, and alternative ways to cope with stress are developed.

If a person is profoundly depressed, hopelessness may not abate for some weeks with psychopharmacotherapy. If the depression was precipitated by social factors, such as rejection by family and friends for being gay, enhancing awareness that being homosexual is not pathological and in fact not uncommon, and establishing connections with a supportive gay community, may engender hope and reduce risk.

Individual and Family Therapy

Individual Therapy

The form of individual therapy and frequency of sessions should be tailored to patients' specific needs. At a time of crisis, daily visits or phone contacts may be needed to obviate self-harm. If exploratory therapy or less directive therapy leads to increased suicidal ideation, a more directive, supportive, or cognitive therapy may be required, and significant others should be called in for further support. Careful records should be kept of relative risk at times of crisis, and problem-specific treatment plans should be outlined.

Decreased risk of suicide or parasuicide is indicated by enhanced self-esteem and perceived ability to control one's environment or both; decreased depression and sensitivity to criticism; and better social adjustment (Sakinofsky & Roberts, 1990). Problem-solving-oriented therapy and sociotherapy should be part of a treatment plan with all suicidal patients (Fremouw, Callahan, & Kashden, 1993).

The outpatient psychotherapy to accompany pharmacological treatment of suicide impulses should focus on development of less self-destructive means of coping with stress, option elaboration, development of social support, amelioration of learned helplessness, and enhancement of self-esteem. Learned helplessness and low self-esteem are natural sequelae of an untreated depression. Cognitive therapy is particularly helpful (Hollon,

1990), and may in fact be the principal modality of treatment when drug therapy is not indicated. In some cases, it may be comparable in effectiveness to therapy with TCAs. It is also an important conjunctive therapy in cases of biologically based depression when employed to minimize likelihood of exacerbation. The success of cognitive therapy is predicated on the assumption that maladaptive information processing and erroneous information play a causal role in the onset of some depressions, in exacerbations of depression, and in the persistence of learned helplessness after the neurovegetative signs of depression remit.

Family Therapy

All illnesses are family illnesses. Cancer and AIDS, for example, have a far-reaching impact on all family members. The family component, however, is probably greatest with psychiatric disorders in which suicide is threatened or has occurred. There are social, psychological, biological, and existential contributing factors and sequelae. This is particularly true in regard to suicidal adolescents and children (Hendin, 1991; Roy, Segal, Centerwall, & Robinette, 1991; deWilde, Kienhorst, Diekstra, & Wolters, 1992). Adolescents are more prone to peer pressure, as seen in suicide epidemics and in the suicides of gay youth, the physically handicapped, and youth with substance abuse. Suicidal behavior and ideation may also relate to parental problems over which children have little control (Pfeffer, 1985). Risk is best managed when family or couple therapy and individual therapy are used in combination with psychopharmacotherapy.

Concurrent Substance Use Treatment

Substance misuse and self-medication of a primary psychiatric disorder lead to increased impulsivity and poor judgment, and thus enhance suicide risk (Bartels, Drake, & McHugo, 1992; Marzuk et al., 1992; Murphy, Wetzel, Robins, & McEvoy, 1992; Ojehagen, Berglund, & Appel, 1992). Over time, substance use can become a problem in itself, requiring both detoxification and a concurrent substance use treatment program of the Twelve Step variety, with a sponsor, home group, and 90 meetings in 90 days. Clonazepam (Klonopin), sometimes supplemented with carbamazepine (Tegretol), is frequently used for alcohol and sedative/hypnotic withdrawal, and clonidine (Catapres) is used for opiate withdrawal. Disulfiram (Antabuse) and naltrexone (ReVia) are used to reduce impulsive alcohol abuse and to reduce alcohol craving in selected patients, respectively.

Medical Consultation

At times, as noted earlier, suicidal ideation is a result of medication or a primary medical/surgical disorder. For instance, if depression and suicidal thoughts are due to use of a hypertensive patient's propranolol (Inderal), the patient's internist should be advised so that the medication can be either reduced or discontinued, and another beta-blocker with less depresso-genic effect or an antihypertensive from another class (e.g., calcium channel blocker) can be chosen.

Outpatient ECT

ECT may be indicated for an acutely suicidal patient to prevent self-harm before psychopharmacotherapy can take effect, for a patient who wishes rapid remission of depressive symptoms while awaiting therapeutic levels of antidepressant therapy, or for a patient whose depression is resistant to pharmacological treatment. It may be solely prescribed on an outpatient basis, or provided after an initial course of treatment in the hospital for maintenance. There are a number of myths regarding ECT use and its side effects. Prospective candidates can have their anxieties assuaged by speaking to someone who has had a successful course of ECT.

Psychoeducation

Teaching patients, families, teachers, clergy, caregivers, and others how to recognize individuals at risk of suicide, and educating them about the roles of medication, therapy, and social support, can reduce patients' risk and can help reduce the anxiety of those wishing to help. Psychoeducation about suicide risk should cover signs of increasing severity of depression, as well as signs of increasing risk of self-harm. Again, weight loss, social isolation, sleep disturbance, impulsivity, decreasing work and school per-formance, and agitation suggest worsening depression; lack of plans for the future and giving away prized possessions indicate evolving plans to die.

Access to Help

Any patient at risk of suicide should be provided with the therapist's phone numbers, the therapist's backup's phone numbers, and a place to call if neither clinician responds in a timely manner. Lack of access to help at a time of despair may result in panic, anger, and impulsive acts.

Realistic Goals

Caregiver and family uncertainty may be reduced when all parties understand that there are limits to what is possible. Most depressions (viz., 70% to 85%) respond predictably to antidepressant therapy, many with the first drug chosen. However, side effects may occur, limiting choice and dosage; risk may also increase in the course of therapy when energy returns before the feelings of hopelessness, helplessness, and worthlessness abate, as noted earlier. In a few instances, ECT for an inpatient or outpatient may be required. Few affective disorders are totally treatment-refractory, although the rate of recovery may be below expectations. Schizophrenia, on the other hand, has the same lifetime risk of suicide as major depression (viz., 10% to 15%) but has a considerably worse prognosis.

Another factor of which patients and their significant others should be aware is that what works at one point in the course of depression treatment may not at another point, and case management may need to be altered. In some instances, time—a long time, by patients' and therapists' standards—is required to allow diminution of the desire to die. Even more time (more than a year) may be required to help patients regain or acquire a lust for life that in itself counters a desire to die.

Record Keeping

Careful records should be kept at all times indicating why a patient was prescribed a particular medication, why dosage changes were made, why a certain type of psychotherapy was chosen, why or why not hospitalization was elected, and what the relative risk of suicide was at *each* visit during a crisis.

HELPING THE SURVIVORS OF SUICIDE

Loss of a loved one to suicide is one of the most painful, if not the most painful, of human experiences. Few people understand that the choice to die by suicide is seldom self-determined, but is usually driven by a distortion of perception by a biochemical defect. However, sometimes a survivor *has* played a role in the person's choice (e.g., a parent's rejection of a child because he or she is gay or has sought a lifestyle different from the parent's); in such a case, guilt may be overwhelming. Survivors are awash in confused feelings—guilt, grief, anger, and despair—which may increase the survivors' own risk of self-inflicted death. Each day they may find themselves playing the game of "if's": "What if I said that? What if I didn't? What if we divorced? What if we didn't?" Survivors may find themselves especially uneasy one day and then realize it is the day of the month a friend or family member committed suicide. Suicide survivor groups help survivors learn both what feelings to expect and how the course of grief usually runs. The pain of losing someone to suicide is never totally ameliorated. It only becomes tolerable as the thread of loss is woven into the fabric of the survivor's life with threads of more happy moments. It is always there, and the survivor's eye always is quick to sight it.

When suicide occurs, those who survive must be supported. The impact of suicide is incomprehensible to most; it is best understood by others who have experienced it. The loss is always painful, never fully forgotten, and unique for everyone (Kovarsky, 1989). Referral to a survivor group should be provided for all who have suffered such a loss. Survivors may not want to exercise the option at the time, but it should be available if the need or wish for it emerges.

SUMMARY

In summary, most suicides are preventable if the psychiatric disorders responsible for clinical symptoms and impulsivity are identified early and treated aggressively via psychopharmacology, and if any attendant (or, in some instances, predominant) psychosocial stress factors are ameliorated through therapy. A clinician is not omnipotent. A profoundly despairing person can lie about plans, and can hoard medicine even if it is prescribed weekly or less often. The best care for potentially suicidal patients consists of initial and recurrent assessment of risk; timely intervention early in the course of the illness responsible for the suicidality; and provision of support for those especially at risk, regardless of symptoms.

REFERENCES

Achte, K. (1988). Depression and suicide. *Psychopathology, 19,* 210–214.
Alessi, N. E., McManus, M., Brickman, A., et al. (1984). Suicidal behavior among serious juvenile offenders. *American Journal of Psychiatry, 141,* 286–287.
Alfonso, C. A., & Cohen, M. A. A. (1994). HIV-dementia and suicide. *General Hospital Psychiatry, 16,* 45–46.

Apter, A., Kutler, M., Levy, J., Plutchik, R., Brown, S.-L., Foster, H., Hillbrand, M., Koch, M. L., & vanPraag, H. M. (1991). Correlates of risk of suicide in violent and nonviolent psychiatric patients. *American Journal of Psychiatry, 148,* 883–887.

Asarnow, J. R., & Carlson, G. (1988). Suicide attempts in preadolescent child psychiatry inpatients. *Suicide and Life-Threatening Behavior, 18,* 129–136.

Asberg, M. (1980). Biochemical abnormalities in depressive illness. In G. Curxon (Ed.), *The biochemistry of psychiatric disturbance.* New York: Wiley.

Asberg, M. (1986). Biochemical aspects of suicide. *Clinical Neuropharmacology, 9*(Suppl. 4), 374–376.

Asberg, M., Eriksson, B., Martensson, B., et al. (1986). Therapeutic effects of serotonin uptake inhibitors in depression. *Journal of Clinical Psychiatry, 40*(Suppl. 4), 23–35.

Asberg, M., Nordstrom, C., & Traskman-Bendz, L. (1986). Biochemical factors in suicide. In A. Roy (Ed.), *Suicide.* Baltimore: Williams & Wilkins.

Asberg, M., Nordstrom, C., & Traskman-Bendz, L. (1990). Cerebrospinal fluid studies in suicide: An overview. *Annals of the New York Academy of Sciences, 487,* 243–255.

Asberg, M., Schalling, D., Traskman-Bendz, L., et al. (1986). Psychobiology of suicide, impulsivity, and related phenomena. In H. Y. Meltzer (Ed.), *Psychopharmacology: A third generation of progress.* New York: Raven Press.

Asnis, G. M., Harkary, R. G., Friedman, J. M., Igbal, N., et al. (1990). The drug-free period: A methodological issue. *Biological Psychiatry, 15*(6), 657–660.

Bartels, S. J., Drake, R. E., & McHugo, G. J. (1992). Alcohol abuse, depression, and suicidal behavior in schizophrenia. *American Journal of Psychiatry, 149,* 394–395.

Beck, A. T., Brown, G., Berchick, R. J., et al. (1990). Relationship between hopelessness and ultimate suicide: A separation with psychiatric outpatients. *American Journal of Psychiatry, 147,* 190–195.

Beck, A. T., Steer, R. A., Beck, J. S., & Newman, C. F. (1993). Hopelessness, depression, suicidal ideation, and clinical diagnosis of depression. *Suicide and Life-Threatening Behavior, 23*(2), 139–145.

Beck, A. T., Steer, R. A., Kovacs, M., & Garrison, B. (1985). Hopelessness and eventual suicide: A 10 year prospective study of patients hospitalized with suicide ideation. *American Journal of Psychiatry, 142,* 559–563.

Black, D. W., Warack, G., & Winokur, G. (1985). The Iowa Record-linkage Study: Suicide or accidental deaths among psychiatric patients. *Archives of General Psychiatry, 42,* 71–75.

Blier, P., deMontigny, C., & Chaput, Y. (1990). A role for the serotonin system in the mechanism of action of antidepressant treatment: Preclinical evidence. *Journal of Clinical Psychiatry, 51*(Suppl.), 4–20.

Braunig, P., Rao, M. L., & Fimmirs, R. (1989). Blood serotonin levels in suicidal schizophrenic patients. *Acta Psychiatrica Scandinavica, 79,* 206–209.

Brent, D. A., Perper, J. A., Goldstein, C. E., Kolko, D. L., et al. (1988). Risk factors for adolescent suicide. *Archives of General Psychiatry, 45,* 581–588.

Brier, A., & Astrachan, B. M. (1984). Characterization of schizophrenic patients who commit suicide. *American Journal of Psychiatry, 141,* 206–209.

Bulik, C. M., Carpenter, L. L., Kupfer, D. V., et al. (1990). Features associated with suicide attempts in recurrent major depression. *Journal of Affective Disorders, 18,* 29–37.

Caldwell, C. B., & Gottessman, I. I. (1990). Schizophrenics kill themselves too: A review of risk factors for suicide. *Schizophrenia Bulletin, 16*(4), 571–589.

Canetto, S. S. (1992). Gender and suicide in the elderly. *Suicide and Life-Threatening Behavior, 22*(1), 80–97.

Casey, P. R. (1989). Personality disorder and suicide intent. *Acta Psychiatrica Scandinavica, 79,* 290–295.

Cheetham, S. C., Crampton, C., Czudek, R., et al. (1986). Serotonin concentrations and turnover in the brains of depressed suicides. *Brain Research, 502,* 332–340.

Clark, D. C., Young, M. A., Scheftner, W. A., et al. (1987). A field test of Motto's risk estimators for suicide. *American Journal of Psychiatry, 144,* 923–926.

Clayton, P. J. (1985). Suicide. *Psychiatric Clinics of North America, 8,* 203–214.

Cohen, L. J., Test, M. A., & Brown, R. L. (1990). Suicide and schizophrenia: Data from a psychiatric community treatment study. *American Journal of Psychiatry, 147,* 602–607.

Conwell, Y., Caine, E. D., & Olsen, K. (1990). Suicide and cancer in late life. *Hospital and Community Psychiatry, 41,* 1334–1339.

Cox, B. J., Direnfeld, D. M., Swinson, R. P., & Norton, G. R. (1994). Suicidal ideation and suicide attempts in panic disorder and social phobia. *American Journal of Psychiatry, 151,* 882–887.

Cox, R. C., & Meltzer, H. Y. (1989). Serotonergic measures in the brains of suicide victims: 5HT2 binding sites in the frontal cortex of suicide victims and control subjects. *American Journal of Psychiatry, 146,* 730–736.

Dassori, A. M., Mezzich, J. E., & Keshavan, M. (1990). Suicidal indicators in schizophrenia. *Acta Psychiatrica Scandinavica, 81,* 409–413.

deWilde, E. J., Kienhorst, C. W. M., Diekstra, R. F. W., & Wolters, W. H. G. (1992). The relationship between adolescent suicidal behavior and life events in childhood and adolescence. *American Journal of Psychiatry, 149,* 45–51.

Diekstra, R. F. W., & Van Egmond, M. (1989). Suicide and attempted suicide in general practice, 1979–1986. *Acta Psychiatrica Scandinavica, 79,* 268–275.

Dilsaver, S. C., Chen, Y.-W., Swan, A. C., Schoaib, A. M., & Krajewski, K. J. (1994). Suicidality in patients with pure and depressive mania. *American Journal of Psychiatry, 151,* 1312–1315.

Egeland, J. A., & Sussex, J. W. (1985). Suicide and family loading for affective disorders. *Journal of the American Medical Association, 254,* 915–918.

Farmer, R. D. T. (1988). Assessing the epidemiology of suicide and parasuicide. *British Journal of Psychiatry, 153,* 16–20.

Fowler, R. C., Rich, C. L., & Young, D. (1986). San Diego Suicide Study: II. Substance abuse in young cases. *Archives of General Psychiatry, 43,* 962–965.

Fremouw, W., Callahan, T., & Kashden, J. (1993). Adolescent suicidal risk: Psychological, problem solving, and environmental factors. *Suicide and Life-Threatening Behavior, 23*(1), 46–54.

Friedman, R. C., Aronoff, M. S., Clarkin, J. F., Corn, R., et al. (1983). History of suicidal behavior in depressed borderline inpatients. *American Journal of Psychiatry, 139,* 1484–1486.

Friedman, S., Jones, J. C., Chernen, L., & Barlow, D. H. (1992). Suicidal ideation and suicide attempts among patients with panic disorder: A survey of two outpatient clinics. *American Journal of Psychiatry, 149,* 680–685.

Fyer, M. R., Francis, A. J., Sullivan, T., Hurt, S. W., et al. (1988). Suicide attempts in patients with borderline personality disorder. *American Journal of Psychiatry, 145,* 737–739.

Garfinkel, B. D., Froese, A., & Hood, J. (1982). Suicide attempts in children and adolescents. *American Journal of Psychiatry, 139,* 1257–1261.

Goldacre, M., & Hawton, K. (1985). Repetition of self-poisoning and subsequent death in adolescents who take overdoses. *British Journal of Psychiatry, 146,* 395–398.

Goldberg, R. J. (1987). Use of constant observation with potentially suicidal patients in general hospitals. *Hospital and Community Psychiatry, 38,* 303–305.

Griffith, E. H., & Bell, C. C. (1989). Recent trends in suicide and homicide among blacks. *Journal of the American Medical Association, 262,* 2265–2269.

Gross-Isseroff, R., Israeli, M., & Bregan, A. (1989). Autoradiographic analysis of tritiated imipramine binding in the human brain postmortem: Effects of suicide. *Archives of General Psychiatry, 46,* 237–241.

Hassam, R., & Tan, G. (1989). Suicide trends in Australia, 1901–1985: An analysis of sex differentials. *Suicide and Life-Threatening Behavior, 19,* 362–380.

Hellerstein, D., Frosch, W., & Kownigsberg, H. W. (1987). The clinical significance of command hallucinations. *American Journal of Psychiatry, 144,* 219–221.

Hendin, H. (1986). Suicide: A review of new directions in research. *Hospital and Community Psychiatry, 37,* 148–154.

Hendin, H. (1991). Psychodynamics of suicide with particular reference to the young. *American Journal of Psychiatry, 148,* 1150–1158.

Hendin, H., & Haas, A. P. (1991). Suicide and guilt as manifestations of PTSD in Vietnam combat veterans. *American Journal of Psychiatry, 148,* 586–591.

Henriksson, M. M., Aro, H. M., Marttunen, M. J., Heikkinen, M. E., Isometsa, E. T., Kvoppasalino, K. I., & Lonnquist, U. K. (1993). Mental disorders and comorbidity in suicide. *American Journal of Psychiatry, 150,* 935–940.

Hollon, S. D. (1990). Cognitive therapy and pharmacotherapy for depression. *Psychiatric Annals, 20,* 249–258.

Husain, S. A. (1990). Current perspective on the role of psychosocial factors in adolescent suicide. *Psychiatric Annals, 20,* 122–127.

Hutchinson, M. P., & Draguns, J. G. (1987). Chronic, early exposure to suicidal ideation in a parental figure: A pattern of presuicidal characteristics. *Suicide and Life-Threatening Behavior, 17,* 288–298.

Isometsa, E. T., Henriksson, M. M., Aro, H. M., & Lonnquist, J. K. (1994). Suicide in bipolar disorder in Finland. *American Journal of Psychiatry, 151,* 1020–1024.

Johnson, J., Weissman, M. M., & Klerman, G. L. (1990). Panic disorder, comorbidity, and suicide attempts. *Archives of General Psychiatry, 47,* 805–808.

Karlinsky, H., Taesk, G., Schwartz, K., Ennis, J., et al. (1988). Suicide attempts and resuscitation dilemmas. *General Hospital Psychiatry, 10,* 423–427.

Keller, M. B. (1990). Depression: Underrecognition and undertreatment by psychiatrists and other health care professionals. *Archives of Internal Medicine, 150,* 946–948.

Kerhof, R., & Bernasco, W. (1990). Suicidal behavior in jails and prisons in The Netherlands: Incidence, characteristics and prevention. *Suicide and Life-Threatening Behavior, 20,* 123–130.

Kovarsky, R. S. (1989). Loneliness and disturbed grief: A comparison of parents who lost a child to suicide or accidental death. *Archives of Psychiatric Nursing, 3,* 86–96.

Kramer, T. L., Lindy, J. D., Green, B. L., Grace, M. C., & Leonard, A. C. (1994). The comorbidity of post-traumatic stress disorder and suicidality in Vietnam veterans. *Suicide and Life-Threatening Behavior, 24*(1), 58–66.

Levine, S., Ancill, R. J., & Roberts, A. P. (1989). Assessment of suicide risks by computer-delivered self-rating questionnaire: Preliminary findings. *Acta Psychiatrica Scandinavica, 80,* 216–220.

Lindberg, L., Tuck, J. R., Asberg, M., et al. (1985). Homicide, suicide and CSF-5HIAA. *Acta Psychiatrica Scandinavica, 71,* 230–236.

Mann, J. J. (1987). Psychological predictors of suicide. *Journal of Clinical Psychiatry, 48,* 39–43.

Mann, J. J., Stanley, M., McBride, P. A., et al. (1986). Increased serotonin 2 and beta 1 receptor binding in the frontal cortex of suicide victims. *Archives of General Psychiatry, 43,* 954–959.

Margo, G. M., & Findel, J. A. (1990). Early dementia as a risk factor for suicide. *Hospital and Community Psychiatry, 41,* 676–678.

Marzuk, D. M., Tardiff, K., Leon, A. C., Stajic, M., Margam, L. B., & Mann, J. J. (1992). Prevalence of cocaine use among residents of New York City who committed suicide during a one-year period. *American Journal of Psychiatry, 149,* 371–375.

McIntosh, J. L. (1992). Epidemiology of suicide in the elderly. *Suicide and Life-Threatening Behavior, 22*(1), 15–35.

McIntosh, J. L., & Jewell, B. L. (1986). Sex difference trends in completed suicide. *Suicide and Life-Threatening Behavior, 16,* 16–27.

Modai, I., Apter, A., Meltzer, H., et al. (1989). Serotonin reuptake by platelets of suicidal and aggressive psychiatric inpatients. *Neuropsychobiology, 21,* 9–13.

Modestin, J., & Kopp, W. (1988). Study on suicide in depressed inpatients. *Journal of Affective Disorders, 15,* 157–162.

Murphy, E., Lindesay, J., & Grundy, E. (1986). 60 years of suicide in England and Wales: A cohort study. *Archives of General Psychiatry, 43,* 969–976.

Murphy, G. E. (1983). On suicide prediction and prevention. *Archives of General Psychiatry, 40,* 343–344.

Murphy, G. E. (1988). Suicide and substance abuse. *Archives of General Psychiatry, 45,* 593–596.

Murphy, G. E., Wetzel, R. D., Robins, E., & McEvoy, L. (1992). Multiple risk factors predict suicide in alcoholism. *Archives of General Psychiatry, 49,* 459–463.

Nordstrom, P., Samuelsson, M., Asberg, M., Trakman-Bendz, L., Asberg-Wistedt, A., Nordin, C., & Bertilsson, L. (1994). CSF 5-HIAA predicts suicide risk after attempted suicide. *Suicide and Life-Threatening Behavior, 24*(1), 1–9.

Ojehagen, A., Berglund, M., & Appel, C. P. (1993). Long-term outpatient treatment in alcoholics with previous suicidal behavior. *Suicide and Life-Threatening Behavior, 23*(4), 320–328.

Papadimitriou, G. N., Linkowski, P., Delarbre, C., & Mendlewicz, J. (1991). Suicide on the paternal and maternal sides of depressed patients with lifetime history of attempted suicide. *Acta Psychiatrica Scandinavica, 83*, 417–419.

Paris, J. (1990). Completed suicide in borderline personality disorder. *Psychiatric Annals, 20*, 19–21.

Paul, S. M. (1986). *Serotonin reuptake in platelets and human brain: Clinical implications.* Paper presented at the WPP Regional Symposium, Copenhagen.

Perez-Stable, E. J., Maranda, J., Munozrf, A., et al. (1990). Depression in medical outpatients: Underrecognition and misdiagnosis. *Archives of Internal Medicine, 150*, 1083–1088.

Pfeffer, C. R. (1985). Suicidal fantasies in normal children. *Journal of Nervous and Mental Disease, 173*, 78–83.

Pfeffer, C. R. (1986). *The suicidal child.* New York: Guilford Press.

Pfeffer, C. R. (1988). Risk factors associated with youth suicide: A clinical perspective. *Psychiatric Annals, 18*, 652–656.

Pfeffer, C. R. (1990). Clinical perspectives in treatment of suicidal behavior among children of adolescents. *Psychiatric Annals, 20*, 143–152.

Pokorny, A. D. (1983). Prediction of suicide in psychiatric patients: Report of a prospective study. *Archives of General Psychiatry, 40*, 249–257.

Prasod, A. J., & Kumar, W. (1988). Suicidal behavior in hospitalized schizophrenics. *Suicide and Life-Threatening Behavior, 18*, 265–269.

Prezant, D. W., & Neimeyer, R. A. (1988). Cognitive predictors of depression and suicide ideation. *Suicide and Life-Threatening Behavior, 18*, 259–264.

Price, L. H., Charney, D. S., Delgado, P. L., et al. (1990). Clinical data on the role of serotonin in the mechanisms of action of antidepressant drugs. *Journal of Clinical Psychiatry, 57*(Suppl. 4), 44–50.

Reich, P. (1989). Panic attacks and the risk of suicide. *New England Journal of Medicine, 321*, 1260–1261.

Rich, C. L., Fowler, R. C., Fogerty, L. A., & Young, J. G. (1988). San Diego Suicide Study: III. Relationships between diagnoses and stress. *Archives of General Psychiatry, 45*, 589–592.

Rich, C. L., Fowler, R. C., Young, J. G., & Blenkush, M. (1986). San Diego Suicide Study: Comparison of gay to straight males. *Suicide and Life-Threatening Behavior, 16*, 448–457.

Rich, C. L., Warsradt, G. M., Nemiroff, R. A., Fowler, R. C., & Young, J. G. (1991). Suicide, stressors, and the life cycle. *American Journal of Psychiatry, 148*, 524–527.

Rich, C. L., Young, J. G., Fowler, R. C., Wagner, J., et al. (1990). Guns and suicide: Possible effects of some specific legislation. *American Journal of Psychiatry, 147*, 342–346.

Robbins, D. R., & Alessi, N. E. (1985). Depressive symptoms and suicidal behavior in adolescents. *American Journal of Psychiatry, 142,* 588–592.

Rosenbaum, M. (1983). Crime and punishment—the suicide pact. *Archives of General Psychiatry, 40,* 979–982.

Rothberg, J. M., Ursano, R. J., & Holloway, H. C. (1987). Suicide in the United States military. *Psychiatric Annals, 17,* 545–548.

Roy, A. (1983). Family history of suicide. *Archives of General Psychiatry, 40,* 971–974.

Roy, A. (1989). Suicide. In H. Kaplan & B. Sadock (Eds.), *Comprehensive textbook of psychiatry* (5th ed., Vol. 5). Baltimore: Williams & Wilkins.

Roy, A. (1994). Recent biologic studies on suicide. *Suicide and Life-Threatening Behavior, 24,* 10–14.

Roy, A., Lamparski, D., DeJong, J., et al. (1990). Characteristics of alcoholics who attempt suicide. *American Journal of Psychiatry, 147,* 761–763.

Roy, A., Pichad, D., DeJong, J., Karoum, F., et al. (1989). Suicidal behavior in depression: Relationship to noradrenergic function. *Biological Psychiatry, 25,* 341–350.

Roy, A., Segal, N. L., Centerwall, B. S., & Robinette, C. D. (1991). Suicide in twins. *Archives of General Psychiatry, 48,* 29–32.

Roy-Byrne, P. P., Post, R. M., Hambrick, D. D., Leverich, G. S., et al. (1988). Suicide and its course of illness in major affective disorder. *Journal of Affective Disorders, 15,* 1–8.

Rudd, M. D. (1989). The prevalence of suicidal ideation among college students. *Suicide and Life-Threatening Behavior, 19,* 173–183.

Rudd, M. D., Cahm, P. F., & Rajab, M. H. (1993).Diagnostic comorbidity in persons with suicidal ideation and behavior. *American Journal of Psychiatry, 150,* 928–934.

Sakinofsky, I., & Roberts, R. S. (1990). Why parasuicides repeat despite problem resolution. *British Journal of Psychiatry, 156,* 399–405.

Scheftner, W. A., Young, M. A., Endicott, J., Coryell, W., et al. (1988). Family history and five year suicide risk. *British Journal of Psychiatry, 153,* 805–809.

Schlebusch, L., & Wessels, W. H. (1988). Hopelessness and low intent in para-suicide. *General Hospital Psychiatry, 10,* 209–213.

Schneider, S. G., Farberow, N. L., & Kruks, G. E. (1989). Suicidal behavior in adolescent and young gay men. *Suicide and Life-Threatening Behavior, 19,* 381–384.

Schneider, S. G., Taylor, S. E., Kemeny, M. E., & Hammen, C. (1991). AIDS-related factors predictive of suicidal ideation of low and high intent among gay and bisexual men. *Suicide and Life-Threatening Behavior, 21(4),* 313–320.

Schou, M., & Weeke, A. (1988). Did manic–depressive patients who committed suicide receive prophylactic or continuation treatment at the time? *British Journal of Psychiatry, 53,* 324–327.

Shafi, M., Carrigan, S., Whittenghill, J. R., & Derrick, A. (1985). Psychological autopsy of completed suicide in children and adolescents. *American Journal of Psychiatry, 142,* 1061–1064.

Shearer, S. L., Peters, C. P., Quaytman, M. S., & Woodman, B. E. (1988). Intent and lethality of suicide attempts among female borderline inpatients. *American Journal of Psychiatry, 145,* 1424–1427.

Shneidman, E. S. (1993). Suicide as psychache. *Journal of Nervous and Mental Disease, 181,* 147–149.

Slaby, A. E. (1986). Prevention, early identification, and management of adolescent suicidal behavior. *Rhode Island Medical Journal, 69,* 463–470.

Slaby, A. E. (1992). Creativity, depression and suicide. *Suicide and Life-Threatening Behavior, 22*(2), 157–166.

Slaby, A. E. (1994a). The neurobiology of suicide. In A. Leenaars, J. T. Maltsberger, & J. Neimeyer (Eds.), *Treatment of suicidal people.* Washington, DC: Taylor & Francis.

Slaby, A. E. (1994b). *Handbook of psychiatric emergencies: Crisis stabilization for the 1990's.* Norwalk, CT: Appleton & Lang.

Slaby, A. E. (1995). Suicide as an indicium of biologically-based brain disease. *Archives of Suicide Research, 1,* 59–73.

Slaby, A. E., & Dumont, L. E. (1992). Psychopharmacotherapy of suicidal ideation and behavior. In B. Bongar (Ed.), *Suicide: Guidelines for assessment, management, and treatment.* New York: Oxford University Press.

Slaby, A. E., & Garfinkel, L. F. (1994). *No one saw my pain: Why teens kill themselves.* New York: Norton.

Smith, K., & Crawford, S. (1986). Suicidal behavior among "normal" high school students. *Suicide and Life-Threatening Behavior, 16,* 313–323.

Soloff, D. H., Lis, J. A., Kelly, T., Cornelius, J., & Ulrich, R. (1994). Risk factors for suicidal behavior in borderline personality disorder. *American Journal of Psychiatry, 151,* 1316–1323.

Spurlock, J. (1990). Adolescent suicide: Introduction. *Psychiatric Annals, 20,* 120–121.

Stafford, M. C., & Weisheit, R. A. (1988). Changing age patterns of U.S. male and female suicide rates, 1934–1983. *Suicide and Life-Threatening Behavior, 18,* 149–163.

Stallines, L. (1990). Suicide mortality among Kentucky farmers, 1979–1985. *Suicide and Life-Threatening Behavior, 20,* 156–163.

Stanley, M., & Mann, J. J. (1983). Increased serotonin-w binding sites in frontal cortex of suicidal victims. *Lancet, i,* 214–216.

Stanley, M., & Stanley, B. (1988). Reconceptualizing suicide: A biological approach. *Psychiatric Annals, 101,* 645–651.

Stanley, M., & Stanley, B. (1990). Postmortem evidence of serotonin's role in suicide. *Journal of Clinical Psychiatry, 51*(Suppl. 4), 22–28.

Steer, R. A., Beck, A. T., Garrison, B., & Lester, D. (1988). Eventual suicide in interrupted and uninterrupted attempts: A challenge to the cry-for-help hypothesis. *Suicide and Life-Threatening Behavior, 18,* 119–128.

Stiffman, A. R. (1989). Suicide attempts in runaway youths. *Suicide and Life-Threatening Behavior, 19,* 147–159.

Sturner, W. Q. (1986). Adolescent suicide fatalities. *Rhode Island Medical Journal, 69,* 171–174.

Tanney, B. L. (1992). Mental disorders, psychiatric patients, and suicide. In R. W.

Maris, A. Berman, J. T. Maltsberger, & R. I. Yufit (Eds.), *Assessment and prediction of suicide.* New York: Guilford Press.

Teicher, M. H., Glod, C., & Cole, J. O. (1990). Emergence of intense suicidal preoccupation during fluoxetine treatment. *American Journal of Psychiatry, 147,* 207–210.

Thompson, J. W., & Walker, R. D. (1990). Adolescent suicide among American Indians and Alaska natives. *Psychiatric Annals, 20,* 129–133.

Traskman, L., Asberg, M., Benlsson, L., et al. (1981). Monoamine metabolites in CSF and suicidal behavior. *Archives of General Psychiatry, 38,* 631–636.

Traskman-Bendz, L., Asberg, N., Nordstrom, P., & Stanley, M. (1989). Biochemical aspects of suicidal behavior. *Progress in Neuropsychopharmacology and Biological Psychiatry, 13,* 335–344.

Traskman-Bendz, L., Asberg, M., & Schulling, D. (1990). Serotonergic function and suicidal behavior personality disorders. *Annals of the New York Academy of Science, 487,* 160–174.

Valzell, L. (1981). *Psychobiology of aggression and violence.* New York: Raven Press.

Van Praag, H. M. (1983). CSF 5-HIAA and suicide in non-depressed schizophrenics. *Lancet, ii,* 977–978.

Van Praag, H. M., & Plutchik, R. (1988). Increased suicidality in depression: Group or subgroup characteristic? *Psychiatry Research, 26,* 273–278.

Virkkunen, M., DeJong, J., Bartko, J., & Linnoila, M. (1989). Psychological concomitants of history of suicide attempts among violent offenders and impulsive fire setters: A follow-up study. *Archives of General Psychiatry, 46,* 604–606.

Wasserman, D., & Cullberg, J. (1989). Early separation and suicidal behavior in the parental homes of 40 consecutive suicide attempters. *Acta Psychiatrica Scandinavica, 79,* 296–302.

Weiden, P., & Roy, A. (1990). *General vs. specific risk factors for suicide in schizophrenia,* Internal report, Hillside Hospital, Long Island Jewish Medical Center, New Hyde Park, NY.

Weishaar, M. E., & Beck, A. T. (1992). Hopelessness and suicide. *International Review of Psychiatry, 4,* 177–184.

Weissman, M. M., Klerman, G. L., Markowitz, S., et al. (1989). Suicidal ideation and attempts in panic disorder and attacks. *New England Journal of Medicine, 321,* 1209–1214.

Yu-Chin, R., & Arcuni, O. J. (1990). Short-term hospitalization for suicidal patients within a crisis intervention service. *General Hospital Psychiatry, 12,* 153–158.

3

Inpatient Standards of Care and the Suicidal Patient: Part I. General Clinical Formulations and Legal Considerations

BRUCE BONGAR
RONALD W. MARIS
ALAN L. BERMAN
ROBERT E. LITMAN
MORTON M. SILVERMAN

Suicidal behaviors are ubiquitous in the hospital setting, and dangerousness to self is the most common reason for admission to a psychiatric unit (Friedman, 1989). As Friedman (1989) points out, the frequency of completed suicide in patients with a history of psychiatric hospitalization is many times that of patients in the general population. A survey of suicides in the Los Angeles area (Litman, 1982) found that 1% of patients being treated in general medical–surgical and/or psychiatric hospitals committed suicide during their hospital treatment. Approximately one-third of these suicides resulted in lawsuits against the hospital. Psychiatric units were the targets of about half of these suits.

After reviewing the malpractice claims data and examining the clinical literature on standards of care for non-hospitalized patients, we detailed in Chapter 1 the essential guidelines for sound assessment, intervention and management procedures in outpatient settings. The present chapter, Part I of a two-part series on inpatient care, continues this discussion through an examination of general standards of inpatient care for the adult suicidal patient. A subsequent chapter, Part II (Chapter 4), on specific danger zones and risk assessment issues in inpatient care, will examine in detail the issues of unit precautions; common mistakes in pharmacotherapy; the effects of managed care; the chronically suicidal patient and detailed considerations for not hospitalizing suicidal patients; the ward milieu; specific recommendations for discharge, pass, and aftercare planning; the role of electroconvulsive therapy; practicalities in ordering a "suicide watch," seclusion and restraint considerations; and finally, workable institutional policies and procedures for competent and reasonable inpatient care.

Fundamentally, the inpatient model we propose here is in accord with Gutheil (1992) that the best solution to the specter of liability following a patient's suicide is for the clinician to have provided well-documented good clinical care that followed acceptable standards of practice; also, that appropriate risk management is the core of a preventive approach to the unfortunate possibility of liability after the suicide of a patient (Gutheil, 1992). However, before proceeding, we must emphasize several points that will guide the discussion in both this chapter, and the subsequent chapter on specific inpatient techniques—namely, that in discussing clinical and legal issues of inpatient care, the law deals with *minimum standards*, not the highest ideals of practice or even optimal practice.

Recently, Monahan (1993) pointed out that for any such rules to be workable, they must be based on guidelines that reflect the minimal standard necessary for competent professional practice and not the ideals to which practitioners might aspire should they have access to unlimited resources. Maris and Berman (1992) pointed out that effective assessment and prediction guidelines must reflect the real world, and not be a "sterile, self-contained game, unrelated to treatment and suicide prevention" (p. 560). Unreasonable standards are an invitation to be sued; effective standards must be based on what we actually expect clinicians and staff to be able to do "in the real resource-constrained world of clinical practice" (Monahan, 1993, p. 247).

If we accept that, at times, the decisions of courts and juries can be seen as arbitrary, inconsistent, and unpredictable—turning as much upon the skill of rival attorneys and expert witnesses as upon the facts of the case—the concept of "standards" must by necessity include enormous amounts of "gray areas." In such a stormy sea, we often have only our training and observations on effective and practical methods to reduce risks to guide our way—recognizing that in each unique case, the practitioner must ultimately rely on his or her best judgment. We recognize, then, that any reasonable standard of care must acknowledge the vital importance of clinical judgment in working with a unique individual; that every decision in clinical practice has both risk and benefit to the patient; and that the task of the clinician, time and again, is to weigh these issues and make a judgment that is competent, prudent, and reasonable—based upon a reasonable amount of decision time for data collection and clinical formulation. We begin our consideration of inpatient guidelines by a review of the goals for the initial intake evaluation.

INITIAL INTAKE EVALUATION GOALS

We begin our consideration of inpatient guidelines with a review of the goals for the initial intake evaluation. A review of case law suggests that an acceptable standard of care requires an initial and periodic evaluation of suicide potential for *all* patients seen in clinical practice. The case law further shows that reasonable care requires that a patient who is "either suspected or confirmed to be suicidal" must be the subject of certain affirmative precautions (Simon, 1988, p. 85). The clinician who fails either to reasonably assess a patient's suicidality or fails to implement an appropriate management plan based on the detection of elevated risk is likely to be exposed to liability if the patient is harmed by a suicide attempt. As Simon notes, "the law tends to assume that suicide is preventable, in most circumstances, if it is foreseeable" (p. 85).

In addition to assessing and hospitalizing patients who present as at high risk of suicide at the initial inpatient admission evaluation, the clinician and staff will have to assess suicide risk in deciding issues of specific treatments, privileges, discharge and so forth. The inpatient staff will also have to deal (sometimes continuously) with the presence of suicidal thoughts, gestures, and impulses, within the context of the therapeutic milieu.

Litman (1957) has taken the position that in cases where the patient can function as an outpatient but is at high risk for suicide, it is the clinician's responsibility to ensure that the risk is made known to all concerned parties (i.e., the family and significant others). The clinician must dispassionately provide the family and significant others with an informed consent as to the risks and benefits of both inpatient and outpatient treatment (Sadoff, 1990). Mental health professionals may wish to consider routinely involving a senior colleague, who is expert in working with the suicidal scenario, for a "second opinion" on this particular decision (see Chapter 2).

When reviewing the clinicians' positions on outpatient care of patients at high suicidal risk, there is a general consensus (with one exception) that the outpatient environment exposes the patient to much greater danger, because the patient is not under 24-hour restrictive care. Thus, courts have typically seen a psychiatric decision to hospitalize as the more usual and customary one for a patient who is at high and imminent risk. Hospitals are usually seen as the environment where maximum protection can best be provided.

However, clinicians should heed the warning of Klerman (1986) that clinicians must carefully examine their own policies and procedures for hospitalizing patients to insure that their decisions are actual risk–benefit decisions, focused on the optimal care and safety of the patient, and not merely defensive reactions based on fear of litigation. Klerman has cautioned further that because of this threat of litigation, the clinician may become so concerned with the question of hospitalization that vital details in therapy are missed. Moreover, the inability of the clinician to deal effectively with the anxiety of the situation may influence the course of the treatment—and not necessarily in ways that are beneficial to the patient.

Therefore, any inpatient standard of care must assume the ability of clinicians to make decisions effectively and appropriately—based on their personal and professional tolerances and competencies, and on the nature of the therapeutic relationship (Bongar, 1991). It is also necessary to emphasize that despite the outpatient psychotherapist's best efforts, the patient may still require voluntary or involuntary hospitalization (Simon, 1988).

THE DECISION TO SEEK INPATIENT CARE

It is essential that clinicians recognize that the decision to hospitalize a patient should not end at the point of admission (Schutz, 1982); rather, the referring clinician should be aware of the type of facility he or she is sending a patient to (e.g., accredited or unaccredited), and needs to make a judgment on it's capability to provide the reasonable level of care necessary to assure the safety of the patient. (Note that in the eyes of the law, the word "reasonable" in this context should reflect the minimal, not optimal, standard for unit precautions necessary to provide competent professional treatment.) Such information might include a working knowledge of unit architecture, safety procedures, pass and discharge policies, milieu treatment, staffing patterns, and past performance of the inpatient unit. In addition to referring the patient to an appropriate hospital, Schutz noted that the therapist must provide adequate information to the institution to allow the professionals there to make a competent and independent assessment of suicide risk for the patient. Moreover, if the mental health professional is the primary inpatient attending clinician, the attending clinician should provide his or her own clear supervision orders in writing to the staff of the hospital at the time of the request for admission. According to Schutz, if the therapist withholds key facts, provides inappropriate supervision orders, or, most importantly, fails to insure that his or her orders were correctly carried out, the therapist may be liable.

GENERAL PRINCIPLES OF INPATIENT MANAGEMENT

The reader is directed to the works of Benensohn and Resnik (1973), Bongar, (1991), Friedman, (1989), Furrow (1980), Litman (1982), Maris, Berman, Maltsberger, and Yufit (1992), Schutz (1982), and Simon (1987, 1988) for additional general risk management policies, standards of care, and safety precautions.

However, it is useful to review the general principles of inpatient management. Simon (1988) noted that intervention in inpatient settings usually requires "screening evaluations; case review by the clinical staff; development of an appropriate inpatient and post-discharge treatment plan, and implementation of that plan" (p. 84).

He further noted that careful documentation of all assessments and management decisions (with careful and timely amendments, responsive to any changes in the patient's clinical circumstances) are usually considered the foundation for clinically and legally sufficient inpatient care. It is important to remember that although the courts have moved in recent years towards a more open door policy, there is still a split in court decisions over the use of this technique. The clinician should assess carefully both local and state standards in his or her area. One's state psychiatric or psychological association, state department of mental health, and so forth, are usually good resources for obtaining this information.

Because hospitals, inpatient attending staff, and other staff have been "put on notice" by the reason for the hospitalization (e.g., a suicide attempt, serious threats, impulses, etc.), affirmative precautions (e.g., one-on-one supervision or inpatient observation) can be extended to the suicidal patient. However, there is "no such thing as a suicide-proof unit" (Simon, 1988, p. 95). The illusion of this possibility can be dangerous to patients and to staff. Jacobs (1989) pointed out that although death is an accepted occurrence in most medical specialities, it is a relatively uncommon event in mental health care. The fact that the possibility of death is ever-present in the treatment of suicide can be a very difficult and discouraging situation in which to work. However, clinicians must not avoid situations where patients seem beyond help or beyond hope. Jacobs recalled that when he was a psychiatric resident at the Massachusetts Mental Health Center, the superintendent used to say, "Hospitals that don't have suicides are turning away sick people" (Jacobs, 1989, p. 331).

Litman (1982) also stated that hospitals should develop formal policies and standards for the inpatient management of suicide; staff should be trained in these policies; and most importantly, quality assurance mechanisms should be in place to insure that these policies are actually being applied, reviewed, and updated. Again, both Litman (1982), Maris and Berman (1992), and Monahan (1993) emphasize that any guidelines must reflect the *minimal standards* necessary for competent professional practice. For example, an unrealistic and unworkable standard might propose that "all records of prior treatment shall be obtained, or that all significant others will be questioned about a patient's history" (Monahan, 1993, p. 247).

GENERAL STANDARDS OF INPATIENT MANAGEMENT

Litman (1982) noted that the standards for reasonable psychiatric care with regard to suicide prevention "are unclearly stated and inconsistently applied" (p. 213). He pointed out that courts have generally tended to hold institutions to standards of care that are equivalent to standards prevailing in the community. The duty of a psychiatric hospital can best be defined "as the generally accepted standard of using reasonable care in the treatment of the patient. If, however, a hospital is on notice that a patient has suicidal tendencies, the hospital also assumes the duty of safeguarding the patient from self-inflicted injury or death" (Robertson, 1988, p. 193). The psychiatric hospital's duty of care is measured by the standards typically in use by such psychiatric hospitals (or by general hospitals with psychiatric units) under similar circumstances. At the same time, as a rule, a general hospital is usually held to a lower standard of care than a psychiatric hospital. However, a general hospital that provides psychiatric care and has a psychiatric floor must adhere to the standards of psychiatric hospitals (Robertson, 1988).

This duty is proportionate to a patient's needs, that is, the facility must provide the care that the patient's history and mental condition dictate as adequate. (Note that these needs may change and fluctuate over the course of the hospitalization.) However, the hospital is not required to guard against or "take measures to avert what a reasonable person under the circumstances would not anticipate as likely to happen" (Robertson, 1988, p. 193). Just as in the liability of the individual clinician, the hospital and staff's liability is based on foreseeability. Still, even when there is a private attending clinician in charge of the patient's care, the hospital and its staff must perform proper observations, make thorough evaluations, and take affirmative precautions if needed.

When litigation ensues, the two issues of foreseeability and causation are typically determined based upon the testimony of expert witnesses as to the performance of the attending clinician(s) and of the hospital and inpatient staff (Litman, 1982).

Robertson (1988) commented that typically the exercise of sound judgment provides a good defense for the hospital. Hospitals have not generally been found to be liable when a doctor has determined in his or her opinion that surveillance was adequate (see *Sklarsh v. United States,* 1961; *Lichtenstein v. Montefiore,* 1977).

As we have already stated, hospitals should formulate written administrative and professional policies concerning the care of suicidal patients. Moreover, these policies need to agree with the guidelines of the American Psychiatric Association and Joint Commission on Accreditation of Hospitals, and to be conventionalized for all hospitals (Litman, 1982).

Litman (1982) cited a number of cases where the following problems were the cause of litigation: a case where the patient was diagnosed as high-risk, but an order for active suicide precautions was not followed correctly (verdict for the plaintiff of $125,000); a case where the suicide attempt was not taken seriously and the physician did not take time to work up the patient adequately or make a complete diagnostic evaluation (verdict for the plaintiff of $150,000); the case of a small remote community hospital with a very small psychiatric unit and only a part-time psychiatrist available (the jury voted 9 to 3 not to impose liability, feeling that this unit should not be held to the high standards of an urban hospital); finally, a case where the clinician had a daily working inpatient therapeutic relationship with the patient, where pass/discharge risks were calculated and the treatment plan was followed, but where the doctor's risk–benefit decision turned out to be in error, that is, while on a pass, the patient jumped to his death. In this last case, Litman believed it was not negligent to have taken a calculated risk.

But perhaps most importantly, Robertson lists the eight most common allegations for a complaint for malpractice following a patient's suicide:

1. Failure to predict or diagnose the suicide.
2. Failure to control, supervise or restrain.
3. Failure to take proper tests and evaluations of the patient to establish suicide intent.
4. Failure to medicate properly.
5. Failure to observe the patient continuously (24 hours) or on a frequent enough basis (e.g., every 15 minutes).
6. Failure to take an adequate history.
7. Inadequate supervision and failure to remove belt or other dangerous objects.
8. Failure to place the patient in a secure room. (1988, pp. 198–199)

VOLUNTARY AND INVOLUNTARY HOSPITALIZATION

Even if it is apparent to the clinician that a suicidal patient needs referral to an inpatient facility, constraints unique to a specific environment can make such placements quite difficult (Maris & Berman, 1992). For example, in Massachusetts, recent rulings by the Department of Mental Health require completion of extensive documentation every 3 hours when a patient is in seclusion or restraint. As a consequence, few private hospitals accept involuntary patients or patients who may require these precautions. In order to admit a patient into a state hospital in Massachusetts, the clinician must obtain approval of a screening team from the patient's mental health catchment area. Some local mental health teams will not give approval without first assessing the patient. The problem is that although these requirements must be met, alternative placement is not guaranteed (Peterson & Bongar, 1989).

Initiating an involuntary hospitalization under a state's civil commitment guidelines may be one of the final options for the suicidal patient who meets the legislated criteria for mental illness and dangerousness, often interpreted as the patient's presenting an imminent danger to self or to others. If a clinician is seeing a suicidal outpatient and makes a gross error in deciding not to seek commitment for the patient meeting the legal criteria, he or she may well be held liable (Simon, 1988).

Simon (1987, 1988) pointed out an additional number of considerations when contemplating hospitalization. For example, clinicians may also need to consider the involvement of law enforcement agencies with a paranoid patient who has become overwhelmed by paranoid thoughts. These patients are not only at risk for suicide, but also for murder–suicide; if they feel that family members or other people in their immediate environment are part of conspiracies against them, paranoid patients may see suicide as the alternative (Allen, 1983).

In the case of suicide, there are two general determinations that must usually be made in civil commitment. The first is whether the person suffers from a disorder or defect that is a diagnosable mental disorder. Fremouw, de Perczel, and Ellis (1990) noted that the definition of mental disorder or defect does not always mean DSM criteria and that such definitions vary from state to state. Second, the person may present a "danger to self." In some jurisdictions, this requires "the identification of a recent overt act and not just an inferred state of dangerousness based on test data or speculation" (Fremouw et al., 1990, p. 95).

However, it is important to reiterate that criteria do vary from state to state. For example, in Texas, the clinician is required to obtain an evaluation by a second clinician and the signature of a justice of the peace to hold a patient against his or her will for 24 hours. Then, even if the patient is sent to a psychiatric screening facility for evaluation for possible hospitalization in the state hospital system, he or she may be released onto the street within 3 days. It is not uncommon to see such patients shortly return with a second suicide attempt (Peterson & Bongar, 1989). Such difficulties obviously create major problems for mental health professionals. Whether clinicians choose to admit it or not, the bureaucratic obstacles to inpatient hospitalization may color judgment about the possible risk of suicide (Peterson & Bongar, 1989).

Also, the concept of the "least restrictive environment" has evolved in the case law, which in theory translates as the idea that "patients should be treated in a facility with the fewest restrictions of liberty possible" (*Wyatt v. Stickney* 1971, cited in Fremouw et al., 1990, p. 95). Recently state courts have recognized the right of "involuntarily committed patients to refuse some types of psychiatric care if they are not in an emergency situation" [*Rennie v. Klein* 1979 and *Rogers v. Okin 1979*] (Fremouw et al., 1990, p. 95).

Other difficulties in hospitalization include the comorbidity of an alcohol or substance misuse diagnosis. Many substance abuse or alcohol treatment units will not accept suicidal patients, and few psychiatric units will accept patients with substance or alcohol abuse problems. These policies are sometimes supported by state laws or regulations (Peterson & Bongar, 1991).

Successful inpatient treatment may require an intense multidisciplinary and multimodal treatment team approach (Friedman, 1989; Maris & Berman, 1992), involving somatic therapies, cognitive-behavioral, psychodynamic, group and family therapies, and so forth, in addition to formal involvement of the interpersonal matrix and an ongoing assessment of the level of psychosocial supports. All of these are part of a well-integrated and unified treatment plan (Friedman, 1989; Maris & Berman, 1992; Peterson & Bongar, 1989). However, we must again emphasize that the above suggestions represent optimal rather than minimal standards, and that with regard to managed care situations, the

> early data suggest that the introduction of managed care itself has led to modifications in professional standards, with marked shifts from inpatient to outpatient treatment. (Appelbaum, 1993, p. 252)

Treatment for both inpatients and outpatients in an acute, overwhelming suicidal state usually takes the form of massive support on the patient's own terms. Psychological interpretation at such vulnerable moments can too easily generate a feeling of lethal distance (Motto, 1979). Motto, however, cautioned that this should not preclude "the use of dynamic understandings, but that such interpretation should be at a level and form that reflects acceptance, caring, and concern rather than intellectual explanation" (p. 5). He also noted that the therapist should be in close contact with the patient's psychosocial support system—family, close friends, priest/minister/rabbi, employer, and other important psychosocial resources—and also should be available to provide support to the interpersonal matrix and advise them in acute situations. The permission to respond to inquiries from friends and relatives, and the dynamics involved, should be clarified as early in treatment as possible. Shneidman (1981) also cautions on the need for an early assessment of the position of the support system vis-a-vis being supportive or unsupportive of life forces and of the patient's survival. See Bongar (1991) and Friedman (1989), and Maris and Berman (1992) for additional specific information.

SELECTED EXAMPLES OF MALPRACTICE ACTIONS INVOLVING INPATIENT MANAGEMENT FOLLOWING A PATIENT'S SUICIDE

The following brief samples of the court decisions on inpatient management illustrate repeatedly the twin criteria of foreseeability and causation. Psychotherapists and hospitals should diligently assess the suicidal potential of their patients and carefully implement affirmative treatments. The risk of suicide should be noted regularly in the management plan and be re-evaluated at each significant juncture in treatment, and whenever important management decisions are to be made (VandeCreek & Knapp, 1983). In addition, a new evaluation should be made whenever family, staff, and other significant others provide new information (see Farberow, 1981, for additional information on this point).

Failure to Use Good Judgment and to Evaluate

In *Kardas v. State* (1965) the wife of a patient who committed suicide filed a suit against the hospital and the patient's physician alleging failure to use good judgment. The physician had determined that the patient's condition did not present a risk of suicide. The instructions of the institute's physicians were that the patient be placed under "close observation." The patient was not permitted to leave the ward except on "accompanied walks," because he was excited at some times and depressed at others. Liability was not found. The court stated that the State, having through its physicians made a diagnosis of no suicidal tendency, was under no duty to guard against suicide and, having been under no duty, could not be held liable in negligence for the patient's death. The state, that is, could not be held liable for what, in retrospect, proved to be an error in judgment by the physician.

Failure to Evaluate and Failure to Observe

In *Smith v. United States* (1977), the widow and children of the patient brought suit against the Veterans Administration psychiatric hospital and its physicians after the patient was allowed to leave a locked ward without being evaluated and then threw himself in front of a train. The complaint alleged that there was both failure to evaluate and failure to observe. The court found liability and stated that prior to the patient's release from the locked ward, the accepted standard of care required that the patient be evaluated by a psychiatrist to determine whether he was sufficiently free from impulsive inclinations. It also was recognized that a proper evaluation by a psychiatrist of the patient on the day he was transferred, the day on which he committed suicide, would have detected the impulsive inclinations that caused the patient to commit suicide. He would not then have been granted the privileges that allowed him to kill himself. The family also alleged physicians were negligent in failing to note that the patient did not return to the hospital at 4:30 P.M., when sign-out privileges ended. If he had been missed at that time and a search had been initiated, he might have been found and returned to the locked ward before his death at 5 P.M.

Negligent Supervision and Failure to Adequately Observe

In *Torres v. State* (1975), the administrator of the patient's estate brought suit against a state hospital and alleged negligent supervision when the patient jumped off a bridge. The court ruled that the suicide was not caused by negligent supervision received at the hospital. The patient was placed in an open ward and granted an honor card that allowed him to leave the ward during daylight hours; nothing in the record indicated that the treatment he received was other than medically sound and proper. The patient never exhibited violent or suicidal tendencies, and the possibility of his committing suicide as a result of his increased freedom was not a foreseeable risk for which the state could be help liable.

Failure to Take Adequate Precautions

In *Dimitrijevic v. Chicago Wesley Memorial Hospital* (1968), the administrator of the patient's estate brought suit against a private hospital after a patient jumped from an 11th-floor window. The complainant alleged that the hospital was negligent in having the patient next to an unguarded window and not transferring him to a section of the hospital with locked doors and windows in accordance with a supervising physician's order. The court did not find liability and stated that unless the attending physician recommended special precautions against the suicide, the hospital was under no duty to take such precautions. The court noted that the evidence was conclusive that the supervising physician, as well as a psychiatric resident neither felt such instructions to be necessary nor gave them. The resident prescribed that the patient remain ambulatory, and the supervising physician was consulted by the hospital's administrator over the need for security precautions. Furthermore, the hospital contacted the supervising physician, who stated that the transfer was not an emergency and could be delayed until there was regular space available. The court concluded that the hospital had a right to rely on the instructions of the doctors.

In *Herold v. State* (1962), the husband of a woman who killed herself brought suit against a state hospital and the attendants when the patient was given a cloth and told to do some dusting. Approximately 10 minutes later, she was found hanging by the dust cloth in the nurses' bathroom. The court found liability and reversed a judgment in favor of the state dismissing a claim for a patient's wrongful death. The court entered judgment in favor of the patient's husband for her wrongful death by suicide. Following the patient's transfer, on the morning of the suicide, there were at least 31 patients in the open ward, with only two attendants present.

In *Zilka v. State* (1967), the administrator of the patient's estate brought suit after the patient died by a self-administered dose of rat poison. The plaintiff alleged that there was a failure to observe and that there was no record of any medical determination that the patient was fit for less restricted freedom than she had in the security ward. The court did not find liability and concluded that a medical determination that the patient was fit for the more unrestricted freedom was made when she was allowed to go home for a week approximately 2 months prior to her death. It also stated that there was no evidence of any suicidal inclinations from that time to the day she died. At any time during the 9-year period when the patient was in and out of the hospital, there was always present the opportunity for her to take her life. The court added that the fact that she did so while in the custody of the state hospital was one of those risks that society must be willing to accept if it is to hold out any hope for the mentally ill.

Negligent Assignment of Privileges

In *Schwartz v. United States* (1964), the administrator of the patient's estate brought suit against a government mental hospital after the patient hanged herself from a tree. The course of treatment for the patient included instituting a program of intensive individual psychotherapy, according the patient freedom of the grounds, and allowing the patient personal articles of clothing while she was unaccompanied on the grounds of the hospital.

The court concluded that the plaintiffs had been unable to show that these medical judgments, all of which were rendered by qualified staff psychiatrists in the performance of their duties at the hospital, were not rendered with the degree of skill and learning ordinarily possessed and exercised by psychiatrists in the locality at that time. It was noted that the patient never manifested a suicidal attempt or gesture while at the hospital. In addition, the plaintiff's witness stated that, in his opinion, granting the patient "grounds" privileges constituted good medical practice.

Failure to Provide Adequate Supervision

In *Wilson v. State* (1961), the husband of a patient sued a state hospital when the patient, who had attempted suicide in the past, jumped to her death using an unlocked laundry chute. The husband alleged that the failure to lock a laundry chute door, which was a violation of the rules of the hospital, resulted in the patient's jumping through chute and killing herself, and was the proximate cause of her death. The court found liability and noted that on the day of the occurrence, the attendant had unlocked the door to permit another patient to throw some bags of laundry down the chute. Some difficulty between other patients in the room distracted the attention of the attendant, and she closed the door without locking it and went to quiet the disturbance. The attendant did not recall leaving the chute unlocked until some 2.5 hours later, when she was informed that the patient was found at the bottom of the chute.

Overview

As all of the above cases show, hospitals should ask themselves the following:

> "Do we treat persons at special risk for suicide?" If yes, then there must be a security area and policies for special management of suicidal persons. (Litman, 1982, p. 220)

Such policies are best determined by a hospital suicide prevention committee that represents the staff and administration (Litman, 1982). Such a committee can establish written guidelines after a survey of the hospital security areas and after talking with staff and patients. It is critical that these policies be incorporated routinely into the training and supervision of all staff and attending, and that there be a regular mandatory review and updating of training and clinical competencies. Litman also stated that a reasonable performance requires that the "patient be evaluated for suicide risk, that a treatment plan be formulated, and that the staff follow the treatment plan according to the hospital's policies" (p. 220). Here, the treatment plan documents reasonable and prudent procedures for the monitoring, management, and aftercare of patients at high risk for continued suicidal behaviors.

CONCLUSION

A review of case law suggests that an acceptable standard of care requires an initial and periodic evaluation of suicide potential for *all* patients seen in clinical practice. Furthermore, well-known authorities and the case law tell us that a demonstration that reasonable care was taken requires that patients suspected or confirmed to be suicidal must be the subject of certain affirmative precautions. The courts will often assume that suicide is preventable in most reasonable circumstances if it is foreseeable.

However, the standards for reasonable psychiatric care with regard to suicide prevention are often perceived by clinicians and hospitals as unclearly stated and inconsistently applied. Generally, the courts have tended to hold institutions to standards of care that are equivalent to standards prevailing in the community. The psychiatric hospital's duty of care is measured by the standards used by psychiatric hospitals (or general hospitals with psychiatric units).

This duty is proportionate to a patient's needs (which means providing the adequate care that the patient's history and mental condition dictate). When litigation ensues, the two issues of foreseeability and causation are typically determined based upon the testimony of expert witnesses' opinions as to the performance of the attending clinician(s), hospital, and inpatient staff. The exercise of sound judgment provides a good defense for the hospital, and hospitals have not generally been found to be liable when a clinician in charge of the patient's care has determined in his or her opinion that surveillance was adequate.

We believe that it is crucial in most cases to involve the family and significant others in an open and candid discussion of the risks and benefits of a voluntary versus involuntary milieu, and the specifics of treatment and discharge/follow-up planning. This is important both to increase the levels of cooperation, and to depict realistically the actual abilities of inpatient facilities to treat the patient, and to protect the patient from self-harm (Slaby, Lieb, & Tancredi, 1986).

The inpatient treatment of the suicidal patient may include somatic therapies, cognitive-behavioral, psychodynamic, group, and family therapies, and so on, as well as formal involvement of the interpersonal matrix and an ongoing assessment of the level of psychosocial supports—all part of a well-integrated and unified treatment/management plan.

Finally, it is essential that all assessment, treatment, and management decisions, case conferences, telephone contacts with screening teams, and with hospitals, the patient, family contact, and all other activities and interactions be meticulously and contemporaneously documented. Both the legal system and an effective clinical standard require that clinicians and hospitals make appropriate and reasonable efforts to foresee elevated suicide risk. Once an elevated risk is determined, clinicians and institutions need to take affirmative precautions. Such precautions should entail balancing and carefully assessing both the risks and benefits of any subsequent management decision. Realistically, we know that psychiatric patients are at risk for completed and attempted suicide while in a psychiatric facility, and during the period following their discharge. In the final analysis, a workable standard of care must always rest on the clinician's exhibiting good judgment that is reasonable and prudent, and that includes timely consultation and documentation. While no empirical evidence exists that good clinical judgment saves lives, the common consensus among experts remains that this is still our best form of suicide prevention.

ACKNOWLEDGMENT

This chapter is reprinted from *Suicide and Life-Threatening Behavior, 23*(3), 245–256, Fall 1993. Copyright 1993 by the American Association of Suicidology. Reprinted by permission. Portions of the chapter are adapted from Bongar (1991). Copyright 1991 by the American Psychological Association. Adapted by permission.

REFERENCES

Allen, N. H. (1983). Homicide followed by suicide: Los Angeles, 1970–1979. *Suicide and Life-Threatening Behavior, 13*(3), 155–165.

Appelbaum, P. S. (1993). Legal liability and managed care. *American Psychologist, 48*(3), 251–257.

Benensohn, H., & Resnik, H. L. P. (1973). Guidelines for "suicide proofing" a psychiatric unit. *American Journal of Psychotherapy, 26,* 204–211.

Bongar, B. (1991). *The suicidal patient: Clinical and legal standards of care.* Washington, DC: American Psychological Association.

Dimitrijevic v. Chicago Wesley Memorial Hospital, 92 Ill. App. 2d 251, 236 N.E.2d 309 (1968).

Farberow, N. L. (1981). Suicide prevention in the hospital. *Hospital and Community Psychiatry, 32,* 99–104.

Fremouw, W. J., de Perczel, M., & Ellis, T. E. (1990). *Suicide risk: Assessment and response guidelines.* New York: Pergamon Press.

Friedman, R. S. (1989). Hospital treatment of the suicidal patient. In D. G. Jacobs & H. N. Brown (Eds.), *Suicide: Understanding and responding. Harvard Medical School perspectives on suicide* (pp. 379–402). Madison, CT: International Universities Press.

Furrow, B. R. (1980). *Malpractice in psychotherapy.* Lexington, MA: Lexington Books.

Gutheil, T. G. (1992). Suicide and suit: Liability after self-destruction. In D. Jacobs (Ed.), *Suicide and clinical practice* (pp. 147–167). Washington, DC: American Psychiatric Press.

Herold v. State, 15 App. Div. 2d 835, 224 N.Y.S.2d 369 (3d Dept.) (1962).

Jacobs, D. G. (1989). Evaluation and care of suicidal behavior in emergency settings. In D. G. Jacobs & H. N. Brown (Eds.), *Suicide: Understanding and responding. Harvard Medical School perspectives on suicide* (pp. 363–377). Madison, CT: International Universities Press.

Kardas v. State, 24 App. Div. 2d 789, 263 N.Y.S.2d 727 (3d Dept.) (1965).

Klerman, G. L. (Ed.). (1986). *Suicide and depression among adolescents and young adults.* Washington, DC: American Psychiatric Press.

Lichtenstein v. Montefiore Hospital & Medical Center, 56 App. Div. 2d 281, 392 N.Y.S.2d 18, (1st Dept.) (1977).

Litman, R. E. (1957). Some aspects to the treatment of the potentially suicidal patient. In E. S. Shneidman & N. L. Farberow (Eds.), *Clues to suicide* (pp. 111–118). New York: McGraw-Hill.

Litman, R. E. (1982). Hospital suicides: Lawsuits and standards. *Suicide and Life-Threatening Behavior, 12*(4), 212–220.

Maris, R. W., & Berman, A. L. (1992). Conclusions and recommendations. In R. W. Maris, A. L. Berman, J. T. Maltsberger, & R. I. Yufit (Eds.), *Assessment and prediction of suicide* (pp. 660–688). New York: Guilford Press.

Maris, R. W., Berman, A. L., Maltsberger, J. T., & Yufit, R. I. (Eds.). (1992). *Assessment and prediction of suicide.* New York: Guilford Press.

Monahan, J. (1993). Limiting therapist exposure to *Tarasoff* liability: Guidelines for risk containment. *American Psychologist, 48*(3), 242–250.

Motto, J. A. (1979). Guidelines for the management of the suicidal patient. *Weekly Psychiatry Update Series Lesson, 3,* 3–7. (Available from Biomedia, Inc., 20 Nassau Street, Princeton, NJ 08540)

Peterson, L. G., & Bongar, B. (1989). The suicidal patient. In A. Lazare (Ed.), *Outpatient psychiatry: Diagnosis and treatment* (2nd ed., pp. 569–584). Baltimore: Williams & Wilkins.

Rennie v. Klein, 462 F. Supp. 1131 (1979).

Robertson, J. D. (1988). *Psychiatric malpractice: Liability of mental health professionals.* New York: Wiley.

Rogers v. Okin, 478 F. Supp. 1342 (1979).

Sadoff, R. L. (1990). Argument for the plaintiff—Expert opinion: Death in hindsight. In R. I. Simon (Ed.), *Review of clinical psychiatry and the law* (pp. 331–335). Washington, DC: American Psychiatric Association.

Schutz, B. M. (1982). *Legal liability in psychotherapy.* San Francisco: Jossey-Bass.

Schwartz v. United States, 226 F. Supp. 84 (D.C. Dist. Col.) (1964).

Shneidman, E. S. (1981). Psychotherapy with suicidal patients. *Suicide and Life-Threatening Behavior, 11*(4), 341–348.

Simon, R. I. (1987). *Clinical psychiatry and the law.* Washington, DC: American Psychiatric Press.

Simon, R. I. (1988). *Concise guide to clinical psychiatry and the law.* Washington, DC: American Psychiatric Press.

Sklarsh v. United States, 194 F. Supp. (E.D.N.Y.) (1961).

Slaby, A. E., Lieb, J., & Tancredi, L. R. (1986). *Handbook of psychiatric emergencies* (3rd ed.). New York: Medical Examination.

Smith v. United States, 437 F. Supp. 1004, (E.D. Pa.) (1977).

Torres v. State, 49 App. Div. 2d 966, 373 N.Y.S.2d 696 (1975).

VandeCreek, L., & Knapp, S. (1983). Malpractice risks with suicidal patients. *Psychotherapy: Theory, Research and Practice, 20*(3), 274–280.

Wilson v. State, 14 App. Div. 2d 976, 221 N.Y.S.2d 354 (3d Dept.) (1961).

Wyatt v. Stickney, 325 F. Supp. 781 (1971).

Zilka v. State, 52 Misc. 2d 891, 277 N.Y.S.2d 312 (1967).

4

Inpatient Standards of Care and the Suicidal Patient: Part II. An Integration with Clinical Risk Management

MORTON M. SILVERMAN
ALAN L. BERMAN
BRUCE BONGAR
ROBERT E. LITMAN
RONALD W. MARIS

The treatment of suicidal inpatients involves the collaboration and coordination of clinician, hospital staff, and hospital administration. As opposed to the outpatient treatment and management of suicidal individuals, the fact of a hospitalization suggests the increased level of suicidality present in the individual and the need to rely upon more structured environments to provide the means and mechanisms to prevent the progression of suicidal behaviors (see Chapter 1). Whereas the outpatient setting constitutes three interlocking systems (patient, clinician, support network), the inpatient setting adds two more interlocking systems (hospital staff and hospital administration), with their own sets of duties, responsibilities, and limitations. Now the clinician is operating in a larger arena, incorporating additional contingencies, contexts, and concerns. For the inpatient treatment of suicidal patients, it is the coordinated interplay between all these systems that maximizes good outcomes.

As has been argued elsewhere (Bar-Levav, 1992; Brent, Kupfer, Bromet, & Dew, 1988; Klerman, 1986; Litman, 1982, 1992; Simon, 1988), the decision to hospitalize a suicidal patient carries its own set of risks (as well as anticipated benefits). Nevertheless, once this decision has been made, the process of providing a standard of care for a suicidal inpatient in this expanded domain requires additional steps and considerations. The purpose of this chapter is to provide clinicians, hospital staff, and hospital administration with perspectives on approaching standards of care commensurate with the appropriate assessment, treatment, supervision, and clinical management of suicidal inpatients.

Predicting suicidal behavior, even in psychiatric inpatients, is very difficult and often not possible on an individual basis (Pokorny, 1992, 1993). Nevertheless, a clinician, armed with significant information, can use his or her best judgment in assigning relative risk of suicidality on an individual basis (Litman, 1992). Two critical pieces of data are the presence or absence of a major psychiatric disorder, and whether there is a prior history of a suicide attempt.

Over the last quarter century, the standards of care for inpatients exhibiting suicidal behaviors have derived from a number of different but related sources: (1) case law (medical malpractice, court-determined professional standards); (2) statutory determined professional standards (set by professional organizations); (3) legal commentary on case law; (4) clinical practice and the teaching of clinical management skills; and (5) reports by forensic suicidologists of cases settled out of court (see Chapter 3).

This present chapter provides a summary and synthesis of trends and consensus positions resulting from these sources. Before embarking on a presentation of the standards of care for inpatient suicidal patients, we briefly review the pertinent terminology, concepts, and legal language that are most relevant to a discussion of the interface between standards of care and clinical risk management.

A word of caution is needed here. As cases come to the attention of forensic suicidologists or enter the legal literature, the standards of care may well expand or even contract (Amchin, Wettstein, & Roth, 1990). Hence, this chapter should not be construed as a static or comprehensive review of standards of care, but rather as an overview of the interface between the legal standards of care currently in place and the clinical risk management of suicidal inpatients. Because we are neither hospital administrators nor responsible for the direct training and supervision of hospital staff, our discussion of these two critical components in the overall coordination of care for suicidal inpatients derives from our own clinical, academic, and forensic work.

DEFINING STANDARDS OF CARE

The evolution of standards of care for inpatient suicidal patients took a dramatic leap in the late 1970s, when there was a shift in case law allowing for the filing of malpractice suits against clinicians when a patient died by self-injury while under the care of the clinician—whether in inpatient or outpatient settings (Wettstein, 1989). Standards of care for the appropriate assessment, treatment, and management of suicidal patients have evolved in the last quarter century as a result of court decisions, settlements out of court, development of clinical risk management concepts and practices, a resurgence in clinical care teaching and practice, the development and validation of new psychotherapies, and the revolution in psychopharmacology.

Despite this process, standards of care have remained an area of enormous ambiguity and vagueness. Case law presents unique case circumstances and contingencies that do not easily translate into generalities. Therefore, there is no universally agreed-upon list of *minimum* standards for the inpatient care of suicidal patients. Nor is there a uniform set of standards that provides an *optimum* standard for the care of all such patients (Berman & Cohen-Sandler, 1982). In fact, even full adherence to an "ideal" standard of care might result in a suicide outcome. In truth, the standard of care, that level of care provided by the mythical "average" practitioner operating in a reasonable and prudent manner, is defined by *opinions* of experts called upon as consultants in a tort action. Like experts, each clinician probably has in mind his or her own set of standards for the care of suicidal patients.

Ideally, in order to operationalize a set of minimum standards as they *currently* exist, one would survey a representative sample of clinicians who routinely provide inpatient clinical services and ask them what their actual clinical practice is in assessing, managing, and treating suicidal patients.

Such a field study has never been conducted and is fraught with its own set of problems, including but not limited to those of validity and reliability.

Much has been written about case law as it relates to suicidal behaviors, and much has been written about the hospital management of suicidal patients (Farberow, 1981; Friedman, 1989; Motto, 1979). Unfortunately, much of case law and reports of cases settled out of court inform us of standards of care and clinical practices that claim failures of omission. Furthermore, the case law in existence is based on a small subset of all malpractice actions initiated, the number of trial cases comprising fewer than 10% of all lawsuits filed (Gutheil, 1992). Much of the clinical risk management literature suggests optimal or ideal standards of conduct. Hence, there is a need for a synthesis between the two. We believe this chapter is the first attempt to clarify the minimal standards of care for the treatment of inpatient suicidal patients, as well as to provide clinical examples to illustrate the translation and expansion of these standards into good clinical practice.

ALLEGED FAILURES OF OMISSION AND COMMISSION

Standards of care refer to those categories of actions that demand attention by the clinician. As outlined below, these actions range from the initial assessment of a patient through aftercare planning following discharge from a hospital. Because there is great variability in how suicidal patients present clinically, the range of suicidal behaviors threatened or enacted, the unique circumstances that define individuals and their clinical contexts, the variability of inpatient settings, and the numerous traditions in training of clinicians, standards of care cannot be so specific that they become restrictive. Standards denote categories of action and suggest broad areas that must be attended to in the care of suicidal patients by "reasonable and prudent practitioners." Hence, standards are categories of actions that must be performed in order to provide the *minimum* standard of care in the assessment, treatment, and management of suicidal patients in inpatient settings.

Many authors (Bongar, 1991; Bursztajn, Gutheil, Hamm, & Brodsky, 1983; Robertson & Simon, 1991; Simon, 1988) have interpreted court-determined professional standards, statutory professional standards, and practice-based professional standards to revolve around two aspects of tort law that contribute to the establishment of negligence: (1) foreseeability, and (2) proximate cause (causation). "Foreseeability" does not refer to predicting suicidal behavior (Maris, Berman, Maltsberger, & Yufit, 1992). Rather, the term reflects simply the clinician's attention to risk assessment. The argument is that a failure to assess the possibility of suicidality leads to a failure to foresee the potential risk for suicide, which then leads to a failure to provide appropriate treatment, environmental interventions, and constraints, and restrictions to prevent suicidal behavior from being enacted (Simon, 1988).

For example, in an inpatient setting, this then could lead to a failure to appropriately or properly supervise the patient (identified as a high-risk individual) and thereby a failure to place the patient in a setting that is secure and safe; or a potential to prematurely discharge a patient when he or she still has high suicidal potential (Doyle, 1990; Friedman, 1989; Litman & Farberow, 1966). These actions could each then be construed as the proximate cause of a subsequent suicidal act.

After a suicide occurs, the typical types of allegations that have been made about clinical omissions include failure to take a history and perform a mental status examination; failure to foresee the potential for suicidal behavior; failure to treat a condition associated with suicidal behaviors; failure to prevent a self-inflicted injury; failure to protect a suicidal patient by providing environmental and custodial safeguards; failure to limit access to means of suicide; failure to write precise clinical orders on charts; and a failure to carry out treatment orders as they are written (Litman, 1967, 1982; Maris, 1992).

After a suicide occurs, the typical types of allegations that have been made about clinical commissions include the early or premature discharge of a patient from an inpatient setting before suicidal risk has sufficiently diminished (i.e., abandonment); prescribing inappropriate medications and/or dosages to treat a diagnosed mental disorder; failing to treat, for example, by not providing 1:1 psychotherapy; and making clinical decisions based exclusively on intuition, without the benefit of available input from objective sources (Sadoff & Gutheil, 1990; Weiss & Dubin, 1992).

Alleged failures (clinical omissions and commissions) in meeting standards of care for suicidal inpatients can be understood as failures in the proper assignment and execution of duties and responsibilities between and among the parties legally held accountable for the clinical welfare of the patient: the clinician, the inpatient staff, and the hospital administration. These failures can be categorized under the two central issues that establish medical negligence in suicide litigation: foreseeability and causation (Bongar, 1991; Simon, 1988). Although these commonly alleged failures are addressed in this chapter, we have designed Tables 4.1–4.3 as aids in distinguishing the duties and responsibilities of the three parties, respectively, as they relate to providing the appropriate standard of care. Furthermore, the tables provide suggested remedies addressing some of the more commonly alleged failures discussed in case law and addressed as complaints in suicide litigation. Our intent is not to provide a comprehensive enumeration of alleged failures and related remedies, or a checklist to ensure the provision of optimal clinical care to suicidal inpatients. Rather, the tables provide guidance for clinicians, inpatient staff, and hospital administrators in how to approach the clinical care of suicidal patients. Not every "remedy" is appropriate for every clinical setting or situation. Not every "alleged failure" is an absolute failure in the clinical care of every patient. The tables are an attempt to bring some order and clarity to the interface and integration of standards of care with clinical risk management and clinical judgment.

STANDARDS OF CARE AND CLINICAL RISK MANAGEMENT

One of the major "gray areas" regarding the implementation of standards of care is the degree to which the clinician understands, practices, and documents the risk–benefit analysis inherent in the clinical decision-making process. Every clinical decision is based on facts, observations, secondary information (from other professionals, family members, etc.), and the clinical experience of the practitioner. A clinical decision or judgment is made as a consequence of weighing all the available objective and subjective data. The operative term here is "available." It is the duty and responsibility of the clinician to make reasonable and prudent efforts to obtain as much data as possible. Failure to attempt to obtain some data (current level of lethality, access to means, response to prior therapeutic interventions) is below the standard of care. The subsequent clinical management decision then becomes the reasonable and prudent course of action that incorporates a risk–benefit assessment of the anticipated consequences of the decision.

The clinical decision is often based on an assessment of the foreseeability of the patient's clinical course of behavior or disorder. The clinical decision itself is a mediating variable, having both its own set of consequences (which are not always foreseeable or predictable) and a consequent effect on the patient's behavior and prognosis.

At every point in the clinical assessment, treatment, and management of a suicidal inpatient, the clinician is faced with risk management decisions, beginning with the initial decision to hospitalize the patient. These decisions are informed by many sources, but may well be influenced by existing standards of care. Clinicians should have reasonable latitude in determining the costs and benefits of particular clinical decisions. However, these clinical decisions should be made according to some documented rationale based on both objective and subjective data (Gutheil, Bursztajn, & Brodsky, 1986; Gutheil, Bursztajn, Brodsky, & Alexander, 1991).

It is very difficult to provide "iron-clad" standards of care that encompass all possible scenarios when dealing with suicidal inpatients. The standards of care developed below are not offered as a "cookbook" or as a substitute for good clinical judgment, but rather as reasonable and prudent guidelines and general checkpoints that inform the provision of good clinical care of suicidal inpatients. The following 10 topics incorporate fundamental standards of care that interface with clinical risk management and clinical judgment in the assessment, treatment, and management of suicidal inpatients.

The Therapeutic Contract

Ralph M., age 37, upon being presented with divorce papers by his wife, made a suicide attempt by overdose and was admitted to the hospital. At intake, he was agitated and guarded, showing poor insight and judgment, marked anxiety, and violent behavior toward self and others. It was noted that he had a prior history of a suicide attempt, depression, and paranoid behavior. Psychosis could not be ruled out. A provisional diagnosis was recorded as bipolar disorder, mixed type. The initial treatment plan recommended 15-minute observational checks, antipsychotic drugs, intensive psychotherapy, and an expected inpatient stay of 3–4 weeks. Two weeks after discharge, Ralph M. attempted to murder his wife and succeeded in killing himself. Suit was brought against the hospital treatment team, alleging a long list of failures in assessment and treatment. When Ralph M.'s treatment charts were examined, the 15-minute observation logs showed no evidence that the patient was seen by either the treating psychiatrist or social worker in either individual or group psychotherapy during the 2-week course of this observation. Additionally, no attempt was made by any member of the treatment team to bring the patient's wife in for either marital therapy or a collateral session regarding the resolvability of the marital crisis.

Hospitalization for purposes of preventing a patient from acting on his or her self-destructive urges implies that the ability of a patient to be responsible for his or her own life has to be carefully evaluated and assessed in a controlled setting. The evaluation includes an assessment of the patient's ability to contribute to his or her own safety, physical and mental well-being, and immediate destiny. Hence, it is incumbent upon the treating clinician and the multidisciplinary treatment team to accept certain responsibilities, roles, and functions on an immediate and short-term basis. It is important to understand these added duties and responsibilities in light of the nature of the "contract" that is implicitly entered into when a patient is admitted to an inpatient unit to protect him or her from self-harm, be it voluntary or involuntary.

One of the common problems is when a therapist relies exclusively on a "suicide contract" with a patient (Drye, Goulding, & Goulding, 1973). The therapist may be feeling relieved that the patient has concurred with an agreement not to harm himself or herself while under the direct care of the therapist. However, the basis of a clinician–patient contract is a solid therapeutic relationship (Simon, 1988). The therapist must know the patient and share a common language with the patient prior to engaging in the formation of a contract. A contract entered into with a patient in a setting such as an inpatient unit, where behaviors may be extreme and risks for acting out have already been acknowledged to be high, must be understood as an enhancement of a therapeutic relationship, not a substitute for one.

As Maris, Berman, and Maltsberger (1992) have pointed out, "any treatment of a suicidal patient that relies on impersonal means alone (e.g., the prescription of psychoactive medication, seclusion, restraint, checks, etc.) is second-rate. . . . The heart of treatment is the relationship with the therapist" (p. 666). Elements of a psychotherapeutic relationship include reasonable and prudent offerings of support; accessibility; empathic exploration of the patient's current life stressors and despair; and close monitoring of the patient's shifting perceptions, affect, mood, and self-concept (see Table 4.1).

Risks and Benefits of Hospitalization

The care of a suicidal patient entails a constant review of the risk–benefit ratio associated with making clinical and administrative interventions.

TABLE 4.1. Commonly Alleged Failures in Meeting Standards of Care for Suicidal Inpatients: Duties and Responsibilities of the Clinician

Alleged failures	Remedies
	A. Foreseeability
1. Appropriately diagnose patient	Obtain history of current and past problems
	Perform physical examination
	Perform mental status exam
	Conduct assessment of suicidality to determine suicidal risk
	Reach tentative diagnosis
	Provide risk–benefit analysis of treatment options to support critical clinical and administrative management decisions
	Consider least restrictive environment options
	Develop initial treatment plan
	Discuss treatment plan with patient
	Obtain informed consent
	Discuss limits of confidentiality with patient
	Communicate treatment plan to all relevant staff by writing orders
	Obtain and review past medical and psychiatric/psychological records when reasonably possible
	Obtain collateral information from patient's support network with patient's consent
	Order appropriate tests and evaluations to establish suicidal intent
2. Appropriately foresee future behavioral problems	Reassess regularly the diagnosis, level of suicidality, and appropriateness of all aspects of the treatment plan
	Communicate regularly with staff in writing and orally
	Reassess regularly the patient's competencies and capacities for complying with the treatment plan
	Be aware of the hospital's policy and procedure manual regarding the management of suicidal patients
	Monitor adherence to the treatment plan by staff
	Read the medical chart entries regularly
	Obtain consultation when indicated
	B. Causation
1. Provide protection against harm	Implement treatment plan
	Monitor treatment plan results
	Provide informed consent about changes in treatment plan
	Discuss confidentiality with patient

(continued)

TABLE 4.1. *(continued)*

Alleged failures	Remedies
2. Control, supervise, observe, and restrain patient	Offer alternative therapeutic approaches and discuss advantages/disadvantages with patient
3. Provide safe, secure, and protective environment	Consider appropriate installation of privileges, restrictions, and precautions Determine frequency of surveillance Remove all known means of self-harm from unit
4. Treat conditions associated with suicidal behaviors (including use of medication and all other appropriate therapeutic modalities)	Consider consultation when indicated Provide plan-specific interventions
5. Carry out treatment orders as written	Monitor adherence to treatment plan
6. Document clinical decisions	Determine frequency of clinical availability Review regularly pass and privilege policies and procedures
7. Communicate among staff	Adhere to hospital manual on policies and procedures
8. Retain patient in hospital until no longer actively suicidal	Arrange for alternative secure environments if prolonged hospitalization is not financially feasible
9. Provide postdischarge plans	Engage in discharge planning Encourage adherence to aftercare plans
10. Provide postdischarge care	Educate patient's support network about risk management Maximize support network's attention to ensuring patient's compliance with aftercare recommendations

Every intervention carries potential risks as well as potential benefits. In constantly monitoring and evaluating the benefits against the risks, the clinician must make an informed judgment. Where appropriate, each judgment needs to be discussed with the appropriate and relevant colleagues associated with the care of the patient (consultants and hospital staff), the patient's support network (family and friends), and, of course, the patient (informed consent). All these judgments need to be documented. These judgments should be competent, prudent, and reasonable. *Competent judgments* are dependent on sufficient experience with and exposure to the theory and practice of evaluating and treating suicidal patients, and being

TABLE 4.2. Commonly Alleged Failures in Meeting Standards of Care for Suicidal Inpatients: Duties and Responsibilities of the Inpatient Staff

Alleged failures	Remedies
A. Foreseeability	
1. Appropriately communicate suicidal risk to each other	Regularly document interactions and observations
	Adhere to the treatment plan
2. Assess changes in suicidal risk	Attend in-service training updates
	Follow the hospital manual of policies and procedures
	Schedule regular treatment team planning meeting
B. Causation	
1. Assess changes in patient's condition	Regularly monitor patient status
	Regularly reassess patient's suicidal risk status
	Take affirmative precautions to protect patient against self-harm
	Communicate observations to responsible staff and clinicians
	Participate in treatment team meetings and case reviews
	Regularly review the treatment plan
	Discuss inpatient management of patient with visitors

aware of the customary standards of care within the therapeutic community in which the treatment occurs. *Prudent judgments* are based on the existing climate in which the treatment occurs and are a function of making risk–benefit assessments. *Reasonable judgments* are based on the availability of clinical data and the application of existing community practice standards.

Although assigning relative risk in these clinical situations is a rather imprecise science, it nevertheless is an important exercise for the clinician, because it is based on and informs ongoing decisions. "Relative risk" is a technical statistical term used by epidemiologists to ascertain the degree to which a particular individual is at risk to express a certain disorder or dysfunction, relative to another individual. Relative risk, as it relates to assessing suicidal behavior, is the end product of considering factors such as prior history of suicidal behavior, presence or absence of a major psychiatric disorder, response to psychotropic medication, level of social support, degree of therapeutic alliance established with primary health care providers, level of behavioral interaction observed on the unit, degree and frequency of verbalization of suicidal thoughts, preoccupation with suicidal plans, and access to suicidal means.

Comprehensive Evaluation

Ralph M. [continued] was referred during the second week of his inpatient hospitalization for psychological evaluation of suicide risk and to "rule out psychosis." The hospital policy was to contract with independent clinical psychologists to provide testing and evaluation services. Ralph was seen by Dr. Cook and given a Minnesota Multiphasic Personality Inventory (MMPI). In spite of the patient's guardedness and high K score, Dr. Cook concluded that the patient was not psychotic and that he "was unlikely to be suicidal in the near future." Plaintiff's experts assessed that the referring questions could not be adequately answered by MMPI results alone (i.e., that projective testing was called for); that the test results should have been invalidated or, at least, seriously questioned, given the validity scale configuration; and that the MMPI provided no conclusive basis for making a suicide risk assessment in either the present or near future.

From our clinical perspective, suicidal behaviors are behaviors that are correlated with a range of psychiatric, psychological, biological, social, and cognitive disorders and dysfunctions. Suicidal behaviors are but one manifestation of underlying distress and disorder in an individual's mental state (Khuri & Akiskal, 1983; Shneidman, 1981, 1992). Ideally, the clinician would investigate the correlated and associated problems that contribute to the suicidal crisis (Tanney, 1992). Such an investigation would include relevant and indicated objective diagnostic tests—psychological, cognitive, biological, physiological, and so forth.

The clinician not only is expected to arrive at an assessment of the conditions that have contributed to the suicidal behaviors, but is also expected to offer some forms of treatment to alleviate them. Assigning a diagnosis often directly determines the course of treatment to be provided. The rationale for the treatment may take many forms, one of which is to remove the underlying etiological or correlated cause for the suicidal behavior, and another of which is to prevent or attenuate the intensity of the factors that contribute to the observed behaviors.

The assumption is that suicidal behaviors do not express themselves in a vacuum. Under optimal conditions, the underlying causes, associated

TABLE 4.3. Commonly Alleged Failures in Meeting Standards of Care for Suicidal Inpatients: Duties and Responsibilities of the Hospital Administration

Alleged failures	Remedies
A. Foreseeability	
1. Appropriately communicate suicidal risk to staff	Ensure uniformity of policies regarding documentation and charting Establish suicide prevention committee
2. Appropriately predict future behavior	Ensure mechanisms for staff to communicate to each other, especially between shifts and across disciplines Develop policies regarding the use of therapeutic modalities for emergency situations Put quality assurance mechanisms in place to ensure that policies and procedures are being applied, reviewed, and updated
B. Causation	
1. Provide protective environment	Ensure regular review and update of hospital policies and procedures Distribute hospital manual on policies and procedures
2. Design and maintain a safe and secure facility	Provide environmental safety checks Ensure secure environment Train all new staff to hospital standards Provide in-service training of current staff and personnel Ensure appropriate credentials for staff working with suicidal patients Enforce documentation of procedures, clinical decision making, clinical activities Provide access to consultants
3. Remove all dangerous means of assisting suicidal behavior from patient's access	Provide guidelines for specific levels of supervision, including seclusion, restraint, 1:1 observation, and transfer to other units

problems, precipitating factors, and predisposing conditions would be enumerated and appropriately addressed (Felner & Silverman, 1989). However, these assessments often take time to complete and cannot be done necessarily in the first 48–72 hours of a hospitalization. During these initial few days of hospitalization, clinical management activities include the acquiring of a relevant prior psychiatric and medical history, especially as it relates to past suicidal behaviors. Efforts to obtain prior treatment and consultative records are indicated. Collateral interviews with family members and significant others are initiated early in the beginning phases of assessment and treatment. The need for clinical and diagnostic consultations from colleagues are reviewed during this phase (Litman, 1992).

Arriving at a working diagnosis is important because it informs the clinician about the potential for intervening psychological states that can influence the movement along the continuum of suicidal behavior. Different psychological states can fluctuate over time and can therefore affect the level of lethality experienced by the patient. For example, a patient with a diagnosis of paranoid schizophrenia may struggle with persecutory delusions, auditory and visual hallucinations, ideas of reference, and other altered states of consciousness that can acutely affect his or her level of suicidal behavior on a moment-to-moment basis. Such a diagnosis raises the level of concern regarding assessing when and if suicidal behaviors may be expressed.

We must keep in mind that all assessments are temporally static, that is, that we cannot predict these changes in the levels of suicidal behaviors nor control the events and factors that contribute to the expression of these affects and behaviors. Even within a fairly controlled environment, the individual clinician has little control over the nature of communications between the patient and others on the ward, family and friends, employers, and other significant individuals in his or her life. Furthermore, the treating clinician must understand that there are often hormonal and biological processes at work that may defy direct and precise observation and intervention. This suggests the importance of maintaining and regularly reviewing daily sleep, diet, medication, weight, temperature, blood pressure, and physical activity records. These realities highlight the importance of frequent follow-up risk assessments after a patient's admission to the inpatient unit.

The Therapeutic Milieu

The suicidal patient is on an inpatient unit for purposes of providing reasonable safety and security. However, the purpose of an inpatient unit is not only to provide reasonable safety and protection from self-harm. Some of the functions of an inpatient hospitalization are evaluation, assessment, management, and treatment of psychiatric disorder, emotional dysfunctions, and acute and chronic behavior that are detrimental to the health and welfare of the individual. Another optimal goal of an inpatient unit is to restore an individual to a prior level of functioning and, ideally, to an improved manner of functioning. These various goals are achieved along a time continuum in direct relationship to the clinical improvement in the patient's ability to manage his or her suicidal behaviors and regain autonomous functioning.

Inpatient psychiatric treatment is designed to evaluate and assess the serious nature of the illness or behaviors in a confined, constricted, and controlled therapeutic environment. However, once a patient begins to improve psychologically, therapeutic efforts need to be addressed to reduce the feeling of being confined, constricted, and controlled. Hospitals are for sick patients. The "zone of danger" is ever-present (Litman, 1989). This overarching issue has direct implications for discharge planning and aftercare (Bongar, 1991).

In our experience, most patients seem to react favorably to being placed in a highly restrictive environment because it lowers their tension state and removes the access to means by which they can enact their self-destructive tendencies. The therapist should not interpret the initial improvement in a patient's overall level of affect and functioning as an indication of immediate and permanent improvement in his or her level of suicidal risk. In our experience, some patients report a return of suicidal preoccupations as a hospitalization lengthens, especially when they do not perceive lasting improvements from therapeutic interventions. The appropriate standard of care includes maintaining vigilance and maintaining the level of concern and care warranted by the need for hospitalization in the first place. It is not often the case that the influence of the therapeutic milieu of an inpatient psychiatric unit is sufficient alone to reduce the threat of suicidal behavior or self-destructive behavior.

If a patient is not observed to respond to this structure and explicit indicators of safety and security, then the clinician's level of concern must be raised to an even higher level of concern, because it indicates the severity of the patient's distress and inability to accurately interpret and respond to his or her environment. Consideration of the involvement of family and friends, when appropriate, in the day-to-day decision making and care of the patient is part of the standard of care.

Hospital Policies and Procedures

Susan S., a 48-year-old female with a long history of unstable relationships, multiple marriages, suicidal overdoses (beginning at the age of 10), and physical abuse, was admitted to inpatient psychiatry after making suicide threats to her husband. She admitted to auditory hallucinations. Her admitting diagnosis was bipolar disorder. Over the course of her 2-week hospitalization, she was placed on and taken off suicide status four times, as her mood and assessed risk were observed to be quite labile. One day after last being taken off suicide observation, she was given a 4-hour pass to her home in the company of her husband. Upon her return to the hospital, several syringes were found in her room. A drug screen was ordered and returned positive for cocaine. Hospital policy stated that "If unauthorized mood-altering drugs [are found in the patient's possession], the patient shall be considered for immediate discharge per order of the physician." The attending psychiatrist ordered the patient's immediate discharge. No attempt was made to consult with or inform the patient's husband regarding her discharge. Within 12 hours of arriving home, Susan S. was dead by self-inflicted injection of insulin and chlorine.

One of the important considerations for the effective management of suicidal patients on hospital inpatient units is to work within the existing policies and procedures. The minimal standard of care is for treatment facilities to have a written policy and procedure manual that outlines the manner in which clinical care is to be provided to patients. These manuals cover the duties and responsibilities of all personnel and all administrative and clinical units in the facility. Therefore, it behooves the treating clinician to be familiar with the hospital's rules and regulations for the care of mentally ill patients, and particularly mentally ill patients exhibiting self-destructive and violent behaviors. The treating clinician should be reasonably aware of the level of training, experience, and expertise of the treating team regarding the ongoing assessment, management, and treatment of patients with suicidal tendencies.

All members of the treatment team should make reasonable efforts to be familiar with the scope and limitations placed on policies and procedures such as seclusion, off-ward privileges, watch/observation protocols, visitation limitations, and possession of personal items. In our experience, there often tends to be confusion on the part of members of the treatment team regarding the implementation and maintenance of difficult suicide watch protocols. In most facilities, there are four suicide watch levels: 1:1 (constant observation); Q15 minutes (observation of behavior every 15 minutes around the clock); Q30 minutes (behavioral observation every 30 minutes around the clock); and general suicide observation/precautions (which are defined variably as maintaining a heightened awareness that the patient has a suicide potential, often operationalized as keeping track of the patient's whereabouts while he or she is awake). These suicide watch levels only refer to staff observations of patient behavior. They do not address routinely questioning the patient about affect, cognition, reality testing, mood, or other variables that may contribute to the evolution or maintenance of suicide behaviors. These behavioral observations are recorded routinely in the patient's chart. Hence, suicide watch levels are only one aspect of the overall therapeutic function of an inpatient hospitalization.

Everyone should be familiar with how all these policies and procedures are operationalized, implemented, and monitored on a day-to-day basis under normal operations (*not* in ideal circumstances). The inpatient team needs to provide feedback to the hospital policy makers for updating and revising policy and procedure manuals in keeping with current practice and treatment realities.

Treatment Planning

Although there is no mandate for documentation of the following, it seems to us that the treating clinician should, under optimal conditions, develop an overall "game plan" regarding the various technologies, techniques, and treatment modalities that are available for addressing the needs of the suicidal inpatient. Here we refer to understanding the strengths and limitations of each of the available resources that can be used by the clinician to thwart the suicidal act. The clinician needs to realize that no one modality, technique, or intervention is sufficient to reduce the suicidal risk. Each has its own benefits as well as limitations. It is the judicious combination of interventions that, as a sum, provides a "plan" for addressing the specific needs of the specific patient at the specific moment he or she is being treated in a specific setting.

Although we advocate constant concern coupled with careful and deliberate management, we also recognize the importance of rewarding improvement in the patient's lability, cognition, and psychological state in response to treatment. Restoring a patient's sense of well-being, self-esteem, self-confidence, and self-worth is a critical element of the therapeutic restoration achieved through an inpatient hospitalization.

Nevertheless, there needs to be a sensitive monitoring of this evolving process throughout the hospital stay. There is no *sine qua non* for when a patient "turns the corner" and moves away from suicidal preoccupations or behaviors. The important point is to document such a change based on good clinical assessment *before* restrictions are lifted and *before* critical decisions are made about restoring to the patient personal privileges and freedom of movement.

At some critical point in the treatment of a suicidal inpatient, the clinician is faced with the dilemma of communicating trust in the patient's ability to manage and monitor his or her own impulses, feelings, and fleeting or chronic suicidal tendencies. This return of autonomy must be weighed and reassessed, and a determination made that the benefits outweigh the risks in terms of taking the next step. One of the final steps in the process of retreat from suicidal behaviors is to signal to the patient that he or she is trusted to manage his or her own affairs.

Monitoring clinical changes in the patient determines the timing of off-ward privileges, off-campus passes, overnight visitations home, discharge planning, and aftercare plans. Ideally, this process should not be governed by insurance or third-party limitations on hospital stay or other external monetary or financial pressures. In reality, and to an ever-increasing extent, insurance benefits are a fact of life that determines the length of hospital stay. The clinician, in consultation with the patient, must judge the patient to be ready to resume responsibility for his or her life before this responsibility is returned to him or her.

We advise the clinician to carefully document the rationale for taking these next steps, based on objective and subjective observations and data. In our experience, it is this critical step in the therapeutic process that can precipitate the reenactment of the suicidal behaviors, for reasons ranging from returning the patient to an unchanged suicidogenic environment to the loss of structure and support provided by the inpatient milieu. Although the physician in charge is legally responsible for the treatment, these decisions ideally are made in cooperation and collaboration with the treatment team, the patient, and the patient's significant support network.

Watch Procedures and Protocols

Mary S. was brought to the hospital subsequent to a multiple drug overdose. In the emergency room, she was combative, loud, and belligerent, and was immediately placed in four-point leather restraints. Once stabilized, she was transferred to inpatient psychiatry. She revealed a long history of instability and emotional lability, family crises, rape, depression, substance dependence (both she and her third husband were crack addicts), multiple suicide attempts, and associated psychiatric hospitalizations with diagnoses ranging from inadequate personality to chronic undifferentiated schizophrenia. On the morning of her second day in inpatient psychiatry, she was observed to be agitated, crying uncontrollably, and screaming in the halls. She was placed in an unlocked quiet room but not on suicide observation. Before a diagnostic evaluation (and treatment plan) could occur, Mary R. hanged herself by a nylon shower curtain in the ward bathroom.

There are real practicalities in ordering a "suicide watch," depending on such variables as the actual architectural design of the inpatient unit, the degree of suicide-proofing of that unit, staffing patterns on the unit, the dependability and reliability of patients on the ward for reporting unusual behaviors in their fellow patients, and the level of sophistication and training of the treatment staff. The reality is that any patient can successfully do serious self-harm if he or she has access to the means and a few uninterrupted minutes to act in a self-destructive manner (Litman, 1992; Maris, 1992). It only takes 4–5 minutes of anoxia (decreased oxygenation of the blood) to cause irreversible brain damage. The reality is that, even when utilizing 1:1 *constant* observation (including when a patient takes a bath or shower, or attends to other personal hygiene), suicide watch procedures are no guarantee of suicide prevention. There is a "down side" regarding the message the clinician and staff may be giving the patient if suicide watch techniques are arbitrarily used or extensively used for long periods of time (Pokorny, 1992). The removal of a sense of trust and mastery from the control of the patient, as evidenced by prolonged 1:1 suicide observation, is a therapeutic and management issue.

Being on 1:1 observation or on 15-, or 30-minute checks is no guarantee that a patient will abstain from self-destructive behaviors. Clinical judgment precedes the clinical risk management decision to place a patient at one of these watch levels, to increase or decrease the level of precautions, or to remove a patient from this degree of close observation. Some believe that these maneuvers can lull the clinician into believing that "the problem has been fixed." In other words, there is a real inherent danger in placing undue emphasis on this treatment modality to the exclusion of all others. Our point is that such precautions are but one element of a coordinated and comprehensive approach to the clinical risk management and treatment of the suicidal patient.

The clinician must understand that all of these modalities—seclusion and restraints, medications, suicide watch and precaution levels, restrictions of movement (i.e., locked wards), restrictions on access to sharp objects and other means of self-destructive behavior—convey meaning to the patient. They also have their utility at different points in the overall treatment plan for the patient. They must be used carefully, with great concern and consideration for their strengths and weaknesses in affecting desired outcomes. Sometimes these modalities can delay the desired goal (i.e., reduction in suicidal behavior), and sometimes they may even precipitate or intensify existing or dormant suicidal behavior.

Clinical Risk Management and Clinical Judgment

The acquisition of clinical judgment regarding the assessment, management, and treatment of suicidal patients is beyond the purview of this chapter (Bongar, 1992; Jacobs, 1992; Maltsberger, 1986; Simon, 1992a, 1992b). Nevertheless, it is important to emphasize that the use of appropriate consultation by more experienced clinicians is always an appropriate option to consider whenever the clinician feels that the problem warrants another perspective (Bongar, 1991; Doyle, 1990).

Clinical risk management and clinical judgment are based on current clinical data, past data, experience, basic knowledge, a working relationship with the patient, an awareness of the milieu in which the therapy is being conducted, the physical environment of the inpatient unit, the evolving psychiatric disorder that has contributed to the patient's suicidal state, the degree of social and familial support available to the patient, the psychological/cognitive level of the patient, and the behavioral assessment of the patient. All of these data must be understood in terms of an evolving system that is undergoing change due to the therapeutic process, the effects of medication, and the benefits of being in a therapeutic inpatient milieu.

In our experience, one area of vulnerability for the clinician is a lack of clarity of thought. The clinician must use his or her clinical judgment to interpret the data against the backdrop of his or her training, experience, and knowledge base. It is incumbent upon the clinician to document the data and the current state of the patient along the relevant domains (i.e., physical, psychological, psychiatric, behavioral), and to logically demonstrate how changes are made in treatment orders or management and treatment approaches. Whenever there is uncertainty in the management process, it is advisable to "think out loud" in the formal clinical record (Bongar, 1991).

Psychopharmacological Agents

One therapeutic modality involves the use of psychopharmacological agents and other psychiatric interventions such as electroconvulsive therapy. Most major psychiatric disorders that are correlated with suicidal behaviors are responsive to the use of psychotropic medications for the relief of the symptoms and for prevention of relapse over time (long-term maintenance). Not all major psychiatric disorders are associated with suicidal behaviors, and not all suicidal behaviors are associated with the presence of psychiatric disorders. Nevertheless, a full investigation of the presence of a psychiatric disorder is warranted when a patient is hospitalized for severe and serious suicidal behaviors. Once a psychiatric disorder is diagnosed, it is important to document the rationale behind the decision to use medications.

If psychotropic medications are indicated, the clinician must demonstrate familiarity with the use and chemical properties of these medications. In short, the clinician must be sensitive to all of the variables that are associated with the beginning phases of psychotropic use, as well as the maintenance, monitoring, and adjustment phases. Such problems include compliance, adherence, and length of time for therapeutic levels to be reached. These medications are not without their own set of side effects and associated contraindications for their use. The use of medications in the management and treatment of a suicidal patient adds yet another layer to the treatment plan, and another layer to the clinical decision-making process (Maris, Berman, & Maltsberger, 1992). The role of medications may complicate as well as complement the treatment plan.

Psychotropic medications may have influences on a wide range of psychological and biological mechanisms, including cognition, memory, affect, psychological states, sleep patterns, hormonal balance, emotional lability, and behavioral levels of agitation and withdrawal. Psychopharmacological drugs are active agents of change in the therapeutic process. This change may not always be in the direction that is anticipated or preferred. Careful and consistent monitoring of the contribution of psychotropic drugs to the overall treatment strategy is critical. To place too much emphasis on the therapeutic benefits of a psychopharmacological agent is to run the risk of oversight and potential disaster. Yet not to medicate, if indicated, is a legal and clinical risk as well. No one intervention, in and of itself, is sufficient to ensure the improvement in the overall level of functioning of a patient across many different and contributory domains of his or her life.

Psychotropic drugs have psychological meaning for the patient who is in psychological pain. These are not innocuous agents without physiological and psychological effects that may be deleterious to the outcome desired. Indications as well as contraindications for placing a patient on medications need to be documented. Decisions not to medicate, to increase or decrease levels of medication, to add or remove adjunctive medications, to switch classes of medications, or to switch medications within the same class (i.e., to change one antidepressant for another antidepressant because the first one did not achieve the desired results in a specified time frame) are important clinical judgments that require appropriate documentation based on both objective and subjective data.

In addition, clinicians should be attentive to changes in suicidal risk status at times of change in the administration of psychotropic medications. The decisions to increase, decrease, add medications, change medications, and so forth are important points of misperception and miscommunication in the clinical setting. It is important to document the patient's understanding of any changes in the administration of psychotropic medications.

There are side effects of any therapeutic intervention, particularly psychotropic medication interventions, which can have negative effects on desired goals. Knowing the degree of effectiveness of prior medication regimens is very important. All these factors must be, as well as possible, monitored, accounted for, and included in any decision-making process that hopes to reduce the risk for continued suicidal behavior. The best possible means of monitoring these fluctuations and their effects on the patient is to be in close and regular contact with the patient, and to ask about the patient's perceptions of the effect of these medications on his or her clinical state.

In a similar manner, the range of psychotherapies often utilized on inpatient units (i.e., behavioral, cognitive, group, family, individual, vocational, etc.) constitute treatments directed at the behavioral or psychological disorder or dysfunction. Here it is important to document in the treatment plan the intended use of these therapeutic modalities. These therapies represent specific interventions targeted at specific behaviors or disorders associated with the patient's suicidal state.

Discharge and Aftercare Planning

Another area that is a touchstone for litigation is that of the process and procedures surrounding discharge and aftercare. It is important to appreciate the significance of the effects of confinement, control, and predictability that characterize the daily routine on an inpatient unit. Decisions about passes, off-ward privileges, discharge planning, and aftercare should be made with appropriate attention to the implicit and explicit effects and influences of being on or off an inpatient psychiatric unit. A clinician should strive to be aware of the patient's reactions, responses, feelings, and perspectives regarding his or her presence on an inpatient unit. Although essential to the acute treatment of a suicidal patient, the structure and function of an inpatient psychiatric unit cannot be relied on solely for the prevention of further suicidal behaviors by a patient. In other words, the clinician has to be careful about placing too much emphasis on the role of the inpatient unit alone in the reduction of the threat of suicidal behavior by the patient (Litman, 1992). The transition process from inpatient to outpatient care is extremely important and always something of a gamble or a risk.

The standard of care here includes explicit statements about what the patient is instructed to do by way of taking medication, and when, where, and with whom the patient's next follow-up appointment is. Ideally, at the point of discharge, the patient's medications have been sufficiently adjusted to fall within a therapeutic range as measured by blood levels and regular clinical assessment. The patient's and his or her family's full compliance and adherence to the clinician's recommendations for follow-up treatment are essential ingredients in optimal discharge planning. Of note is that suicides can occur within relatively short time frames following discharges from inpatient units (Bongar, 1991; Litman, 1992; Simon, 1992a). Sometimes it is alleged that such tragedies are due, at least in part, to inconsistent monitoring through a period of aftercare risk and to poor communication with significant family members or friends.

SUMMARY

The legal literature and decisions pertaining to malpractice litigation following suicide attempts and suicide completions on hospital inpatient units suggest that there are common points on the continuum of care that must be addressed by clinicians, hospital staff, and hospital administration. The clinician working in an inpatient setting must attend to the following four general clinical risk management strategies: (1) attention to the therapeutic alliance; (2) regular assessment of the patient's competencies and capabilities for cooperation and collaboration with the treatment plan; (3) consultation with other clinicians and specialists; and (4) documentation of significant information and decisions in the patient's record (Amchin et al., 1980; Bursztajn et al., 1983; Gutheil, 1992; Gutheil, Bursztajn, Hamm, & Brodsky, 1983; Wettstein, 1989). These four strategies interface with the standards of care for suicidal inpatients as outlined in each of the 10 main topic areas.

Hospital staff participate in the clinical care of the patient, follow the treatment plan, adhere to hospital policies and procedures regarding the management and supervision of suicidal patients, and communicate regularly to each other and to other critical personnel responsible for the patient's care.

The hospital administration, in a reasonable and prudent manner, provides a safe, secure, and protective physical environment. This may be accomplished through reasonable efforts to "suicide-proof" inpatient units, providing updated hospital policy and procedure manuals, providing regular in-service training, and appropriate staffing of units ensuring adequate and appropriate staff-to-patient ratios (Benensohn & Resnik, 1973; Farberow, 1981; Simon, 1988).

CONCLUSION

The best that we can do is to reasonably reduce the risk for suicidal behaviors. Although we cannot predict well who will commit suicide, we *can* engage in both reasonable and prudent risk management and intervention practices that translate into reasonable standards of care for acutely ill patients. In order to prevent further occurrences of suicidal behavior, we must rely on clinical judgment for providing appropriate constraints and restraints when the patient is unable to take full responsibility for himself or herself. Clinical judgment is based on a sound knowledge base, prior experience and training with these matters, and thorough assessment of suicidal potential (Maris, Berman, Maltsberger, & Yufit, 1992). Standards of care are based on all the available facts and circumstances relevant to each individual patient. They are subject to change as scientific knowledge and medical technology advance and patterns of practice evolve (American Medical Association, 1993).

The clinician must always keep in mind that suicidal behaviors may well be impulsive, irrational, unpredictable, situationally based, reactive, reactionary, or opportunistic. The appropriate utilization of existing standards of care on inpatient units can assist in limiting the conditions under which such behaviors can occur.

ACKNOWLEDGMENT

This chapter is reprinted from *Suicide and Life-Threatening Behavior, 24*(2), 152–169, Summer 1994. Copyright 1994 by the American Association of Suicidology. Reprinted by permission.

REFERENCES

Amchin, J., Wettstein, R. M., & Roth, L. H. (1990). Suicide, ethics, and the law. In S. J. Blumenthal & D. J. Kupfer (Eds.), *Suicide over the life cycle. Risk factors, assessment and treatment of suicidal patients* (pp. 637–663). Washington, DC: American Psychiatric Press.

American Medical Association, Council on Scientific Affairs. (1993). Adolescents as victims of family violence. *Journal of the American Medical Association, 270*(15), 1850–1856.

Bar-Levav, L. (1992). The risk of hospitalizing suicidal patients: A personal perspective. *Jefferson Journal of Psychiatry, 10*(2), 43–49.

Benensohn, H. S., & Resnik, H. L. P. (1973). Guidelines for "suicide proofing" a psychiatric unit. *American Journal of Psychotherapy, 27*(2), 204–211.

Berman, A. L., & Cohen-Sandler, R. (1982). Suicide and the standard of care: Optimal vs. acceptable. *Suicide and Life-Threatening Behavior, 12*(2), 114–122.

Bongar, B. (1991). *The suicidal patient: Clinical and legal standards of care.* Washington, DC: American Psychological Association.

Bongar, B. (Ed.). (1992). *Suicide: Guidelines for assessment management and treatment.* New York: Oxford University Press.

Brent, D. A., Kupfer, D. J., Bromet, E. J., & Dew, M. A. (1988). The assessment and treatment of patients at risk for suicide. In A. J. Frances & R. E. Hales (Eds.), *Review of psychiatry* (Vol. 7, pp. 353–385). Washington, DC: American Psychiatric Press.

Bursztajn, H., Gutheil, T. G., Hamm, R. M., & Brodsky, A. (1983). Subjective data and suicide assessment in the light of recent legal developments: Part II. Clinical uses of legal standards in the interpretation of subjective data. *International Journal of Law and Psychiatry, 6*(3–4), 331–350.

Doyle, B. B. (1990). Crisis management of the suicidal patient. In S. J. Blumenthal & D. J. Kupfer (Eds.), *Suicide over the life cycle. Risk factors, assessment, and treatment of suicidal patients* (pp. 381–423). Washington, DC: American Psychiatric Press.

Drye, R. C., Goulding, R., & Goulding, M. (1973). No-suicide decisions: Patient monitoring of suicidal risk. *American Journal of Psychiatry, 130*(2), 171–174.

Farberow, N. L. (1981). Suicide prevention in the hospital. *Hospital and Community Psychiatry, 32,* 99–104.

Felner, R. D., & Silverman, M. M. (1989). Primary prevention: A consideration of general principles and findings for the prevention of youth suicide. In Alcohol, Drug Abuse, and Mental Health Administration (Ed.), *Report of the Secretary's Task Force on Youth Suicide: Vol 3. Prevention and intervention in youth suicide* (DHHS Publ. No. ADM 89-1623, pp. 23–30). Washington, DC: U.S. Government Printing Office.

Friedman, R. S. (1989). Hospital treatment of the suicidal patient. In D. G. Jacobs & H. N. Brown (Eds.), *Suicide: Understanding and responding. Harvard Medical School perspectives on suicide* (pp. 379–402). Madison, CT: International Universities Press.

Gutheil, T. G. (1992). Suicide and suit: Liability after self-destruction. In D. Jacobs (Ed.), *Suicide and clinical practice* (pp. 147–167). Washington, DC: American Psychiatric Press.

Gutheil, T. G., Bursztajn, H., & Brodsky, A. (1986). The multidimensional assessment of dangerousness: Competence assessment in patient care and liability prevention. *Bulletin of the American Academy of Psychiatry and Law, 14*(2), 123–129.

Gutheil, T. G., Bursztajn, H., Brodsky, A., & Alexander, V. (1991). *Decision making in psychiatry and the law.* Baltimore: Williams & Wilkins.

Gutheil, T. G., Bursztajn, H., Hamm, R. M., & Brodsky, A. (1983). Subjective data and suicide assessment in the light of recent legal developments: Part I. Malpractice prevention and the use of subjective data. *International Journal of Law and Psychiatry, 6*(3–4), 317–329.

Jacobs, D. (Ed.). (1992). *Suicide and clinical practice.* Washington, DC: American Psychiatric Press.

Khuri, R., & Akiskal, H. S. (1983). Suicide prevention: The necessity of treating contributory psychiatric disorders. *Psychiatric Clinics of North America, 6*(1), 193–207.

Klerman, G. L. (Ed.). (1986). *Suicide and depression among adolescents and young adults.* Washington, DC: American Psychiatric Press.

Litman, R. E. (1967). Medical–legal aspects of suicide. *Washburn Law Journal, 6,* 395–401.

Litman, R. E. (1982). Hospital suicides: Lawsuits and standards. *Suicide and Life-Threatening Behavior, 12*(4), 212–220.

Litman, R. E. (1989). Suicides: What do they have in mind? In D. Jacobs & H. N. Brown (Eds.), *Suicide. Understanding and responding. Harvard Medical Shool perspectives on suicide* (pp. 143–156). Madison, CT: International Universities Press.

Litman, R. E. (1992). Predicting and preventing hospital and clinic suicides. In R. W. Maris, A. L. Berman, J. T. Maltsberger, & R. I. Yufit (Eds.), *Assessment and prediction of suicide* (pp. 448–466). New York: Guilford Press.

Litman, R. E., & Farberow, N. L. (1966). The hospital's obligation toward suicide-prone patients. *Hospital, 40,* 64–68.

Maltsberger, J. T. (1986). *Suicide risk: The formulation of clinical judgment.* New York: New York University Press.

Maris, R. W. (1992). Forensic suicidology: Litigation of suicide cases and equivocal deaths. In B. Bongar (Ed.), *Suicide: Guidelines for assessment, management, and treatment* (pp. 235–252). New York: Oxford University Press.

Maris, R. W., Berman, A. L., & Maltsberger, J. T. (1992). Summary and conclusions: What have we learned about suicide assessment and prediction? In R. W. Maris, A. L. Berman, J. T. Maltsberger, & R. I. Yufit (Eds.), *Assessment and prediction of suicide* (pp. 640–672). New York: Guilford Press.

Maris, R. W., Berman, A. L., Maltsberger, J. T., & Yufit, R. I. (Eds.). (1992). *Assessment and prediction of suicide*. New York: Guilford Press.

Motto, J. A. (1979). Guidelines for the management of the suicidal patient. *Weekly Psychiatry Update Series Lesson, 3*, 3–7. (Available from Biomedia, Inc., 20 Nassau Street, Princeton, NJ 08540)

Pokorny, A. D. (1992). Prediction of suicide in psychiatric patients: Report of a prospective study. In R. W. Maris, A. L. Berman, J. T. Maltsberger, & R. I. Yufit (Eds.), *Assessment and prediction of suicide* (pp. 105–129). New York: Guilford Press.

Pokorny, A. D. (1993). Suicide prediction revisited. *Suicide and Life-Threatening Behavior, 23*(1), 1–10.

Robertson, J. D., & Simon, R. I. (1991). The psychiatrist in the courtroom: Suicide litigation. In R. I. Simon (Ed.), *Review of clinical psychiatry and the law* (Vol. 2, pp. 423–451). Washington, DC: American Psychiatric Press.

Sadoff, R. L., & Gutheil, T. G. (1990). Expert opinion: Death in hindsight. In R. I. Simon (Ed.), *Review of clinical psychiatry and the law* (Vol. 1, pp. 329–339). Washington, DC: American Psychiatric Press.

Shneidman, E. S. (1981). Psychotherapy with suicidal patients. *Suicide and Life-Threatening Behavior, 11*(4), 341–348.

Shneidman, E. S. (1992). A conspectus of the suicidal scenario. In R. W. Maris, A. L. Berman, J. T. Maltsberger, & R. I. Yufit (Eds.), *Assessment and prediction of suicide* (pp. 50–64). New York: Guilford Press.

Simon, R. I. (1988). *Concise guide to clinical psychiatry and the law*. Washington, DC: American Psychiatric Press.

Simon, R. I. (1992a). Clinical risk management and suicidal patients: Assessing the unpredictable. In R. I. Simon (Ed.), *Review of clinical psychiatry and the law* (Vol. 3, pp. 3–63). Washington, DC: American Psychiatric Press.

Simon, R. I. (Ed.). (1992b). *Clinical psychiatry and the law* (2nd ed.). Washington, DC: American Psychiatric Press.

Tanney, B. L. (1992). Mental disorders, psychiatric patients, and suicide. In R. W. Maris, A. L. Berman, J. T. Maltsberger, & R. I. Yufit (Eds.), *Assessment and prediction of suicide* (pp. 277–320). New York: Guilford Press.

Weiss, K. J., & Dubin, W. R. (1992). Psychiatric hospital liability for suicide. In R. I. Simon (Ed.), *Review of clinical psychiatry and the law* (Vol. 3, pp. 115–128). Washington, DC: American Psychiatric Press.

Wettstein, R. M. (1989). Psychiatric malpractice. In A. Tasman, R. E. Hales, & A. J. Frances (Eds.), *Annual review of psychiatry* (Vol. 8, pp. 392–408). Washington, DC: American Psychiatric Press.

5

Psychopharmacological Treatment of Suicidal Inpatients

MARK J. GOLDBLATT
MORTON M. SILVERMAN
ALAN F. SCHATZBERG

In this chapter we focus on the psychopharmacological treatment of patients hospitalized as a result of suicidal behaviors, or with psychiatric disorders that are closely associated with suicidal behaviors. Following a brief overview of the biochemistry of suicide, we review current standards of care in the pharmacological management of psychiatric disorders and behavioral dysfunctions associated with the range of suicidal behaviors most often encountered in hospital settings.

Large-scale empirical studies of consecutive suicides emphasize the correlation between mental illness and suicide (Robins & Murphy, 1959; Dorpat & Ripley, 1960; Barraclough, Bunch, Nelson, & Sainsbury, 1974). Robins and Murphy (1959) reported that 94% of 134 cases of completed suicide were found to have psychiatric diagnoses at the time of death. Just over 50% of these were due to primary depression, and almost 33% were associated with chronic alcoholism. Although there are a number of mental disorders associated with suicide, depression and alcohol-related disorders are generally most closely tied to self-destructive behavior. Panic disorder and panic attacks, bipolar disorders, and cocaine-related disorders are diagnoses that also correlate significantly with suicide and are reviewed in this chapter.

In clinical practice, most hospitalized patients have expressed some degree of suicidality, resulting in the need for admission to a psychiatric facility. Suicide may be considered a lethal component of the underlying psychiatric illness. In this chapter we focus on the appropriate use of medication to treat the underlying psychiatric illness and alleviate the accompanying suicidal component.

BIOCHEMISTRY OF SUICIDE

In recent years increasing attention has been paid to the psychobiology of suicide, with particular emphasis on the examination of two neurotransmitters (serotonin and dopamine) and of the hypothalamic–pituitary–adrenal (HPA) axis. This research has pointed to a number of biochemical features that may be common to the seemingly disparate group of psychiatric disorders with which higher incidences of suicide are associated; it may also provide the basis for developing specific treatment approaches for some suicidal patients.

The role for serotonin as a unifying factor in suicidal behavior was originally proposed by Asberg and colleagues, who reported an association between suicidal behavior and low levels of cerebrospinal fluid (CSF) 5-hydroxyindoleacetic acid (5-HIAA) in depressed patients (Asberg, Traskman, & Thoren, 1976). These observations have been replicated and expanded by reports that violent types of suicide in particular were associated with low CSF 5-HIAA levels (Traskman et al., 1981). In addition, markedly impulsive patients with character disorders have been shown to have low CSF 5-HIAA levels (Linnoila et al., 1983). And levels of 5-HIAA have been shown to be lower in the brains of completed suicides (Beskow et al., 1976).

Investigators have also explored tritiated imipramine binding in platelets as a model for serotonin receptor function. Several groups have reported decreased imipramine binding in the platelets of depressed patients, particularly those with psychotic features (Paul et al., 1981). Meltzer et al. (1981) have reported decreased serotonin transport in the platelets of depressed patients.

Mann et al. (1986) reported a significant increase in the mean number of serotonin-2 receptors (and beta-adrenergic receptors) binding in the frontal cortices of suicide victims. This research supports the hypothesis that suicide completed by violent methods is associated with altered presynaptic serotonin receptor activity, which generates compensatory up-regulation of the postsynaptic serotonin receptor sites. In addition, there may be a concomitant increase in postsynaptic noradrenergic activity. In this study, decreased norepinephrine and serotonin levels were implicated as contributing factors in suicidal behavior.

Furthermore, when hospitalized patients with severe major depressive disorder are treated with antidepressant drugs and electroconvulsive therapy (ECT), tritiated imipramine binding sites are increased, but this may be unrelated to clinical response (Wagner, Aber-Wistedt, & Bertilsson, 1987). Zimelidine, a serotonin uptake inhibitor, has been reported to have more effect on reducing suicidal thoughts than amitriptyline in the early stages of treatment, further suggesting that serotonin may play a primary role in this behavior (Montgomery, McAuley, et al., 1981).

A number of studies have pointed to the curious coupling of serotonin and dopamine systems in various regions of the brain. High-order correlations between CSF homovanillic acid (HVA) and 5-HIAA in depressed patients have been reported in several studies (Aber-Wistedt, Wistedt, & Bertilsson, 1985). The role of dopamine in suicidal character-disordered patients has been inferred from studies on the use of dopamine receptor blockers to decrease suicidal behavior in such patients. Montgomery and Montgomery (1983) reported on the use of flupenthixol, a dopamine receptor blocker, in patients with personality disorders (mainly borderline or histrionic) who had a history of multiple suicide attempts. They raised the possibility that the effect of reducing suicidal behavior in personality disorders is mediated via the dopamine system. They also noted lower levels of CSF HVA, the metabolite of dopamine, in depressed patients with a history of suicidal acts. More recently, Soloff et al. (1986) reported that haloperidol decreased suicidality in borderline patients. Thus, blocking postsynaptic dopamine receptors appears helpful in decreasing suicidality in personality-disordered patients.

HPA axis has been a major focus of research in depressive disorders. Elevated 24-hour urinary free cortisol and dexamethasone nonsuppression are common features of depressed patients. A number of years ago, suicidal behavior was reported to be associated with elevated 24-hour urinary 17-ketosteroids—an observation that has been more recently confirmed by others (Bunney & Fawcett, 1965; Fawcett et al., 1987). Nemeroff et al. (1988)

have reported decreased corticotropin-releasing factor (CRF) receptor activity in the brains of suicide victims, suggesting that elevated CRF may also play a role in suicidality in depression. Cortisol and dexamethasone have been reported to decrease serotonin or 5-HIAA levels in the frontal cortex of rats, perhaps by stimulating alternate synthetic pathways (Green & Curzon, 1968). Conversely, enhanced postsynaptic serotonin activity or sensitivity has been implicated in increased cortisol levels in depressed patients. These data suggest that cortisol and serotonin may be intimately tied to each other, particularly in suicidal depressives.

In depressed subjects, cortisol levels are highest in those with psychotic features—a subgroup that has been reported to be at increased risk for completing suicide (Schatzberg, Rothschild, et al., 1983). Several groups have reported that psychotic depressives demonstrate not only extremely elevated plasma cortisol levels, but high plasma dopamine levels too (Rothschild et al., 1987). Others have reported generally higher CSF HVA and 5-HIAA in psychotic depressives (Agren & Terenins, 1985), although low HVA and 5-HIAA levels have been reported in a subgroup of older psychotic depressives with suicidal ideation (Brown et al., 1987). Glucocorticoids have been reported to increase plasma dopamine and HVA in normal controls, again pointing to possible negative consequences of hypercortisolemia (Rothschild et al., 1984; Wolkowitz et al., 1985). The role of elevated HVA or 5-HIAA in suicidal behavior in psychotic depressives has not been well studied, but findings to date suggest that low or high extremes in serotonin or dopamine (i.e., low 5-HIAA/HVA or high 5-HIAA) may each play a role in different suicidal psychiatric patients.

TREATMENT OF SUICIDAL PATIENTS

All patients undergoing psychiatric evaluation should be assessed as to their level of psychic pain and extent of suicidal ideation, intent, and/or plans. This assessment takes place within the context of the psychiatric interview; the clinician notes the patient's psychopathology and personality structure, as well as any concurrent medical illness or use of medication, and available social and interpersonal support systems. This assessment process is more fully described elsewhere (Maris, Berman, Maltsberger, & Yufit, 1992).

In general, somatic therapies should be aimed at treating symptoms of the underlying psychiatric condition. This occurs within the context of the overall therapeutic and psychoeducational approach to the illness. Medication should be delivered in the context of a positive physician–patient relationship—one that includes mutual respect and conveys a sense of hopefulness. The clinician should not expect to dissuade a patient from his or her hopelessness; rather, the clinician must win the patient's cooperation to undergo a course of treatment. This requires a supportive approach and the building of a working alliance. The clinician's communication of the proposed treatment and expectation that the patient will respond are crucial. The potential for side effects of current medications must be acknowledged, as well as their potential lethality when taken in overdose. However, once treatment has begun, all efforts should be expended to ensure a full trial and prevent undertreatment.

Psychopharmacological evaluation includes a careful review of previous medication trials, with particular attention to specific medication type, dosage, duration of treatment, and history of compliance. Inquiry should also be made as to any history of allergies or complicating medical illness. Family histories of psychopathology, of response to somatic therapies, and of suicidal behaviors are also important.

Prevention of suicidal behavior depends on the appropriate treatment of the underlying psychiatric disorders. What follows is specific consideration of the somatic treatments of depression, delusional depression, bipolar disorders, schizophrenia, alcohol-related disorders, cocaine-related disorders, panic disorder/panic attacks, and borderline personality disorder.

Depression

The National Institute of Mental Health (NIMH) Extramural Collaborative Study of Depression revealed that substantial undertreatment of depressed patients was common, even in academic medical settings. The generally low dosages of somatic treatment and the variability of treatment regimens were attributable to individual medical practitioners' decision making (Keller et al., 1986). Fewer than half of the medication trials that "refractory" depressed patients received were reported to be adequate in dosage or duration (Schatzberg, Cole, et al., 1983).

In the past, the pharmacological treatment of seriously depressed patients began with a tricyclic antidepressant (TCA). More recently, selective serotonin reuptake inhibitors (SSRIs) have become increasingly popular. More and more clinicians are using SSRIs as first-line treatments for depression, given their effectiveness and low incidence of side effects.

Fluoxetine is one of this relatively new group of antidepressant drugs that selectively inhibits the reuptake of serotonin. Its side effect profile is generally more favorable than that of TCAs; it appears to facilitate weight loss in some patients, and does not potentiate seizures in humans. Fluoxetine has a long half-life and appears relatively safe even when taken in overdose. Because it is relatively new, broader clinical use will be needed to more fully delineate this medication's side effect profile and safety limits. However, data from Reimherr et al. (1984) point to its being particularly effective in patients who have failed on TCAs.

Shortly after fluoxetine was introduced to the market, a small number of case reports (e.g., Teicher, Glod, & Cole, 1990) noted the emergence of suicidal ideation in patients taking fluoxetine. A great deal of publicity in the mass media surrounded such reports, and some observers hypothesized that fluoxetine may trigger emergent suicidal and homicidal ideation in a small proportion of patients taking this medication. Further study has clarified that there is no "increased risk of suicidal acts or emergence of substantial suicidal thoughts among depressed patients" associated with the treatment of fluoxetine (Beasley et al., 1991, p. 685). The American College of Neuropsychopharmacology Task Force's review of suicidal behavior and psychotropic medication concluded:

> New generation low-toxicity antidepressants, including SSRIs, may carry a lower risk for suicide than older TCAs. There is no evidence that antidepressants such as the SSRIs, for example fluoxetine, trigger emergent suicidal ideation over and above rates that may be associated with depression and other antidepressants. What is clear is that most patients receive substantial benefit from treatment with this drug and related antidepressants. (Mann, Goodwin, O'Brien, & Robinson, 1993, p. 182)

Other new agents—both SSRIs and "atypical" antidepressants—have proven to be valuable additions to the antidepressant armamentarium. Sertraline (Zoloft), paroxetine (Paxil), bupropion (Wellbutrin), venlafaxine (Effexor), and nefazodone (Serzone) are antidepressants that have been recently approved by the U.S. Food and Drug Administration (FDA). They appear to be equally effective in the treatment of depression and usually are well tolerated, with relatively few side effects.

Trazodone, a mixed serotonin reuptake and receptor blocker, is another alternative for the treatment of depressed patients. An additional advantage is that it is less lethal than TCAs when taken in overdose. Clomipramine, a new TCA, exerts a considerable effect on blocking serotonin reuptake and thus may prove to be a useful alternative treatment for suicidal patients, but this has not been well tested.

If patients are not responding to a course of antidepressant medication, the clinician must assess whether an adequate trial has been achieved. The response to TCAs is often slower than one might wish—up to 4 weeks at therapeutic levels. SSRIs can take up to 8 or 10 weeks to achieve effectiveness. Quitkin et al. (1984) concluded in their review of a series of studies on TCAs in depressed patients that relatively few patients demonstrate significant improvement after only 2 weeks of therapy, and many require as long as 6 weeks to respond. The necessary time course for treatment response remains in considerable debate. The physician should remain responsive to the clinical picture of the individual patient, as well as to the effects that the psychiatric illness may have on the potential for suicidal behaviors.

If only a limited clinical response is noted with a TCA after 6 weeks, the physician should consider increasing the dosage, since some patients metabolize medication rapidly and may require higher doses to respond. Obtaining plasma levels may be helpful for adjusting the dosage of TCAs or for determining the adequacy of a trial. For nortriptyline, a curvilinear relationship has been described, with a critical range of 50 to 150 ng/ml representing a "therapeutic window"; levels above and below this range are frequently associated with poorer responses (Asberg et al., 1971). In endogenously depressed patients, Glassman, Perel, and Shostak (1977) reported a sigmoidal relationship between response and imipramine plus desipramine levels: Clinical response increased with plasma levels up to 250 ng/ml and leveled off thereafter.

For some patients, adding lithium carbonate or liothyronine (Cytomel) to a TCA can bring about a clinical response. If these additions are not effective, the physician is faced with the option of either changing the medication within the same class of drug, moving on to another class of antidepressant, or trying ECT.

Monoamine oxidase inhibitors (MAOIs) block the intraneuronal action of monoamine oxidase, the enzyme that degrades various neurotransmitters, including norepinephrine, dopamine, and serotonin. MAOIs have been reported to be particularly effective in refractory depressed patients, hysteroid dysphorics, and atypical depressives. Clinicians frequently worry that suicidal patients on MAOIs may kill themselves by ignoring their special diets or using proscribed agents. Although case studies have been reported in the literature, we have seldom seen this occur. Generally, even suicidal patients are frightened by the potential pain and sequelae of hypertensive reactions, so that this becomes an unattractive method of self-harm. Rather, MAOIs are often very effective for some suicidal depressives and should be strongly considered.

ECT has generally been shown to be the most broadly effective treatment of depression. ECT should be considered for any seriously depressed patient who has failed to respond to other treatments, or for those with psychotic features. In patients with compromised physical states because of anorexia, catatonia, or psychosis, and in patients with pronounced suicidal ideation/behavior, ECT should be considered early in treatment.

Delusional Depression

Suicide risk is five times higher in delusional than in nondelusional depressions. Robins (1986) reported that 19% of 134 subjects who committed suicide had also been psychotic—a finding that has been confirmed by others. Roose et al. (1983) found that delusionally depressed patients were five times more likely than nondelusionally depressed patients to commit suicide. In our experience, these patients are among the most difficult to treat. They hide the degree of their cognitive disturbance, become frozen or distant, and are difficult to assess for true suicidal risk. Responding to their paranoia, these patients often are afraid of their medication and may be noncompliant with treatment, or may "tongue" their medication. Clinicians should be wary in accepting any assurances about control of suicidal behavior in delusionally depressed patients.

Increased activity of dopamine has been hypothesized as playing a role in delusional depression. These patients respond better to neuroleptic–TCA treatment or to ECT than to TCAs alone (Spiker et al., 1981; Avery & Lubrano, 1979). Better responses to the combination of neuroleptic and TCA than to a TCA alone do not appear to reflect the increased plasma levels of either the TCA or the neuroleptic. Responsiveness of this condition to other antidepressants (e.g., fluoxetine, trazodone, or phenelzine) or to combinations of these agents with antipsychotics has not been well studied.

Bipolar Disorders

Although mania is usually associated with mood elevation and euphoria, several authors have described patients with manic features including affective lability, irritability, anger, and severe dysphoria characterized by depression and anxiety (Post et al., 1989). This is referred to as a "mixed episode" in DSM-IV.

The mainstay of treatment is lithium carbonate. Antipsychotic medications are also helpful in the acute management of a mixed state. Other drugs that are frequently used are carbamazepine (Tegretol) and valproic acid (Depakene). The treatment of these patients may become complicated at times. In some cases they appear to have a relatively poor response to treatment with lithium carbonate, as compared with "pure" manics (Secunda et al., 1986). Post, Uhde, Roy-Byrne, and Joffe (1987) have suggested that this group of patients may show a relatively better therapeutic response to carbamazepine.

Occasionally, it is difficult to distinguish agitated depression from an irritable, dysphoric manic state. The most notable feature in the clinical treatment is that dysphoric manic patients become worse when treated with antidepressant medication.

Schizophrenia

Although schizophrenic disorders are primarily considered to involve difficulties with cognition and thinking rather than with mood, suicide is a serious and unfortunately common complication of this disorder. More than 20% of patients hospitalized for schizophrenia will attempt suicide at some time. The majority of schizophrenic suicides occur among outpatients, usually soon after discharge from the hospital (Caldwell & Gottesman, 1992).

Some schizophrenic patients who commit suicide demonstrate increased agitation or psychosis at the time of their suicidal action. In this subgroup, adequate treatment with antipsychotic medication is essential. Depression in the schizophrenic population is particularly difficult to define or study. The consensus in the literature is that suicidal schizophrenic patients are more likely than nonsuicidal schizophrenic patients to be depressed. However, it is often difficult to distinguish depression from the "negative symptoms" of schizophrenia. Initially, it was believed that antidepressant treatment of the symptoms resulted in an exacerbation of the schizophrenic condition. However, more recent studies have argued that some of these symptoms respond to treatment with TCAs or alprazolam. These drugs are considered worth a trial. Trazodone has been reported to be less likely to promote psychotic decompensation than are other antidepressants. In severe cases, ECT and lithium carbonate can also be considered.

Early studies that were aimed at trying to separate the impact of adequately treated schizophrenia from concomitant depression suggested that neuroleptics (in particular, depot preparations) gave rise to severe depressive moods and therefore facilitated suicide (DeAlarcon & Carney, 1969). Later studies contradicted this finding (Niturad & Nicholschi-Oproiu, 1978). There have, however, been reports of two patients who attempted suicide to relieve severe akathisia (Shear, Frances, & Weiden, 1983). Thus, selecting the "right" drug for schizophrenic patients may be less relevant than developing effective approaches to side effects. It is important to obtain a detailed drug history from the patient, family, and past caregivers, in order to clarify which drugs the patient has received and how he or she has responded to medication over time.

Clozapine, risperidone, and olanzepine are new additions to the treatment armamentarium for schizophrenia. They are structurally different from the more common antipsychotics. In early studies, clozapine has been shown to decrease suicidality in neuroleptic-resistant schizophrenic patients, and has been associated with improvement in depression and hopelessness (Meltzer & Okayli, 1995). Although more studies are indicated to asses the role of the atypical antipsychotic medications in suicidal patients, these new drugs have already proven to be highly valued for their improved response in treatment-refractory psychosis.

Thioridazine is approved by the FDA for use in moderate to marked depression with anxiety or agitation. However, there is no evidence that any neuroleptic is generally superior to standard antidepressants for the treatment of depression. Thioridazine should probably be avoided in sexually active young males, because it may produce retrograde ejaculation.

If a patient dislikes the first few doses of a particular antipsychotic, some physicians advocate trying one or two others to see whether the patient will feel less distressed and be more cooperative with the treatment. Lower rather than higher dosages of a particular drug should be tried first; there is no evidence that daily dosages greater than the equivalent of 15 mg of haloperidol or 400 mg of chlorpromazine are more effective than are lower dosages. For patients who do not begin to improve on an adequate dose of an antipsychotic medication, a different antipsychotic drug can be tried, or a switch can be made to one of the newer antipsychotics, clozapine, risperidone, or olanzepine. Pragmatically, more than 2 weeks without response in a markedly psychotic patient, and 5–6 weeks in a patient with milder symptoms, generally indicate a consideration of a change in medication regimen. Shifting the chemical class of antipsychotic would be a reasonable strategy, but this has not been well studied.

Clozapine, an atypical neuroleptic, does offer an alternative treatment for patients who have failed on standard neuroleptics. Risperidone, a unique serotonergic–dopaminergic antagonist is also an alternative for refractory patients as well as for newly diagnosed ones. Sometimes the addition of a different class of drug, such as lithium or a TCA, may be effective. Depot preparations ensure compliance in patients who are not responding, especially those who do not seem to be responding to adequate doses.

The risk of tardive dyskinesia as a result of conventional neuroleptic medication makes the long-term use of these drugs worrisome. It is currently not possible to predict which patients will develop tardive dyskinesia. However, the best available data suggest a rate of development of dyskinesia of about 3% to 4% over the first 4 or 5 years of exposure. Elderly women and patients with affective disorders appear at greater risk than schizophrenic patients (Gardos & Casey, 1984).

Suicide is a considerable risk in schizophrenic patients. The illness is debilitating, and a patient may be easily demoralized by the cycles of decompensation and recompensation. However, interventions aimed at reducing psychosis and at alleviating distress and depressive/negative symptoms should help to decrease the likelihood of untoward outcomes.

Alcohol-Related Disorders

Alcohol and drug abuse/dependence and affective disorders are commonly associated with suicide. The lifetime risk for suicide is approximately 15% for patients with alcoholism as compared to 1% in the general population. Alcohol misuse increases the risk for suicidal behavior for both alcoholic and nonalcoholic populations, being associated with 50% of all suicides and 5% to 27% of suicides in alcoholics (Robins et al., 1984).

Alcoholics can suffer from other psychiatric illnesses as well, and depression is particularly common. Serotonin represents a possible link between alcoholism and depression. Sellers, Naranjo, and Peachey (1981) have reported that serotonin reuptake blockers reduce alcohol consumption in heavy drinkers. Weingartner, Buchsbaum, and Linnoila (1983) reported that zimelidine, a relatively specific serotonin reuptake blocker, attenuates the impairing effects of ethanol on learning and memory. Thus, serotonin activity may provide a link between suicidality in alcoholic and depressed patients. Prospective studies on the use of SSRIs in treatment for suicidal alcoholics seem reasonable, as does this approach on a clinical basis. Eventually, SSRIs may be included in an overall approach to the treatment of alcohol-related disorders. However, at this point there is no substitute for treatment programs aimed at abstinence, vocational rehabilitation, and psychoeducation.

Cocaine-Related Disorders

Misuse of illicit substances is associated with an increased risk of suicidal behavior. The San Diego Suicide Study, conducted from 1981 to 1983, found that substance abuse was associated with 58% of suicides in young adults, and that substance abuse was the primary diagnosis in 39% of all cases (Fowler, Rich, & Young, 1986). Of particular concern was the finding that suicide risk appears to be highly correlated with misuse of multiple drugs, (Marzuk & Mann, 1988). Although alcohol is the most commonly misused substance, it is often taken in combination with various illicit drugs, including marijuana, hallucinogens, opiates, and cocaine.

The precise causative mechanisms by which psychoactive drug use promotes suicidal behavior remain unclear. Data from the NIMH Epidemiological Catchment Area (ECA) study showed that the risk of panic attacks was greater for identified cocaine users. The estimated relative odds (13) were greatest among cocaine users who reported no marijuana use during the follow-up interval (Anthony, Tien, & Petronis, 1989). In a related report based on the full ECA data set, Petronis, Samuels, Moscicki, and Anthony (1990) conducted multivariate conditional-logistics regression analyses on data collected during a 1- to 2-year follow-up period, to identify potential personal and behavioral risk factors for suicide attempts. They found that being a user of cocaine was associated with increased risk of making a suicide attempt (estimated relative odds = 62), but illicit use of marijuana, sedative/hypnotics, or sympathomimetic stimulants was not. Depression was associated with increased risk of suicide attempt (relative odds = 41), as was active alcoholism (relative odds = 18).

A recent study showed that approximately 20% of completed suicides among residents of New York City had used cocaine within days of their death (Marzuk et al., 1992). After controlling for demographic variables and ethanol use, these investigators found that individuals who committed suicide with firearms were twice as likely to have used cocaine as those who used other methods. There appears to be a relationship between cocaine use, anxiety, and panic attacks, which requires further study. Clinicians should routinely inquire about all types of substance misuse and should advocate interventions aimed at abstinence.

Panic Disorder and Panic Attacks

Follow-up studies of patients with panic disorder, dating back to 1982, have reported significantly increased rates of unnatural mortality, most resulting from suicide (Coryell, Noyes, & Clancy, 1982; Coryell, 1988; Allgulander & Lavori, 1991). Using data from the ECA survey, Weissman, Klerman, Markowitz, and Ouellette (1989) reported that 20% of community members surveyed who met criteria for a diagnosis of panic disorder reported a history of suicide attempts (odds ratio for suicide attempts compared to other disorders was 2.62). In addition, 12% of those who experienced panic attacks, but who failed to meet full criteria for a DSM-III diagnosis of panic disorder, were reported to have a history of suicide attempts. A reanalysis of the data found that 7% of respondents with uncomplicated panic disorder reported a history of suicide attempts (odds ratio = 5.4) (Johnson, Weissman, & Klerman, 1990).

These ECA findings have been criticized from a methodological perspective (Clark & Kerkhof, 1993; Appleby, 1994), as well as from a clinical perspective, because of the presence of comorbidity (particularly depression); this may have accounted for the high prevalence of suicidal ideation and attempts in the cohort reporting panic attacks and panic disorder (Fawcett et al., 1990: Beck, Steer, Sanderson, & Skeie, 1991). Nevertheless, other studies have also found an increased rate of suicide attempts in patients with panic disorder (Lepine, Chignon, & Teherani, 1993; Korn et al., 1992).

Many clinicians now believe that panic attacks appear to be one of several contributing factors that are associated with an increased risk of suicide attempts and completions when they are associated with other psychiatric disorders, especially major affective disorder (Clark & Fawcett, 1992; Appleby, 1994). This underscores the importance of rapid, appropriate treatment for patients with panic attacks and panic disorder, especially when they occur in association with other DSM-IV Axis I or II disorders.

The initial treatment of panic disorder and panic attacks is either with alprazolam (Xanax) or with antidepressants such as imipramine, desipramine, phenelzine, or fluoxetine. Patients with panic attacks generally require lower doses of antidepressants, in the range of 50 mg of imipramine per day. Alprazolam is generally useful in the range of 0.25 mg three times a day up to several milligrams per day for severe cases.

Borderline Personality Disorder

Borderline personality disorder (BPD) is characterized by impulsivity; unstable and intense interpersonal relationships; inappropriate, intense anger; identity disturbance; affective instability; self-destructive acts; and a chronic sense of emptiness. Generally, patients with BPD are not marked responders to psychopharmacological treatments; however, medication may alleviate certain key symptoms.

One report of 58 personality disorder patients who were treated with mianserin or placebo noted no significant reduction in the number of suicidal acts during the 6-month treatment period (Montgomery, Roy, & Montgomery, 1981). However, in a double-blind study of flupenthixol versus placebo, there was a significant reduction over placebo in the number of suicidal acts in the patients treated with flupenthixol at 4, 5, and 6 months (Montgomery et al., 1979). Although various underlying mechanisms are probably involved, flupenthixol's effect on dopamine systems may be inferred to be involved in decreasing suicidal behavior in BPD and other personality disorders.

Soloff et al. (1986) reported that haloperidol produced significant improvement on a broad spectrum of symptom patterns, including depression, anxiety, hostility, paranoid ideation and psychoticism, in borderline patients. In contrast, amitriptyline was found to be minimally effective, with some improvement noted in areas of depressive content. On a composite measure of overall symptom severity, haloperidol was found to be superior to both amitriptyline and placebo, with no difference noted between amitriptyline and placebo. Goldberg et al. (1986) also reported a therapeutic benefit of thiothixene over placebo in treating some selected symptoms of BPD. Significant drug–placebo differences were found on illusions, ideas of reference, psychoticism, obsessive–compulsive symptoms, and phobic anxiety, but not on depression. The mean daily dosage was lower than that used in outpatient schizophrenics.

Although there are at least two studies that have indicated that phenothiazines are helpful in reducing suicidal and other symptoms in borderline patients, there is still much debate about how and whether to use them. Gunderson (1986) has noted that neuroleptics should be reserved for borderline patients who present with sustained and severe symptoms of the kind described above—that is, illusions, ideas of reference, and psychoticism. For borderline patients without these symptoms, or those in whom symptoms are either acute, reactive, or nonsevere, drugs are less likely to be useful and may present unnecessary risks of harmful side effects. This area requires further study.

Two other treatment strategies that may be helpful in BPD patients are MAOIs and anticonvulsants. The MAOIs may be most useful in treating anxiety with related depression in patients with personality disorders. As noted above, phenelzine has been shown to be efficacious in hysteroid dysphorics and atypical depressions with pronounced anxiety. Recently, Cowdry and Gardner (1986) noted that carbamazepine was effective in decreasing the self-destructive behavior of borderline patients, compared to other drug regimens; however, self-destructive behaviors in this group were by no means eliminated. Still, further studies on this approach appear warranted. Recent studies about the effects of SSRIs on BPD patients are encouraging, but more work needs to be done to clarify their potential role for these patients.

CONCLUSION

The suicidal patient represents a challenge to the practitioner. Treatment must begin with a careful assessment of the patient's psychological condition, physical status, and suicidal potential. Thereafter, an organized approach to treating the underlying condition can be undertaken. This approach should include consideration of proven psychotherapeutic interventions and the prescription of appropriate medications in adequate trials (appropriate both in duration and in amount of drug administered). Biological and psychopharmacological studies suggest that SSRIs may prove particularly helpful for alcoholic and depressed patients with suicidal behavior. They also suggest that neuroleptics have an important place in treating schizophrenic patients, and may also play a major role in the treatment of patients with BPD and those with psychotic depression.

ACKNOWLEDGMENT

Portions of this chapter are adapted from Goldblatt and Schatzberg (1990). Copyright 1990 by American Psychiatric Press, Inc. Adapted by permission.

REFERENCES

Aber-Wistedt, A., Wistedt, B., & Bertilsson, L. (1985). Higher CSF levels of HVA and 5-HIAA in delusional compared to nondelusional depression. *Archives of General Psychiatry, 42,* 925–926.

Agren, H., & Terenins, L. (1985). Hallucinations in patients with major depression: Interactions between CSF monoaminergic and endorphinergic indices. *Journal of Affective Disorders, 9,* 25–34.

Allgulander, C., & Lavori, P. W. (1991). Excess mortality among 3302 patients with "pure" anxiety neurosis. *Archives of General Psychiatry, 48,* 599–602.

Anthony, J. C., Tien, A. Y., & Petronis, K. R.(1989). Epidemiologic evidence on cocaine use and panic attacks. *American Journal of Epidemiology, 129,* 543–549.

Appleby, L. (1994). Panic and suicidal behavior. *British Journal of Psychiatry, 164,* 719–721.

Asberg, M., Cronholm, B., Sjoquist, F., et al. (1971). Relationship between plasma level and therapeutic effect of Nortriptyline. *British Medical Journal, 7,* 331–334.

Asberg, M., Traskman, L., & Thoren, P. (1976). 5-HIAA in the cerebrospinal fluid: A biochemical suicide predictor? *Archives of General Psychiatry, 33,* 1193–1197.

Avery, D., & Lubrano, A. (1979). Depression treated with imipramine and ECT: The De Carolis study reconsidered. *American Journal of Psychiatry, 136,* 559–562.

Barraclough, B., Bunch, J., Nelson, B., Sainsbury, P. (1974). A hundred cases of suicide: Clinical aspects. *British Journal of Psychiatry, 125,* 355–373.

Beasley, C. M., Dornseif, B. E., Bosomworth, J. C., et al. (1991). Fluoxetine and suicide: A meta-analysis of controlled trials of treatment for depression. *British Medical Journal, 303,* 685–692.

Beck, A. T., Steer, R. A., Sanderson, W. C., & Skeie, T. M. (1991). Panic disorder and suicidal ideation and behavior: Discrepant findings in psychiatric outpatients. *American Journal of Psychiatry, 148,* 1191–1195.

Beskow, J., Gottfries, C. G., Roos, B. E., et al. (1976). Determination of monoamine and monoamine metabolites in the human brain: Postmortem studies in a group of suicides and in a control group. *Acta Psychiatrica Scandinavica, 53,* 7–20.

Brown, R. P., Keilip, J., et al. (1987, May). *CSF monoamine and depressive subtypes.* Paper presented at the 140th annual meeting of the American Psychiatric Association, Chicago, IL.

Bunney, W. E., Jr., & Fawcett, J. A. (1965). Possibility of a biochemical test for suicide potential. *Archives of General Psychiatry, 13,* 232–239.

Caldwell, C., & Gottesman, I. I. (1992). Schizophrenia—a high risk factor for suicide: Clues to risk reduction. *Suicide and Life-Threatening Behavior, 22,* 479–493.

Clark, D. C., & Fawcett, J. (1992). An empirically based model of suicide risk assessment for patients with affective disorder. In D. Jacobs (Ed.), *Suicide and clinical practice* (pp. 55–74). Washington, DC: American Psychiatric Press.

Clark, D. C., & Kerkhof, A. J. F. M. (1993). Panic disorders and suicidal behavior. *Crisis, 14,* 2–5.

Coryell, W. (1988). Panic disorders and mortality. *Psychiatric Clinics of North America, 11,* 433–440.

Coryell, W., Noyes, R., & Clancy, J. (1982). Excess mortality in panic disorder. A comparison with primary unipolar depression. *Archives of General Psychiatry, 39,* 701–703.

Cowdry, R. W., & Gardner, D. C. (1986). Pharmacotherapy of borderline personality disorder. *Archives of General Psychiatry, 45,* 111–119.

DeAlarcon, R. M., & Carney, M. W. (1969). Severe depressive mood changes following slow release intramuscular fluphenazine injection. *British Journal of Psychiatry, 3,* 564–567.

Dorpat, T. L., & Ripley, H. (1960). A study of suicide in the Seattle area. *Comprehensive Psychiatry, 1,* 349–359.

Fawcett, J., Scheftner, W. A., Fogg, L., et al. (1987). Acute vs. long term clinical predictors of suicide. *CME syllabus and proceedings summary, American Psychiatric Association annual meeting* (pp. 206–207). Washington, DC: American Psychiatric Press.

Fawcett, J., Scheftner, W. A., Fogg, L., et al. (1990). Time-related predictors of suicide in major affective disorder. *American Journal of Psychiatry, 147,* 1189–1194.

Fowler, R. C., Rich, C. L., & Young, D. (1986). San Diego Suicide Study: II. Substance abuse in young cases. *Archives in General Psychiatry, 43,* 962–965.

Gardos, G., & Casey, D. (1984). *Tardive dyskinesia and affective disorders.* Washington, DC: American Psychiatric Press.

Glassman, A. H., Perel, J. M., & Shostak, M. (1977). Clinical implications of imipramine plasma levels for depressive illness. *Archives of General Psychiatry, 34,* 197–204.

Goldberg, S. C., Schulz, S. C., Schulz, P. M., et al. (1986). Borderline and schizotypal personality disorders treated with low-dose thiothixene vs. placebo. *Archives of General Psychiatry, 43,* 680–686.

Goldblatt, M. J., & Schatzberg, A. F. (1990). Somatic treatment of the adult suicidal patient: A brief surgery. In S. J. Blumenthal & D. J. Kupfer (Eds.), *Suicide over the life cycle: Risk factors, assessment, and treatment of suicidal patients* (pp. 425–440). Washington, DC: American Psychiatric Press.

Green, A. R., & Curzon, G. (1968). Decrease of 5-hydroxytryptamine in the brain provoked by hydrocortizone and its prevention by allopurinol. *Nature, 220,* 1095–1097.

Gunderson, J. G. (1986). Pharmacotherapy for patients with borderline personality disorder. *Archives of General Psychiatry, 43,* 698–700.

Gutheil, T. G. (1992). Suicide and suit: Liability after self-destruction. In D. Jacobs (Ed.), *Suicide and clinical practice* (pp. 147–167). Washington, DC: American Psychiatric Press.

Johnson, J., Weissman, M. M., & Klerman, G. (1990). Panic disorder, comorbidity and suicide attempts. *Archives of General Psychiatry, 47,* 805–808.

Keller, M. B., Lavori, P. W., Klerman, G. L., et al. (1986). Low levels and lack of predictors of somatotherapy received by depressed patients. *Archives of General Psychiatry, 43,* 458–466.

Korn, M. L., Kotler, M., Macho, A., et al. (1992). Suicide and violence associated with panic attacks. *Biological Psychiatry, 31,* 607–612.

Lepine, J. P., Chignon, J. M., & Teherani, M. (1993). Suicide attempts in patients with panic disorder. *Archives of General Psychiatry, 50,* 144–149.

Linnoila, M., Virkkunen, M., Scheinin, M., et al. (1983). Low cerebrospinal fluid 5-hydroxyindoleacetic acid concentration differentiates impulsive from nonimpulsive violent behavior. *Life Sciences, 33,* 2609–2614.

Mann, J. J., Goodwin, F. K., O'Brien, C. P., & Robinson, D. S. (1993). Suicidal behavior and psychotropic medication: Accepted as a consensus statement by the ACNP Council, March 2, 1992. *Neuropsychopharmacology, 8,* 177–183.

Mann, J. J., Stanley, M., et al. (1986). Increased serotonin 2 and beta adrenergic receptor binding in the frontal cortices of suicide victims. *Archives of General Psychiatry, 43,* 954–959.

Maris, R. W., Berman, A. L., Maltsberger, J. T., & Yufit, R. I. (Eds.). (1992). *Assessment and prediction of suicide.* New York: Guilford Press.

Marzuk, P. M., & Mann, J. J. (1988). Suicide and substance abuse. *Psychiatric Annals, 18,* 639–645.

Marzuk, P. M., Tardiff, K., Leon, A. C., Stajic, M., Morgan, E. B., & Mann, J. J. (1992). Prevalence of cocaine use among residents of New York City who committed suicide during a one-year period. *American Journal of Psychiatry, 149,* 371–375.

Meltzer, H. Y., Arora, R. C., et al. (1981). Serotonin uptake in blood platelets of psychiatric patients. *Archives of General Psychiatry, 38,* 1322–1326.

Meltzer, H. Y., & Okayli, G. (1995). Reduction of suicidality during clozapine treatment of neuroleptic-resistant schizophrenia: Impact on risk–benefit assessment. *American Journal of Psychiatry, 152,* 183–190.

Montgomery, S. A., et al. (1979). Maintenance therapy in repeat suicidal behavior: A placebo controlled trial. In *Proceedings of the 10th International Congress for Suicide Prevention, Ottawa* (pp. 227–229).

Montgomery, S. A., & Montgomery, D. B. (1983). Psychopharmacology and suicidal behavior. In J. M. Davis & J. W. Maas (Eds.), *The affective disorders* (pp. 309–315). Washington, DC: American Psychiatric Press.

Montgomery, S. A., McAuley, R., Rani, S. J., et al. (1981). A double-blind comparison of zimelidine and amitriptyline in endogenous depression. *Acta Psychiatrica Scandinavica,* (Suppl. 290), 314–327.

Montgomery, D., Roy, D., & Montgomery, S. (1981). Mianserin in the prophylaxis of suicidal behavior: A double blind placebo controlled trial. In *Proceedings of the 11th International Congress for Suicide Prevention, Paris.*

Nemeroff, C. B., Owens, M. J., Bissette, G., et al. (1988). Reduced corticotropin releasing factor binding sites in the frontal cortex of suicide victims. *Archives of General Psychiatry, 45,* 577–579.

Niturad, A., & Nicholschi-Oproiu, L. (1978). Suicidal risk in the treatment of outpatient schizophrenics with long-acting neuroleptics. *Aggressologie, 19,* 145–148.

Paul, S. M., Rehavi, M., Skolnick, P., et al. (1981). Depressed patients have decreased binding of tritiated imipramine to platelet serotonin "transporter." *Archives of General Psychiatry, 38,* 1315–1317.

Petronis, K. R., Samuels, J. F., Moscicki, E. K., & Anthony, J. C. (1990). An epidemiologic investigation of potential risk factors for suicide attempts. *Social Psychiatry and Psychiatric Epidemiology, 25,* 193–199.

Post, R. M., Rubinow, D. R., Uhde, T. W., et al. (1989). Dysphoric mania: Clinical and biological correlates. *Archives of General Psychiatry, 46,* 353–358.

Post, R. M., Uhde, W. T., Roy-Byrne, P. P., & Joffe, R. T. (1987). Correlates of antimanic response to carbamazepine. *Psychiatry Research, 21,* 71–83.

Quitkin, F. M., Rabkin, J. G., Ross, D., et al. (1984). Duration of antidepressant drug treatment: What is an adequate trial? *Archives of General Psychiatry, 41,* 238–245.

Reimherr, F. W., Wood, D. R., Byerley, B., et al. (1984). Characteristics of responders to fluoxetine. *Psychopharmacology Bulletin, 20,* 70–72.

Robins, E. (1986). Psychosis and suicide. *Biological Psychiatry, 21,* 665–672.

Robins, E., & Murphy, G. E. (1959). Some clinical considerations in the prevention of suicide based on a study of 134 successful suicides. *American Journal of Public Health, 49,* 888–889.

Robins, L. N., Helzer, J. E., Weissman, M. M., et al. (1984). Lifetime prevalence of specific psychiatric disorders in three sites. *Archives of General Psychiatry, 41,* 947–958.

Roose, S. P., Glassman, A. H., Timothy-Walsh, B., et al. (1983). Depression, delusions and suicide. *American Journal of Psychiatry, 140*(9), 1159–1162.

Rothschild, A. J., Langlais, P. J., Schatzberg, A. F., et al. (1984). Dexamethasone increases plasma free dopamine in man. *Journal of Psychiatric Research, 18,* 217–223.

Rothschild, A. J., Schatzberg, A. F., Langlais, P. J., et al. (1987). Psychotic and nonpsychotic depressions: Comparison of plasma catecholamine and cortisol measures. *Psychiatry Research, 20,* 143–153.

Schatzberg, A. F., Cole, J. O., Cohen, B. M., et al. (1983). Survey of depressed patients who have failed to respond to treatment. In J. M. Davis & J. W. Maas (Eds.), *The affective disorders* (pp. 73–85). Washington DC: American Psychiatric Press.

Schatzberg, A. F., Rothschild, A. J., Stahl, J. B., et al. (1983). The dexamethasone suppression test: Identification of subtypes of depression. *American Journal of Psychiatry, 140,* 1231–1233.

Secunda, S. K., Katz, M. M., Swann, A. C., et al. (1986). Mixed mania: Diagnosis and treatment. In A. C. Swann (Ed.), *Mania: New research and treatment* (pp. 79–94). Washington, DC: American Psychiatric Association Press.

Sellers, E. M., Naranjo, C. A., & Peachey, J. E. (1981). Drugs to decrease alcohol consumption. *New England Journal of Medicine, 305,* 1255–1262.

Shear, M., Frances, A., & Weiden, P. (1983). Suicide associated with akathisia and depot fluphenazine treatment. *Journal of Clinical Psychopharmacology, 3,* 235–236.

Soloff, P. H., George, A., Nathan, S., et al. (1986). Progress in pharmacotherapy of borderline disorders: A double-blind study of amitriptyline, haloperidol and placebo. *Archives of General Psychiatry, 43,* 691–700.

Spiker, D. G., Hanin, I., Cofsky, J., et al. (1981). Pharmacological treatment of delusional depressives. *Psychopharmacology Bulletin, 17,* 201–202.

Teicher, M. H., Glod, C., & Cole, J. O. (1990). Emergence of intense suicidal preoccupation during fluoxetine treatment. *American Journal of Psychiatry, 147,* 207–210.

Traskman, L., Asberg, M., Bertilsson, L. J., et al. (1981). Monoamine metabolites in CSF and suicidal behavior. *Archives of General Psychiatry, 38,* 631–636.

Wagner, A., Aber-Wistedt, A., & Bertilsson, L. (1987). Effects of antidepressant treatments on platelet tritiated imipramine binding in major depressive disorder. *Archives of General Psychiatry, 44,* 870–877.

Weingartner, H., Buchsbaum, M. S., & Linnoila, M. (1983). Zimelidine effects on memory impairments produced by ethanol. *Life Sciences, 33,* 2159–2163.

Weissman, M. M., Klerman, J. L., Markowitz, J. S., & Ouellette, R. (1989). Suicidal ideation and suicide attempts in panic disorder and attacks. *New England Journal of Medicine, 321,* 1209–1214.

Wolkowitz, O. M., Sutton, M. E., Doran, A. R., et al. (1985). Dexamethasone increases plasma HVA but not MHPG in normal humans. *Psychiatry Research, 16,* 101–109.

6

Clinical Psychopharmacotherapy with Hospitalized Patients: A Forensic Perspective

MORTON M. SILVERMAN

I focus in this chapter on the patient who is hospitalized for treatment of a suicidal behavior, or for a psychiatric disorder that is highly associated with the onset of suicidal behaviors. The present perspective is one of suggesting standards of care for the psychopharmacological assessment and management of patients with suicidal behaviors, or patients at high risk for the expression of suicidal behaviors. Other chapters in this book have addressed the specific psychopharmacological treatment of psychiatric disorders and behavioral dysfunctions associated with the range of suicidal behaviors most often encountered in hospital settings. My aim is not to discuss which drugs to use in which doses for which disorders (see Goldblatt & Schatzberg, 1990, portions of which are adapted in Chapter 5). The focus here is on standards of care pertaining to the use of medications with suicidal individuals seen in inpatient settings.

It is also beyond the scope of this chapter to discuss the indications for hospitalization of patients who have the potential for self-destruction; this subject is likewise covered in depth elsewhere (see Bongar, 1991; Slaby,

1994; Goldblatt, 1994; and Chapter 3, this volume). However, the topic of postdischarge planning when a patient is on a psychotropic medication is addressed here because this subject has not received sufficient attention to date.

Finally, it is not my purpose here to review the signs and symptoms for each of the major disorders and dysfunctions commonly associated with suicidal behaviors. Again, the focus here is on reviewing the contextual issues surrounding the benefits and limitations of psychotropic medications for hospitalized suicidal patients, and the steps that the clinician needs to review in the process of medicating a suicidal patient. Although suicidal ideation, intent, or action may be transient, impulsive, or unpredictable (concealed) in a clinical setting, I start with the assumption that clinicians are working with hospitalized patients who have already expressed suicidal behaviors, or who have psychiatric or medical diagnoses often associated with suicidality. The focus is thus on inpatients for whom suicidal risk is a component of their underlying clinical manifestation of disease, or in whom acute suicidal behaviors have appeared as a consequence of being treated for a disorder or disease. In either case, the objective is the appropriate use of medications to alleviate, diminish, ameliorate, or eradicate the suicidal component of their illness.

A MODEL FOR PSYCHOPHARMACOLOGICAL INTERVENTIONS

Although there is no definitive protocol for psychopharmacological intervention with a suicidal patient, certain steps logically follow each other and parallel the commonly accepted approach to the evaluation, treatment, and management of psychiatric patients. Figure 6.1 is a general flow chart for psychopharmacological interventions, based on the standard sequence of steps used to evaluate, treat, and manage psychiatric patients.

Table 6.1 is an elaboration of the key components in a psychopharmacological intervention. Although it is far from exhaustive, it lists some specifics that are believed to be essential components in the assessment, treatment, and management of patients placed on psychotropic medications. In the first four categories, it provides the key elements of a comprehensive evaluation for the use of psychopharmacological agents. It is not enough just to document the patient's prior and current history of medication usage (types, doses, frequency, duration, responses, etc.). It is also

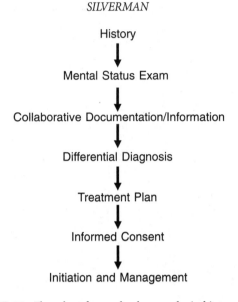

FIGURE 6.1. Flow chart for psychopharmacological intervention.

necessary to inquire about the patient's psychological response to the medications, and the degree of his or her compliance and adherence to drug regimens. A patient's past or current experiences with medications may well foreshadow the future relationship with medications prescribed.

Conducting a complete mental status examination is critical to establishing a diagnosis, as well as establishing a baseline of mental and emotional functioning upon which all future assessments are compared. One of the goals of psychopharmacological intervention is to restore the patient to his or her former level of functioning prior to the onset of illness. Establishing the characteristics, signs, and symptoms of the patient's current illness not only guides the clinician as he or she chooses an appropriate intervention, but also serves as a foundation upon which to monitor change over time, gauge response to pharmacological intervention, and evaluate movement toward recovery. Needless to say, conducting a thorough suicide assessment, including a detailed understanding of prior suicidal behaviors, is essential to providing optimal assessment and care.

Furthermore, it is important to ask the patient whether family members have had similar psychiatric disorders (including suicidal behaviors), and, if so, whether they have responded to various classes of psychotropic medications (including dosages and outcomes). Not only is it important to seek this information from the patient, but it is important to secure inde-

TABLE 6.1. Key Components in a Psychopharmacological Intervention

History:	Known allergies
	Family history of diagnoses and responses to medications
	Medical conditions and current medications
	Prior reaction to drugs—side effects and adverse reactions
	Prior drug trials—names of drugs, amounts, frequency, duration
	Presence of chronic diseases of liver, kidney, heart
	Recent changes in physical status
Mental status exam:	Cognitive status
	Assessment of reliability
	Adherence and compliance history
	Drug abuse and overdose history
	Impulsivity and violence history
	Concerns/fears about medications and their effects
	Current stressors
	Documentation of onset, course, frequency, duration, intensity of symptoms
Collaborative data:	Family history of psychopathology
	Family history of physical illnesses
	Family history of response to psychotropic medications
Diagnoses:	Full consideration of Axis I–V disorders
Treatment plan:	Discussion of goals, means, and plan
	Goals of psychopharmacological treatment
	Expected benefits/outcomes of proposed regimen
Informed consent:	Providing literature regarding medications
	Documentation of discussion re: use of medications
	Signing of appropriate forms
Management:	Observation for side effects and adverse reactions
	Documentation of changes in symptoms
	Monitoring of therapeutic blood levels (if applicable)

pendent, collaborative documentation of a family history of psychopathology (especially suicidality), physical illnesses, and response to psychotropic medications. The choice of a specific medication may well be dictated by whether first-degree relatives have had positive responses to the same medication in the past.

Even when psychopharmacological interventions are warranted and a specific class of medications is indicated, it is incumbent upon the psychopharmacologist to document the expected goals of the treatment, for the benefit of other members of the treatment team. Furthermore, the responsible approach to the medication of inpatients with suicidal thoughts and behaviors includes the documentation of a full and frank discussion with the patient (and significant others) of the proposed psychopharmacological intervention—its expected benefits and its possible side effects.

Maybe the most important components of the psychopharmacotherapeutic intervention with a suicidal patient are the initiation phase of medication use and the longer-term management of the drug therapy. It is evident that the decision to use medications for the treatment of suicidal thoughts and behaviors is often based on the short-term goal of reducing or eliminating the acute intent or desire for self-destructiveness. Hence, the psychopharmacologist may well be working under less than optimum conditions when attempting to quickly reverse a situation that, by definition, is life-threatening. The choice of medications, the dosages used, the frequency and route of administration, and the level of side effects to be tolerated may well be dictated by the individual circumstances created by the interaction of patient, underlying disease, comorbid disorders, and setting.

The longer-term management of patients on psychotherapeutic medications requires regular and periodic evaluations which are designed to review goals of treatment, to assess costs and benefits, and to monitor side effects. These are opportunities to inquire about the development of other disorders or dysfunctions (and their treatment) that might interact with the current regimen. Hence, longer-term management incorporates routine reevaluation, periodic medication adjustment and alteration procedures, and regular monitoring for adherence and compliance.

PSYCHOPHARMACOTHERAPY
OF THE SUICIDAL PATIENT

The approach to the pharmacotherapy of suicide is fraught with some ambiguity and uncertainty, because we only possess minimal knowledge about the interrelationships between and among those thoughts, desires, and actions that constitute the domain of suicidality (Linehan, 1986; Maris, 1992). Despite the best efforts of researchers and theoreticians alike, we lack a "road map" for the causal unfolding of suicidal ideations, intents, attempts, or completions. Although we know much about statistical associations among identifiable risk factors (genetic, familial, societal, biological, demographic, etc.), we lack the precision to predict which sets of risk factors under which conditions for which individuals will result in the expression of suicidal ideations or behaviors (Pokorny, 1992).

Similarly, we are far from elucidating the precise biochemical and neurological pathways that predispose individuals to the expression of suicidality, let alone those that result in the precipitation of these predispositions into actions. Nevertheless, we do have some clues based on strong findings that support the biochemical and neurobiological bases of suicidal behaviors (Linnoila et al., 1983; Mann et al., 1989; Mann & Arango, 1992; Pandey et al., 1995; Mann, Goodwin, O'Brien, & Robinson, 1993; Asberg, Schalling, Traskman-Bendz, & Wagner, 1987). Hence, it seems warranted to conduct (or at least consider conducting) a psychopharmacological evaluation for any patient at risk for suicidal behaviors (Arango & Mann, 1992).

One of the difficult dilemmas when evaluating the suicidal behavior or potential for self-destruction of a patient is to determine what may be the source or etiology of the current suicidality. If one assumes that all behaviors (and specifically suicidal behaviors) have a direct relationship to factors in the biopsychosocial sphere of the patient, then one must try to understand the suicidal behaviors in relation to these conditions, situations, or contributing factors. Table 6.2 outlines six medical or psychiatric conditions that are frequently associated with the expression of suicidal ideation, intent, plans, or behaviors. Again, this list is far from exhaustive; however, for the purposes of this discussion, it addresses the range of options confronting the clinician who is trying to decide whether psychotropic medications may be indicated as part of the overall treatment of a suicidal patient. It is rare that suicidal ideations, intent, plans, or attempts occur in isolation or arise *de novo* in patients. Most often they are associated with some current or recent event or condition in a patient's biopsychosocial sphere.

It is frequently a challenge to the clinician to determine the source of a patient's suicidality. Suicidality may emerge as a consequence of a depressed psychological state, secondary anxiety, command hallucinations, delusional thought processes, confusion/delirium from an organic mental process, or disorientation secondary to anti-inflammatory medications or chemotherapy. It is therefore incumbent upon the clinician and psychopharmacologist to understand the context in which the suicidal thoughts and behaviors are emerging. The decision to act and the choice of psychopharmacotherapeutics should depend upon the careful assessment and regular review of the etiology of the suicidal symptoms.

TABLE 6.2. Relation between Suicidal Behaviors and Other Psychiatric/Medical Conditions: A Psychopharmacological Perspective

Suicidal behaviors may be associated with one or more of the following:

1. Onset/exacerbation of an underlying psychiatric disorder
   Schizophrenia
   Bipolar disorders
   Major depressive disorder
   Substance use disorders

2. Current life stressor that overwhelms the at-risk patient
   Sudden loss/bereavement
   Marital disruption
   Economic change

3. Treatment of a psychiatric disorder
   Adverse reaction to psychotropic medications (e.g., agitation)
   Emergence of suicidality as depression improves

4. A physical condition (underlying medical condition)
   Hypothyroidism
   Brain tumor
   Cancer
   Decreased peripheral blood flow (i.e., delirium, dementia)

5. Medical treatment (i.e., adverse reactions to drug treatment)
   Chemotherapy for cancer
   Reserpine for hypertension management
   Corticosteroids for treatment of immune system disorders
   High-dose antibiotics for treatment of resistant infections

6. An inherited predisposition toward suicidal behavioral patterns in response to stressors in the biopsychosocial domain

Often this determination dictates the decision to use psychotropic medications. If the decision is in the affirmative, then the choice of medication is related to the etiological and correlative factors identified. For example, if the suicidality of the patient is transient and secondary to an acute stressor, then the clinician may choose not to treat the patient with medications or to treat with a medication that is known to be effective for short time periods (i.e., time-limited). Such medications include the anxiolytics and minor tranquilizers.

If the suicidal behavior is a consequence of the chronic and ongoing use of other medications for the treatment of chronic medical or psychiatric disorders, then the clinician is faced with the choice of adjusting, altering, or changing the primary medication for the treatment of the primary disorder (and thus, ideally, eliminating the "suicidal side effects" of the current medication), or of adding another medication to reduce or eliminate the suicidal component associated with the primary treatment of the chronic disorder. For example, some psychotropic medications used for the treatment of major psychiatric disorders (e.g., schizophrenia and bipolar disorders) can cause depression, agitation, and neuroleptic-induced akathisia (Gardos & Casey, 1984; Shear, Frances, & Weiden, 1983; DeAlarcon & Carney, 1969). These unpleasant and disruptive side effects can contribute to the expression of suicidal behaviors in at-risk patients. When these suicidal symptoms arise, the clinician must first reevaluate the current medications for safety, efficacy, and effectiveness. Then a decision needs to be made regarding how to directly address the presence of suicidal thoughts, plans, or behaviors.

Just as a patient may suffer from more than one physical disease concurrently, so may a patient suffer from more than one psychiatric disorder at the same time. It is not an easy decision to enter into the polypharmaceutical approach to the treatment of suicidal behaviors, because it requires a broad understanding of pharmacokinetics, pharmacodynamics, and the growing literature on drug–drug interactions. "Pharmacokinetics" refers to the biological actions of absorption, distribution, metabolism, and elimination of drugs by the body; "pharmacodynamics" refers to the mechanisms of action of the drugs in the body (Preskorn, 1993).

As more potentially psychoactive medications move from prescription status to over-the-counter status, and as patients thus have freer access to more medications, the potential for drug–drug interactions increases. One drug may potentiate or attenuate the mechanism of action of another drug (pharmacodynamics) or affect the metabolism and/or elimination of another drug (pharmacokinetics). One inherent danger in the multiple-drug approach to the treatment of suicidal behaviors is for the clinician to forget to ask about the use of over-the-counter drugs, such as sedatives/hypnotics, antihistamines, "cold" tablets, and analgesics. These drugs have the potential to interact with prescription drugs, and thus to create a risk of adverse reactions, such as delirium, confusion, anxiety, or agitation.

The focus of this chapter is on the psychopharmacological evaluation of inpatients who express suicidal ideation, intent, plans, or behaviors. As discussed above, the common scenario is the evaluation either of patients who are hospitalized because of a primary medical or psychiatric disorder and subsequently develop suicidal behaviors, or of patients who are hospitalized because of their imminent/acute suicidality. Table 6.3 outlines suicidal warning signs, symptoms, and situations that are often present in inpatients. The list is not exhaustive or definitive, but rather suggestive of the range of presentations warranting a consideration of immediate psychotropic intervention. The potential psychopharmacological interventions include anxiolytics, sedatives/hypnotics, mood stabilizers, antipsychotics (neuroleptics), antidepressants, and hormones. The appearance of these signs and symptoms must be first understood in relation to the preexisting psychiatric or medical disorder, and thought must be given to the reassessment of the current treatment plan for the primary disorder. Only after a review is made of the total treatment plan can the addition of medications directed at the suicidal component of the illness be considered.

Table 6.4 outlines a sequence of psychopharmacotherapeutic interventions for suicidal behaviors. This sequence is not exhaustive; rather, it suggests a way of proceeding that should keep the patient and treatment team aware of and involved in the interventions as they unfold. Medications should be seen as an adjunct to or component of the total treatment plan. Because the administration and management of medications require special knowledge and training, it is imperative that the psychopharmacologist understand the importance of communication (often through documentation) with the total treatment team. Total reliance on the use of medications to alter suicidal behaviors is inappropriate and often unjustified, on the part of both the psychopharmacologist and the treatment team. Recognition and appreciation of respective roles and responsibilities in the total approach to the care of the suicidal inpatient are key to a successful outcome.

TABLE 6.3. Some Suicidal Warning Signs, Symptoms, and Situations Requiring Consideration of Immediate Psychopharmacological Intervention

Command hallucinations
Paranoid or persecutory delusions
Depression with psychotic features
Depression with suicidal ideation/intent
Substance abuse or dependence with a history of impulsivity/violence
Acute agitation/anxiety with suicidal ideation/intent
Panic disorder with marked agitation/anxiety
Clearly stated intent for self-injury
Clearly stated plans to die
Difficult-to-manage psychotic and/or manic episodes

TABLE 6.4. Psychopharmacotherapeutic Intervention Sequence for Suicidal Behavior

Medication trial considerations are documented.

Pros and cons of various medications are discussed with patient.

Informed consent is obtained.

Initiation of medication trial is begun slowly and with monitoring of side effects and adverse symptoms.

Blood levels of active metabolites are requested, if available.

Justifications are documented for discontinuing, decreasing, or increasing dosages beyond recommended/accepted levels.

Endpoints are established (goals of symptom reduction are clarified).

Justifications are documented for adjunctive somatic therapies (additions of other psychoactive medications).

Adequate trials are undertaken (time frames match or exceed current recommendations).

Benefits of alternative approaches are documented if reevaluation of medication regimen is warranted.

POSTDISCHARGE PLANNING

Ideally, postdischarge planning occurs at the stage of inpatient treatment when the patient has reached stability and is found to be responding positively to the *total* therapeutic regimen, including, but not limited to, the psychopharmacological agents prescribed. Even here, it is important to measure "good response" across a number of variables, both objective and subjective. Objective variables include side effect profile, blood levels (when applicable), symptom checklist scores, behavioral observation scales, sleep monitoring, and the like. Subjective measurements include the patient's self-observation and reporting of mood, energy level, eating and sleep patterns, thought processes, medication side effects, outlook, hopefulness, and so forth. The observations and feedback of family members, friends, and significant others are important adjuncts to the trained observations of the hospital staff.

Unfortunately, postdischarge planning may come too soon in the process of inpatient stabilization, assessment, treatment, and management. Recent changes in third-party health insurance coverage (i.e., managed care programs and utilization review procedures) have necessitated post-discharge planning for suicidal patients at the point right after stabilization or assessment—at times even before treatment has begun or been normalized. This has added tremendous pressures to inpatient treatment teams to be more efficient and efficacious. Consequently, postdischarge planning has taken on an added dimension—one not far removed from some of the activities and maneuvers that occur in the outpatient setting when a patient is initially begun on a treatment plan, with or without the use of medications. These developments make various components of the planning process all the more important: involving significant others in the overall treatment (or postdischarge) plans, closely monitoring patient compliance, developing and monitoring alliances, clarifying roles and responsibilities, assessing informed consent, providing materials to read about the illness and the function and role of medications, developing contingency plans for emergencies or therapeutic setbacks, discussing availability, and setting goals (see Bongar, 1991, and Chapter 4, this volume).

When a patient has been started on psychotropic medications, it is essential to establish systems of close monitoring and frequent evaluation, for purposes of both assessment and adjustment. Evaluation must consist of both objective *and* subjective measurements, as discussed above. A common error is to rely too heavily on any one measurement of stability, improvement, or even worsening of the condition being treated. Once again, there is no substitute for the role of experience and training in informing the clinical judgment of the primary clinician. Nevertheless, I feel that some general guidelines may serve all medicated patients well in the postdischarge planning process. These standards of care are outlined in Table 6.5.

A few points need to be highlighted here. Of particular importance is the increasing frequency of "split therapy," in which a physician is solely responsible for medication consultation, management, and/or monitoring, and a nonphysician is primarily or solely responsible for providing psychotherapy in one or more of its many forms—individual (insight, supportive, cognitive-behavioral, educational), group, family, and/or couple/marital. Hence, there is a split in duties and responsibilities between the psychopharmacologist and the psychotherapist. Herein lies many potential pitfalls for the coordinated, collaborative, and cooperative care of the suicidal patient after discharge. The roles and function of professional communication become paramount. The treating clinicians' ability to communicate between and among themselves rests with the patient's consent for release of information. The process of communication is labor-intensive and time-dependent. All parties must have a common reference point (the patient), which may well be shifting over time (ideally, in the agreed-upon direction), as well as a common language to discuss their observations, insights, and recommendations.

Although expertise is assigned on the basis of training, experience, and commonly accepted roles and responsibilities, it is not acceptable for one member of the team to profess ignorance of the activities or modes of

TABLE 6.5. Postdischarge Planning: Standards of Care

Document the lethal dose amounts for all drugs prescribed (the LD50 as well as the equivalent in milligrams/kilograms for the patient).

Document the therapeutic blood level range (if applicable) that is being sought.

Document whether the generic or brand name is being prescribed, and whether the patient knows the distinctions (to avoid confusion).

Document prior reactions or side effects to *all* known medications.

Document known drug–drug interactions with over-the-counter drugs the patient may also use (e.g., antihistamines, analgesics, anti-inflammatory agents, etc.), or other medications the patient may be prescribed (e.g., antibiotics, antihypertensives, antihistamines, antiarrhythmia drugs, etc.).

Prescribe medications in small quantities (i.e., amounts that are not potentially lethal if consumed all at once).

Develop methods (i.e., specify responsible persons, timetable, recording locations, etc.) to monitor medication usage and response.

Establish guidelines and schedules for usage—time of day, amounts to be taken, contingency plans for missed doses.

Discuss any dietary or exercise restrictions or contraindications.

Discuss expectations regarding length of time to be on medications(s).

Review therapeutic ranges of medication(s).

Discuss common side effects and how to manage them.

Discuss unusual or infrequent side effects and how to manage them.

Discuss potentially life-threatening signs and symptoms associated with the medication(s) and how to respond to them.

Determine who is to be ultimately responsible for the administration of the medication—the therapist, the psychopharmacologist, the patient, and/or the family.

therapeutic interventions of the other professionals involved in the care of the suicidal patient. In short, psychopharmacologists need to be familiar with the psychotherapies, and psychotherapists need to be aware of the common psychopharmacological interventions for the major disorders and dysfunctions associated with suicidal behaviors. In addition, psychotherapists need to be familiar with the side effect profiles of the medications their patients are prescribed, and to be comfortable with conversing with prescribing physicians. When there is split therapy, there is an added obligation among all the involved parties to "bridge the gap" on both a regular and an as-needed basis.

One of the inherent dangers in postdischarge planning scenarios is that patients have often not benefited from a full trial on a medication because of limitations placed on their hospital stays. Such limitations can result from many causes and have been discussed above. The dangers are that patients may have only partial responses to medications at this point in their treatment, and that these responses (sometimes even being ascribed to a placebo effect) may not be sustained over time. This leaves the

patients vulnerable to relapse even when they ostensibly are being appropriately medicated. Another danger is that medications (usually antidepressants), in their early phases of onset, may serve to "energize" patients just
enough to allow them the physical and psychic energy to become self-
destructive, before the full intended benefit of the medication "kicks in" to
relieve the underlying despair and pain associated with the suicidal process
(Gutheil, 1992). Hence, discharging an undermedicated patient carries
inherent risks for patient and clinician alike.

Full and frequent discussions about the goals of psychopharmacological therapy and a schedule of regular contacts (in person, by phone, by
pager, etc.), must be essential parts of postdischarge planning. It is always
prudent to record the nature and extent of the patient's participation in
these discussions. Needless to say, the patient's capacity to participate in
such a treatment plan needs to be specifically assessed and documented
(Gutheil, Bursztajn, & Brodsky, 1986). In fact, such a clinical exercise and
documentation should be undertaken whenever a change in treatment plan
or strategy is undertaken.

Another maneuver that is often employed is one of prescribing only
small (nonlethal) amounts of potentially lethal, yet therapeutic, medications to suicidal patients. The logic is quite simple: If one assumes that in
many cases clinicians cannot predict suicide with any degree of certainty
(Pokorny, 1992), and that many suicidal acts have an impulsive, contextual
nature/component that is often outside clinicians' immediate purview, then
the most efficient and efficacious preventive intervention is to limit the
lethality of the available means for committing self-harm. This translates
into the practice of only prescribing small amounts of medications (usually
not exceeding a week's supply of medications or a total amount equivalent
to less than a lethal dose, based on a milligrams/kilograms calculation).
This practice also has the added benefit of ensuring that there is regular
contact between patient and physician generally, and that close monitoring
of the specific pharmacological effects of the medication is possible.

However, there are a number of notable problems with this approach.
One has to do with the implied message of trust. This is both a psychotherapeutic and a psychopharmacological issue, and, as suggested above, it
takes different forms depending upon whether there is "split therapy" or
not.

Another implication has to do with concepts of autonomy and freedom, and the extension of the concept of the least restrictive environment
to a postdischarge (or outpatient) treatment setting. Here the clinician is

dealing with the role of impulsivity as a factor in the *expression* of suicidal behaviors. At issue is where the impulsivity "resides"—with the patient or with the underlying illness. If it "belongs" to the illness, then the physician can form an alliance with the patient against the illness and its impulsive nature (which results in the risk of suicide). A therapeutic maneuver, then, is for physician and patient to agree to restrict the availability of medications to thwart the patient's impulse to harm himself or herself with the medications, while at the same time agreeing that the continued use of the medication is essential to diminish or eradicate the underlying illness that "generates" the impulsivity (Gutheil, 1985).

Yet another implication relates to a message about the severity of the illness, as well as the intensity and immediacy of the suicidal risk. Given the discussion above, it should not be surprising to a patient that the short-term plan following hospital discharge is to ensure frequent contacts for purposes of medication evaluation, monitoring, and adjustment. There is no good rationale for stockpiling medications during this initial postdischarge medication adjustment phase.

A final scenario involves the mutual self-deception by patient and physician that the risk of suicide is "under control" because the total amount of medication available is insufficient to result in death (Gutheil, 1992). There then develops a dangerous "cushion" for the physician, who may now no longer be as diligent or direct in assessing suicidal impulses and preoccupations on a regular and routine basis. The patient may feel temporary "relief" that the physician has not given him or her a means for self-destruction, but it does not prevent the patient from harboring self-destructive tendencies or acquiring access to other means of self-destruction.

LIABILITY ISSUES IN THE MEDICATION
OF SUICIDAL PATIENTS

At least two negative outcomes place the clinician who is involved in medicating suicidal patients at potential risk for suit: (1) when it is alleged that a patient who dies by suicide was not adequately evaluated for treatment with medication; and (2) when it is alleged that the medication prescribed may be somehow related to a suicide. This second negative outcome is based on the assumption that improper, inappropriate, or inadequate medication regimens may have propelled the patient toward suicide, or that the medication may have been used as the means for committing suicide (which suggests that its potential for lethality was not being properly monitored or appreciated by the clinician). The first situation, that of a patient's committing suicide while under the care of a treating physician, has been explored and discussed elsewhere (Bongar, 1991; Ruben, 1990; Gutheil, 1992; Maltsberger, 1992; Simon, 1992; Berman & Cohen-Sandler, 1983). The focus here is on situations where the prescribed medication is implicated in the suicidal act.

In my opinion, a clinician often finds himself/herself "in the middle" as the mediating agent "orchestrating" a match between the available medications and the therapeutic needs of the client. This requires the clinician/agent to be exceedingly knowledgeable about both ends of the spectrum. On the one hand, the responsible clinician must be familiar with the fields of psychopharmacology, pharmacodynamics, and pharmacokinetics. The clinician must be aware of the currently available classes of pharmaceutical agents that are approved for the treatment of those conditions most often associated with suicidality. The clinician must be familiar with the descriptions of the medications as they appear in such standard reference texts as the *Physicians' Desk Reference* (*PDR*, 1997), or in the full package inserts that often accompany drug starter kits. The physician must be familiar with the most common contraindications for usage, side effects, adverse reactions, and drug–drug interactions associated with the use of the medication. The clinician must be familiar with other factors as well, including starting doses, therapeutic dosage ranges, time frames for achieving initial relief of symptoms, half-life metabolism times, frequency and timing of administration, and (of course) potentially lethal dosage ranges.

The clinician must also be familiar with combinations of psychotropic medications that can enhance or potentiate each other's effects to achieve better clinical responses overall. In some cases, the combination of two or more psychotropic medications is required in order to achieve a desired therapeutic response. Knowledge of which combinations seem to work best together is dependent upon the clinician's remaining current in the rapidly changing field of clinical psychopharmacology.

From the other perspective, the clinician must be clear about the underlying disorder/disease that the patient is suffering from; the target signs and symptoms that may be precipitating a current suicidal crisis and/or predisposing a patient toward a probable future suicidal behavior; the immediacy and timing needed for initiation of a medication trial to relieve or attenuate symptoms associated with a suicidal crisis; and the current physical and mental context in which the patient resides. The clinician must also know the following about the patient: his or her ability to understand the illness and the associated signs/symptoms, prior experiences with and knowledge about the use of medications, resistance to being placed on medications, past level of adherence and compliance to therapeutic regimens, current willingness to adhere to a medication trial, family history of similar psychiatric disorders and response to psychopharmaceuticals, and understanding of the role of medication in the overall approach to treating the current disorder.

Furthermore, the clinician must arrive at a clinical judgment about the doctor–patient relationship and the degree of therapeutic alliance that exists. This entails an assessment of the patient's competence and capacity to engage in the treatment. This consideration is always essential, but it is particularly necessary as the patient moves toward the postdischarge planning phase, when quantities of prescribed medications as well as other substances (alcohol, tobacco, other licit and illicit drugs of abuse) will be more readily available to the patient in an outpatient context.

In my opinion, the prescribing of potentially lethal medications to a patient with a known history of, or a high degree of risk for, suicidality involves a "sacred trust" between patient and physician. This trust, at a minimum, suggests that the patient trusts the physician to prescribe the most reasonable and prudent medication regimen that will assist the patient's recovery (after a careful weighing and frank discussion of all the pros and cons relevant to its administration). This covenant also suggests that the physician trusts the patient to respect the use of the medication for the purposes intended, and that the medication is understood to be but one component of an overall treatment plan that requires the patient's concurrence, involvement, and ownership. It is my belief that this trust can only be broken by mutual consent, following mutual exploration and discussion of alternative options. It is beyond the scope of this discussion to review psychoanalytic thought on the meaning of the physician's prescribing medications to the patient, although such thinking may have relevance to the long-term psychodynamic treatment of suicidal patients on medication (Dulit & Michels, 1992; Maltsberger & Buie, 1974; Hendin, 1987; Maltsberger, 1992).

A related subject is the hypothesized role of psychotropics as "chemical restraints" that serve to prevent the patient from "getting in touch" with his or her psychic pain or despair, thus impeding the psychotherapeutic healing process in a psychotherapy context. Another version of the argument sees these "drugs" as "chemicals" that serve to alter the patient's "personality." A third variation argues that psychotropic drugs inappropriately "block" an individual from acting on his or her inherent desires or wishes, even when he or she may be blatantly self-destructive. The general argument is that a competent individual should not be "drugged" in order to prevent the person from "being himself or herself," and thus acting on feelings, even when they are self-destructive. My perspective is that these issues need to be explored with the patient and his or her support network in the context of discussing the pros and cons of medication in the clinical setting.

CONCLUSIONS

The decision to place any patient on psychotropic medications should never be made hastily or without sufficient forethought. There are many potential negative consequences to placing a patient on psychotropics—stigmatic, financial, legal, psychological, and physiological—as well as positive therapeutic consequences. The decision to place a suicidal patient on medications engenders additional degrees of concern and complications (safety, security, sense of hope, sense of failure, risk, etc.).

To date, suicide and the state of being suicidal are understood as behavioral manifestations of underlying psychological or physiological disorder, disease, dysfunction, or distress. The suicidal behavior may be a consequence of the underlying disorder or dysfunction, or a reaction to its presence. The medications that are presently available fall within different functional and therapeutic classes. Some are curative (i.e., they directly address and eradicate the underlying disease agent or process); some are palliative (i.e., they lessen or moderate the intensity of the underlying disease agent or process); some are ameliorative (i.e., they improve or make better the symptoms of the underlying disease process); and some are stabilizing (i.e., they maintain or limit the fluctuations of the underlying disease agent or process).

Hence, depending upon a clinician's diagnoses, formulation of the problem (i.e., the relationship between the suicidal behaviors and the associated disease or dysfunction), and treatment goals, medications may or may not be a part of the treatment plan. Their presence must be understood within the total context of the patient's illness (or comorbid illnesses) and subsequent treatment plan. Their relative significance must also be clarified, so that the appropriate weighting of role, function, and importance is assigned. Their potential benefits and possible limitations must be elucidated as well. The treatment goals and outcomes must take into account their presence.

In the development and implementation of a treatment plan, a reasonable and prudent clinician will not rely solely on the response of the suicidal patient to the use of psychopharmacological agents. Nor will a responsible and competent clinician fail to consider the adjunctive use of psychotropic medications in the overall evaluation and treatment of a suicidal patient. As is true of any other component in the total armamentarium for the treatment of suicidal patients, each psychotropic medication must be understood in regard to its potential for good and for harm on an individual basis in the context of individual circumstances. Such considerations include the dynamics of pharmacological tolerance, dependence, and abuse liability. If used prudently and appropriately, many psychopharmacological agents have an important role to play in the overall treatment of the suicidal patient.

Psychopharmacological interventions cannot be accomplished in isolation. The assessment, treatment, and management of suicidal patients placed on psychopharmacological agents must be conducted in the context of constant awareness and monitoring of the following: psychotherapeutic interventions; the role of family members; the patient's behavior on the unit; changes in life stressors and in support systems; exacerbation of physical conditions (e.g., diabetes, rheumatoid arthritis, hypertension); onset of physical disorders (e.g., cancer, myocardial infarction, emphysema); compliance and adherence with the physician's recommendations, therapeutic interventions, maneuvers, and adjustments; and degree of therapeutic alliance.

ACKNOWLEDGMENT

I wish to acknowledge the invaluable assistance of the Suicide Information and Education Centre (SIEC), in Calgary, Alberta, Canada, which provided literature search and retrieval services.

REFERENCES

Arango, V., & Mann, J. J. (1992). Relevance of serotonergic postmortem studies to suicidal behavior. *International Review of Psychiatry, 4,* 131–140.
Asberg, M., Schalling, D., Traskman-Bendz, L., & Wagner, A. (1987). Psychobiology of suicide, impulsivity, and related phenomena. In H. Y. Meltzer (Ed.), *Psychopharmacology: The third generation of progress* (pp. 655–668). New York: Raven Press.

Berman, A. L., & Cohen-Sandler, R. (1983). Suicide and malpractice: Expert testimony and the standards of care. *Professional psychology: Research and practice, 14,* 6–19.

Bongar, B. M. (1991). *The suicidal patient: Clinical and legal standards of care.* Washington, DC: American Psychological Association.

DeAlarcon, R. M., & Carney, M. W. (1969). Severe depressive mood changes following slow release intramuscular fluphenazine injection. *British Journal of Psychiatry, 3,* 564–567.

Dulit, R. A., & Michels, R. (1992). Psychodynamics and suicide. In D. Jacobs (Ed.), *Suicide and clinical practice* (pp. 43–54). Washington, DC: American Psychiatric Press.

Gardos, G., & Casey, D. (1984). *Tardive dyskinesia and affective disorders.* Washington, DC: American Psychiatric Press.

Goldblatt, M. J. (1994). Hospitalization of the suicidal patient. In A. A. Leenaars, J. T. Maltsberger, & R. A. Neimeyer (Eds.), *Treatment of suicidal people* (pp. 153–166). Washington, DC: Taylor & Francis.

Goldblatt, M. J., & Schatzberg, A. F. (1990). Somatic treatment of the adult suicidal patient: A brief survey. In S. J. Blumenthal & D. J. Kupfer (Eds.), *Suicide over the life cycle: Risk factors, assessment, and treatment of suicidal patients* (pp. 425–440). Washington, DC: American Psychiatric Press.

Gutheil, T. G. (1985). Medicolegal pitfalls in the treatment of borderline patients. *American Journal of Psychiatry, 142,* 9–14.

Gutheil, T. G. (1992). Suicide and suit: Liability after self-destruction. In D. Jacobs (Ed.), *Suicide and clinical practice* (pp. 147–167). Washington, DC: American Psychiatric Press.

Gutheil, T. G., Bursztajn, H., & Brodsky, A. (1986). The multidimensional assessment of dangerousness: Competence assessment in patient care and liability prevention. *Bulletin of the American Academy of Psychiatry Law, 14,* 123–129.

Hendin, H. (1987). Youth suicide: A psychosocial perspective. *Suicide and Life-Threatening Behavior, 17,* 151–165.

Linehan, M. M. (1986). Suicidal people: One population or two? *Annals of the New York Academy of Sciences, 487,* 16–33.

Linnoila, M., Virkkunen, M., Scheinin, M., et al. (1983). Low cerebrospinal fluid 5-hydroxyindoleacetic acid concentration differentiates impulsive from nonimpulsive violent behavior. *Life Sciences, 33,* 2609–2614.

Maltsberger, J. T. (1992). The psychodynamic formulation: An aid in assessing suicide risk. In R. W. Maris, A. L. Berman, J. T. Maltsberger, & R. I. Yufit (Eds.), *Assessment and prediction of suicide* (pp. 25–49). New York: Guilford Press.

Maltsberger, J. T., & Buie, D. H. (1974). Countertransference hate in the treatment of suicidal patients. *Archives of General Psychiatry, 30,* 625–633.

Mann, J. J., & Arango, V. (1992). Integration of neurobiology and psychopathology in a unified model of suicidal behavior. *Journal of Clinical Psychopharmacology, 12*(2), 2S–7S.

Mann, J. J., Arango, V., Marzuk, P. M., et al. (1989). Evidence for the 5-HT hypothesis of suicide: A review of post-mortem studies. *British Journal of Psychiatry, 155*(Suppl. 8), 7–14.

Mar   ', & Robinson, D. S. (1993). Suicidal
           ı. *Neuropsychopharmacology, 8,* 177–

Mari: suicide attempts to completed sui-
           T. Maltsberger, & R. I. Yufit (Eds.),
           '62–380). New York: Guilford Press.
Pande   al. (1995). Platelet serotonin-2A
    r(for suicidal behavior. *American*
    Jo
Physici   . Montvale, NJ: Medical Econom-
    ics
Pokorny   chiatric patients: Report of a
    pro   ı, J. T. Maltsberger, R. I. Yufit
    (Ed   105–129). New York: Guilford
    Pre:
Preskorn   tropic agents: Why and how
    they   '*Psychiatry, 54*(Suppl. 9), 3–7.
Ruben, H   tice. In S. J. Blumenthal & D.
    J. Ku   *sk factors, assessment, and*
    treati   *ashington*, DC: American
    Psych
Shear, M.,   ıssociated with akathisia and
    depot   *nical Psychopharmacology, 3,*
    235–236.
Simon, R. I. (1992). *Clinical psychiatry and the law* (2nd ed.). Washington, DC:
    American Psychiatric Press.
Slaby, A. E. (1994). Psychopharmacotherapy of suicide. In A. A. Leenaars, J. T.
    Maltsberger, & R. A. Neimeyer (Eds.), *Treatment of suicidal people* (pp. 141–
    152). Washington, DC: Taylor & Francis.

7

Legal Issues and Risk Management in Suicidal Patients

WENDY L. PACKMAN
ERIC A. HARRIS

OVERVIEW: PSYCHOLOGY AND THE LAW

Mental health professionals are increasingly discovering that their practice is related to the field of law. No longer can clinicians in contemporary practice consider clinical and legal issues mutually exclusive (Conner, 1994). With the increase in malpractice suits and disciplinary complaints against mental health professionals, and the impact of these claims on potential participation in the rapidly industrializing managed care system, it has become vitally important for clinicians to be familiar with the aspects of the law that directly affect their practices.

Mutual understanding is difficult, however, because the systems of psychology and law differ in their fundamental assumptions, goals, and methods (Hess, 1985). Both psychology and the law are concerned about regulating human conduct, but there are clear differences between the two systems. "Law proscribes in an authoritative fashion while psychology describes natural law or phenomena" (Hess, 1985, p. 75). Law is adversarial and seeks particular truth in a case by way of ordeal or trial (Hess, 1985).

Psychology takes a nonadversarial approach to the truth, preferring a collaborative model in which all involved parties pool data and share insights (Gutheil & Appelbaum, 1991). The law focuses heavily on individual's rights; mental health professionals tend to concern themselves exclusively with patients' needs (Gutheil & Appelbaum, 1991). Legal training teaches attorneys to disregard affective responses to cases, whereas clinical education trains mental health practitioners to prioritize affective responses.

Both professions are concerned about human behavior. Clinicians primarily focus on their interactions with their patients. Their goal is to help change maladaptive behavior patterns and alleviate psychological pain. From a legal perspective, the therapeutic enterprise is viewed in the context of the whole series of interactive enterprises taking place in society. The legal system balances clinical objectives against other competing societal interests, such as privacy and public safety. Courts sometimes determine that clinical concerns are outweighed by other interests. For example, in the *Tarasoff* decision (*Tarasoff v. Board of Regents of the University of California*, 1976), the California Supreme Court decided that the interest in public safety outweighed the interest in therapeutic confidentiality. At other times, courts have held that the importance of maintaining a patient's confidentiality outweighs the societal interest of informing family members of a patient's suicide potential (*Bellah v. Greenson*, 1978).

When it comes to liability risk, lawsuits against mental health professionals after patients attempt or commit suicide are becoming more common (Conner, 1994). Many clinicians are frightened by litigation because they do not understand the legal perspective or the operation of the legal system. In addition, practitioners often encounter attorneys in adversarial situations, where at least one of an attorney's roles is to discredit a clinician's testimony and credibility. The adversarial process tends to generate anxiety and anger about the legal system. Many clinicians respond to these uncomfortable feelings with denial and avoidance; they are often panic-stricken when a lawsuit is filed or a subpoena arrives. If litigation ensues, the clinician's initial response is crucial. During this emotional and traumatizing time, it is essential to remain calm and objective.

In a similar vein, Gutheil (1992) has noted that the primacy of suicide in mental health litigation should not lead to practitioners' responding with "fear, defensive practice, or other adversarializing reactions" (p. 166). The approach we propose is in accord with Gutheil (1992), who holds that the best solution to the specter of liability following a patient's suicide is for the clinician to have provided good clinical care that followed acceptable standards of practice. Gutheil also maintains that appropriate risk management is the core of a preventive approach to the unfortunate possibility of liability after the suicide of a patient. Dealing with legal complexities is a manageable task if the clinician incorporates a number of risk management procedures into his or her practice. The time for a clinician to think through difficult issues regarding risk management and assessment is not when the subpoena arrives or when a patient makes a suicidal gesture; instead, general policy choices should be made and reflected upon before the need arises (Monahan, 1993).

In this chapter, we first discuss general principles of malpractice for mental health professionals, outline theories of negligence involving suicide, and provide selected examples of malpractice actions. Next, we suggest risk management strategies that can substantially reduce one's exposure to malpractice liability. We conclude with a discussion of legal liability and risk management in a managed care environment.

MALPRACTICE LIABILITY FOR SUICIDAL PATIENTS

Suicide has been found to be the emergency situation most frequently encountered by mental health professionals (Schein, 1976). Empirical studies have shown that the average practicing clinical psychologist has a 20% chance of losing a patient to suicide at sometime during his or her professional career, with the odds climbing to greater than 50% for psychiatrists (Chemtob, Hamada, Bauer, Kinney, & Torigoe, 1988; Chemtob, Hamada, Bauer, Torigoe, & Kinney, 1988). According to Pope (1989), the costs of suicide cases rank second among those of all malpractice actions against psychologists (after sexual abuse), accounting for 11.2% of the total damages and 5.8% of the suits brought. The subject of suicide is a source of extraordinary stress for clinicians, for it is one of the few fatal consequences of psychiatric illness (Nemiah, 1982). A suicide attempt or a successful suicide can be a devastating experience, generating feelings of loss, helplessness, guilt, anger, and personal failure (VandeCreek & Young, 1989).

The majority of malpractice cases involving patient suicide that go to trial involve clinical activities related to inpatient care (see Chapter 3, this volume). A review of reported cases gives the impression that it is rare for an outpatient clinician to be held liable for a patient suicide. Investigators have noted, however, that outpatient clinicians today are as likely as inpatient clinicians to be the targets of a suit (see Jobes & Berman, 1993, and Chapter 12, this volume). In fact, there are numerous lower court cases where malpractice is actually found, but most lower courts' decisions are not reported. The situation is made even more difficult by the fact that many cases either are settled prior to trial or are not appealed. Although there is little case law, it is reasonable to assume that courts will require outpatient clinicians to comply with professional standards in identifying suicidal risk and taking appropriate actions to prevent a patient from making a suicide attempt.

Essential Elements of Malpractice for Mental Health Professionals

Malpractice is classified in legal terms as a tort action. A "tort" is a civil wrong committed by one individual (the defendant), which has caused some injury to another individual (the plaintiff). In the common law, there is a set of torts—assault, battery, false imprisonment—that covers cases of intentional injury (Pound, 1978). "Negligence," another ground of tort liability, is a principle of duty to answer for injuries that result from failure to meet a legal standard of conduct governing affirmative courses of action (Pound, 1978). In malpractice litigation, negligence is the predominant theory of liability. "Malpractice" is a negligent act committed by a professional that harms another (Stromberg et al., 1988). The negligence of clinicians can be described as doing something they should not have done (act of commission) or not doing something they should have done (act of omission) (Simon, 1992).

In a cause of action based on malpractice against a mental health professional, the elements of proof are the same as in other medical and malpractice actions generally. The plaintiff must establish four elements: (1) that a duty of care was owed by the professional to the plaintiff; (2) that the professional violated the applicable standard of care (breach of duty); (3) that the plaintiff suffered a compensable injury; and (4) that the plaintiff's injury was caused in fact and proximately caused by the defendant's substandard conduct (Prosser, 1971). Each of these four elements must be demonstrated by the plaintiff by a preponderance of the evidence and "may be remembered by the **4D** mnemonic: Dereliction of–Duty–Directly causing–Damages" (Rachlin, 1984, p. 303).

A central issue in any malpractice case is the determination of the standard of care. The "standard of care" is a legal duty owed by mental health professionals to their patients, once a therapist–patient relationship has been established. If a mental health professional acts or fails to act in such a way that the resulting care is below this standard, then the duty of care is said to be breached. If a patient suffers injury as a proximate result of that breach of care, then that action can be considered malpractice.

In the courtroom, mental health professionals are generally held to their respective professions' standards of care, as determined by expert witnesses. Psychiatrists are held to the levels of skill and care provision of a professionally qualified psychiatrist; psychologists are held to those of a professionally qualified psychologist. Thus, the customary practices of each profession generally set the standard of care (Furrow, 1980).

In actual practice, the outcome of malpractice litigation may rest less on the **4D** elements than on two other important factors—the mental health professional's level of control over his or her patient, and the adequacy of documentation. Generally, the more control a clinician or facility has, the more likely a court is to find the clinician or facility responsible for the consequences. Stromberg et al. (1988) point out that clinicians are more likely to be found liable in the cases of suicidal inpatients. In such cases, the underlying assumption is that hospital-based clinicians have greater observational capabilities and control over their patients. In the case of an outpatient, the clinician is likely to be held liable if "similarly situated practitioners would have provided more care" or controlled the patient better (p. 467). Whether clinicians treat inpatients or outpatients, they have a duty to take steps to prevent suicide if they can reasonably anticipate the danger. The central issue is whether the clinician "should have predicted that the patient was likely to attempt suicidal behavior, and (assuming there was an identifiable risk) whether the therapist did enough to protect the patient" (Stromberg et al., 1988, p. 467).

Another important variable is adequacy of documentation. If a plaintiff's lawyer can show that a practitioner was sloppy or careless in any area of professional practice, even if it is a part of practice that is not germane to the litigation, the plaintiff is likely to win the lawsuit. Poor-quality notes or inadequate history taking may be viewed as sloppy practice by a jury.

For example, in *Abille v. United States* (1980), a psychiatrist was found liable when a patient committed suicide after being transferred from a suicide watch status to a lower level of precaution, and the psychiatrist lacked adequate notes to explain the rationale for the decision. At the time of the patient's reclassification, no notation was made by the psychiatrist explaining the transfer. Such notes were also required by hospital regulations. Although the court acknowledged that a reasonable psychiatrist might have determined that the patient could be reclassified with safety, without notes there was concern that the decision was made negligently. According to the court, the psychiatrist's "failure to maintain contemporary notes, orders, or other records adequately recording and explaining his action in reclassifying [the patient] fell below the applicable standard of care" (*Abille v. United States*, 1980, p. 708).

Theories of Liability in Suicide Cases

Lawsuits involving suicide typically fall into one of three fact patterns: A clinician and/or institution is sued (1) following an inpatient suicide, with survivors claiming that the practitioner failed to provide adequate care and supervision; (2) after a recently released inpatient commits suicide, with survivors claiming that the decision to release was negligent; and (3) after an outpatient commits suicide, with survivors contending that if the clinician had provided adequate treatment, the suicide would not have occurred (VandeCreek, Knapp, & Herzog, 1987).

Given that current case law provides a limited view of the overall malpractice picture, it is difficult to discern clear legal guidelines for what constitutes an adequate standard of care for the suicidal patient. In both inpatient and outpatient suicide cases, courts typically struggle with two central issues—foreseeability and causation (Simon, 1988). Courts tend to focus on whether the mental health professional should have predicted the suicide, whether there was sufficient evidence for an identifiable risk of harm, and whether the practitioner did enough to protect the patient (VandeCreek et al., 1987).

Foreseeability involves a comprehensive and reasonable assessment of risk (Jobes & Berman, 1993). Assessment of risk is not synonymous with prediction, because mental health practitioners are not able to "predict" suicidal behaviors reliably and validly without a high number of false-positive identifications (Berman & Jobes, 1991). However, mental health practitioners are able to assess the relative degree of risk, basing clinical judgments on the presence of known risk factors as well as other evaluations of mental status and diagnosis (Jobes & Berman, 1993). The primary role of risk evaluation is to spur competent clinical management, which in turn optimizes treatment (Bongar, 1991).

Reasonable care involves the appropriate implementation of precautions or interventions based on the preceding assessment of risk (Jobes &

Berman, 1993). It also includes the development of a treatment plan, consideration of hospitalization, consideration of medication, and the need for a "second opinion" through consultation (Bongar, 1991). Detailed documentation of assessment, treatment, consultative procedures, process, and outcome must be maintained (Bongar, 1991).

In short, clinicians are not required to predict suicide, but are asked to identify elevated risk. This is a two-step process: (1) assessing the relative degree of risk for suicide, and (2) implementing a treatment plan to reduce or eliminate the risk. A clinician who either fails to reasonably assess a patient's suicidality or fails to implement an appropriate management plan based on the detection of elevated suicidal risk is likely to be exposed to liability if the patient is harmed by a suicide attempt. "The law tends to assume that suicide is preventable, in most circumstances, if it is foresee-able" (Simon, 1988, p. 85).

The courts have followed several theories in imposing liability on mental health professionals in suicide cases (Robertson, 1988). The following items are the most common allegations in a complaint for malpractice following a patient's suicide:

1. Failure to predict or diagnose the suicide.
2. Failure to control, supervise or restrain.
3. Failure to take proper tests and evaluations of the patient to establish suicide intent.
4. Failure to medicate properly.
5. Failure to observe the patient continuously (24 hours) or on a frequent enough basis (e.g., every 15 minutes).
6. Failure to take an adequate history.
7. Inadequate supervision and failure to remove belt or other dangerous objects.
8. Failure to place the patient in a secure room. (Robertson, 1988, pp. 198–199)

Some Examples of Malpractice Actions

Early Release of Patient

In *Bell v. New York City Health and Hospitals Corporation* (1982), a psychiatrist was found liable for the premature release of a patient. The appellate court cited several factors in its finding that the patient's early release was negligent and not a valid exercise of professional judgment. First, the defendant psychiatrist acknowledged that the decision to release the patient turned on a determination of whether the patient presented a risk to himself. Nonetheless, the defendant failed to inquire into the nature of the patient's auditory hallucinations, even though a nurse had recorded her observations concerning the hallucinations for 3 days prior to discharge. Second, the defendant failed to request prior treatment records. Third, the defendant did not take notice of the patient's chart, which showed that on the day prior to release, the patient had to be placed in restraints (an indication of assaultive tendencies). Finally, the defendant did not communicate with the hospital staff. In short, the decision to release the patient was not "a professional judgment founded upon careful examination" (*Bell v. New York City Health and Hospitals Corporation*, 1982, p. 796).

In contrast, when a clinician makes a reasonable assessment of danger and believes that a risk no longer exists, he or she is not held liable for the postdischarge death of a patient (Fremouw, de Perczel, & Ellis, 1990).

Failure to Commit Patient

The issues in other cases are whether the clinician did a thorough examination and history, took adequate precautions, and exercised sound judgment (Robertson, 1988). In several instances, courts have reinforced the principle that mental health professionals cannot be held liable for errors in judgment when they have exercised the care and skill customarily exercised by the average qualified professional.

For example, in *Paradies v. Benedictine Hospital* (1980), the appellate court did not impose liability on a psychiatrist for failing to keep a patient in a hospital under involuntary-commitment statutes. The patient had been admitted as an informal patient and had a right to be discharged upon demand, pursuant to state mental health laws. In the psychiatrist's opinion, the decedent was not a danger to himself or others and did not meet criteria for involuntary admission. The court stated that "[i]f liability were imposed on the physician each time the prediction of the future course of a mental disease was wrong, few releases would ever be made and the recovery of a vast number of patients would be impeded" (*Paradies v. Benedictine Hospital*, 1980, p. 178).

Similarly, in *Dillmann v. Hellman* (1973), the court granted summary judgment in favor of a defendant psychiatrist when a patient jumped out of a window of a psychiatric hospital. The patient had been hospitalized for 9 days when the psychiatrist determined that she was sufficiently well to be transferred to a less secure portion of the hospital. The plaintiff's only argument was that the psychiatrist erred in her judgment and was therefore negligent. The court reinforced the established principle that physicians cannot ensure results and cannot be held liable for honest errors in judgment made while pursuing methods, procedures, and practices within accepted standards of care.

A contrary result was reached in *Psychiatric Institute v. James Allen* (1986), where the court awarded damages to the parents of a 13-year-old child who committed suicide while hospitalized at the institute. The child, Daniel Allen, was hospitalized originally at Children's Hospital as an emergency patient when his private psychiatrist felt he was in danger. During the original hospitalization, Daniel was treated for suicidal ideation. He was transferred to the defendant institution when it was determined that he needed extended care. He remained there until October 1980. At the time of discharge (for eye surgery), he had improved somewhat psychiatrically but still needed extended psychiatric care. Approximately 6 months later, Daniel was readmitted to the defendant institution with a diagnosis of aggressive conduct disorder. The treatment plan included monitoring antisocial, aggressive, sexual, and self-destructive behavior. During the hospitalization, Daniel had severe difficulty. He hit walls, tried to remove putty from safety windows, and asked nurses whether it hurt to starve yourself.

At trial, evidence was introduced showing that the defendant checked off a box stating that there had been no prior suicide attempts by Daniel. In addition, the defendant failed to obtain the prior records from Children's Hospital showing that Daniel had suicidal ideation, frequently spoke about suicide, and was self-destructive. Furthermore, the defendant did not consider Daniel suicidal. The plaintiff's expert found the following deviations from the accepted standard of care:

1. Failure to obtain prior records.
2. Failure to be informed of all relevant history.
3. Failure to communicate properly.
4. Failure to take adequate action in response to the comment, "Does it hurt to starve yourself[?]"
5. Failure to consider suicide precautions. (Robertson, 1988, p. 194)

Failure to Provide Adequate Supervision

In *Wilson v. State* (1961), the husband of a patient brought an action against a state hospital after the patient jumped to her death through an unlocked laundry chute. The husband claimed that the failure to lock the laundry chute door resulted in the patient's jumping through the chute and was thus the proximate cause of her death. The court imposed liability, noting that on the day of the incident, the hospital attendant had unlocked the door to allow another patient to throw some laundry bags down the chute. A disturbance between other patients in the room broke out and distracted the attendant; she shut the chute door without locking it and went to settle the disturbance. The attendant did not remember leaving the chute un-locked until 2½ hours later, when she was told that the patient was found at the bottom of the chute.

Failure to Take Adequate Protective Measures

The clinician must take adequate precautions against patient suicide—pre-cautions that are consistent with accepted psychotherapeutic practices and based on his or her knowledge and assessment of the patient (see *Meier v. Ross General Hospital*, 1968; *Topel v. Long Island Jewish Medical Center*, 1981). This theory is illustrated by *Dinnerstein v. State* (1973), where the court held that a mental health professional is liable when a treatment plan overlooks or neglects the patient's suicidal tendencies.

In *Topel v. Long Island Jewish Medical Center* (1981), liability was not established against a psychiatrist for a patient's suicide by hanging, al-though it was alleged that the defendant failed to take adequate precautions. In this case, the psychiatrist decided to have a paranoid, depressed, agitated, suicidal 48-year-old policeman seen every 15 minutes rather than observed constantly. According to the *Topel* court, the psychiatrist's decision was a matter of professional judgment for which he could not be held liable. The psychiatrist based his decision on the following factors: the victim's reac-tion to constant surveillance, the gesture-like nature of his prior suicidal indications, the rehabilitative aspects of open-ward treatment, and the enhanced probability of obtaining the victim's consent to electroconvulsive therapy in the more relaxed open-ward atmosphere. In the court's view, these were all factors that the defendant could properly consider and weigh in reaching his professional judgment.

Although only a few reported cases have dealt with outpatient suicide, the principles are the same as for inpatient cases. That is, clinicians must use reasonable care in the diagnosis of suicidal intent and in the develop-ment and implementation of the treatment plan (VandeCreek & Knapp, 1989). In *Bellah v. Greenson* (1978), the parents of Tammy Bellah (who died after an overdose of pills) brought an action against their daughter's out-patient therapist. The lawsuit was based on simple negligence and on the negligent performance of a contract with the patient's parents, in which the psychiatrist allegedly agreed that he would prevent harm to the patient. The court found that the complaint stated a sufficient cause of action by alleging the existence of a psychiatrist–patient relationship, knowledge by the psychiatrist of the patient's suicidal propensity, and the psychiatrist's failure to take adequate steps to prevent the suicide.

The court also noted that the nature of the precautionary measures that could or should have been taken by the psychiatrist presented a factual question to be resolved by the trier of fact. Although the court did not impose a *Tarasoff*-type duty to warn relatives of potential suicide risk, it remains an option that clinicians should consider seriously when patients present as at risk (Fremouw et al., 1990).

Failure to Diagnose Properly

Another theory of liability is the failure to diagnose properly. That is, if the clinician had taken ordinary and accepted care in making a diagnosis, he or she would have ascertained that the patient was suicidal (see *Dillmann v. Hellman*, 1973).

Liability of Hospitals

A review of the liability of hospitals is beyond the scope of this discussion (see Robertson, 1988; Bongar, 1991). However, mental health professionals should know that malpractice actions for inpatient suicides can be directed against them or the hospital or both (VandeCreek & Knapp, 1983). Malpractice actions can be brought against mental health practitioners within the hospital setting, provided that they have staff or hospital privileges (Bongar & Greaney, 1994). The mental hospital's duty in the care of a patient can best be defined as the generally accepted standard that reasonable care must be used in the treatment of a patient (Robertson, 1988). "If, however, the hospital is on notice that a patient has suicidal tendencies, then the hospital also assumes the duty of safeguarding the patient from self-inflicted injury or death" (Robertson, 1988, p. 193). Thus, the issue of foreseeability is critical in judging the hospital's behavior.

Conclusions from Case Law

Practitioners are most likely to be found liable when inpatients become suicidal, because it is thought that hospital-based practitioners can control and observe inpatients (Stromberg et al., 1988). Liability will be imposed if a reasonably prudent practitioner would have provided more care or would have controlled the patient better. Mental health professionals who primarily treat outpatients are less likely than hospital-based practitioners to be found liable for patients' self-inflicted injuries and suicides (Stromberg et al., 1988). Courts recognize that outpatient therapists have fewer options for monitoring or controlling the behavior of outpatients (VandeCreek et al., 1987).

Courts have generally been sympathetic to the difficulties mental health professionals face in predicting suicides. Thus, liability has rarely been found unless there was clear, observable suicidal behavior or actual verbal threats, or unless the professional's general level of professional conduct was considerably below community standards (*Ross v. Central Louisiana State Hospital*, 1980). Professionals have been held liable, however, for failing to take adequate precautions to manage patients. Thus, if a therapist's treatment plan ignores, neglects, or overlooks evidence of suicidal tendencies, a court can impose liability on the practitioner or the hospital. The more obvious the suicidal intent, psychosis, or depression, the greater will be the clinician's liability for failure to take this information into account in designing a treatment plan (VandeCreek et al., 1987).

RISK MANAGEMENT PROCEDURES DESIGNED TO MINIMIZE LIABILITY

Coping with malpractice litigation and legal complexities is a manageable task if risk management procedures are integrated into clinical practice. The risk management procedures that we discuss below are designed to reduce the risk of suicide malpractice cases. They will also help practitioners cope with utilization review report requests, ethics committees, licensing boards, and other bodies.

Knowledge of Legal and Ethical Responsibilities

The first step is recognizing risk before it becomes a problem. This requires a good working knowledge of one's ethical and legal responsibilities. Thus, clinicians should be familiar with the laws, regulations, and ethical principles that govern professional practice in their jurisdiction. Two especially important issues are confidentiality and informed consent.

Confidentiality

"Confidentiality" refers to the patient's right not to have communications that are given in confidence disclosed to outside parties without the patient's authorization (Simon, 1988). The clinician's duty to maintain confidentiality is not absolute, and there are situations where breaching confidentiality is both legal and ethically valid (Bongar, 1991). Simon (1988) notes that a competent patient's request for maintaining confidentiality must be honored unless the patient is a clear danger to self or others.

It is important that clinicians understand the legal rules in their jurisdiction related to breaching confidentiality when patients are a "danger to self." In some states, the legal duty to warn third parties exists only if a threat or danger of physical harm toward others exists (Simon, 1988). In California, the attempt to apply the *Tarasoff* standard to therapists treating suicidal outpatients has not been successful (*Bellah v. Greenson*, 1978). As noted above, the *Bellah* court refused to extend the duty to protect to suicidal cases. In other states (e.g., Massachusetts and Florida), statutory waiver of confidential information is allowed when a patient seriously threatens self-harm.

We believe that clinicians have a professional duty to take affirmative steps to prevent patients from hurting themselves. Such affirmative measures may necessitate communicating with family members about the specifics of a patient's case (Simon, 1992). Research indicates that it may be advisable to warn the members of the patient's support system about the patient's suicide potential, and to increase their involvement in the patient's treatment and management (VandeCreek & Knapp, 1989). The involvement of the support system can promote the patient's recovery (Bongar, 1991).

In our view, the clinician's best course of action is to develop a well-thought-out policy on breaching confidentiality before being required to implement it. The critical point is to inform patients of the exceptions that exist to confidentiality before the onset of therapy. Clinicians need to talk with patients about what will happen if their risk reaches a certain level. That is, will the clinicians breach confidentiality in order to notify people in the patients' environment who may be able to protect them?

By way of example, a clinician might say the following to a prospective patient (college student) at the outset of therapy:

> "I want you to know that if I believe you are a serious suicidal risk, I am going to get in touch with your parents and your roommates. I am

going to contact these people because, in my judgment, your safety is more important than your confidentiality when you are suicidal. I really want you to know about this now, at the beginning of treatment, so that we do not have any misunderstandings."

If the college student later becomes suicidal and the clinician breaches confidentiality, it is a very different situation than if that issue had not been discussed and the clinician calls the patient's parents. In essence, a mental health professional should rehearse with patients, in advance, what is likely to happen if the risk gets to a certain level. With this approach, patients will not feel betrayed if it becomes necessary to breach confidentiality.

Informed Consent

The doctrine of informed consent is a main source of tension between the medical and legal professions (Malcolm, 1986). Before 1950, courts did not really concern themselves with the information doctors gave to patients. All that was required was that doctors not provide any information that they should have known was false (Malcolm, 1986). This general expectation gradually developed into an affirmative duty upon a physician to disclose certain information to a patient (*Hunt v. Bradshaw*, 1955). Generally, courts adhered to a professional standard of disclosure; thus, the determination of what risks warranted disclosure was left to the judgment of members of the medical profession (King, 1986). A new lay standard was enunciated in *Canterbury v. Spence* (1972). There, the court held that a physician was required to disclose any information about a proposed treatment or its alternatives that a reasonable person in the patient's circumstances would find material to the decision either to undergo or to forgo treatment. The court feared that arrogating to the medical profession the decision concerning what information to disclose might be a derogation of the patient's right to self-determination (King, 1986).

   In the area of informed consent, the parameters for the extent of the information to be disclosed, as well as the considerations that influence disclosure, continue to be shaped and defined by case law. Generally speaking, regardless of the standard of disclosure, a mental health professional is only expected to know of risks and other information that a similarly situated reasonable practitioner would be expected to know (King, 1986).

   In the debate over informed consent, physicians and mental health professionals usually present the greatest opposition to the doctrine, while legal professionals strongly support it (Malcolm, 1986). Supporters view the relationship between clinician and patient as one between unequal bargaining partners and feel that the inequality is due to the clinician's special knowledge (Malcolm, 1986). The clinician should be made to disclose his or her special knowledge to the patient in order that they will become equal bargaining partners. An increased feeling of participation by the patient in the decision making process may engender a feeling of trust in the clinician and strengthen the therapeutic alliance (Stone, 1990). Opponents of the informed consent doctrine argue that the inequality of knowledge is impossible to overcome. Unless the patient is a physician or mental health professional, the patient will never be able to give a consent that is truly informed (Malcolm, 1986).

This debate has led to a confusing resolution in the courts. In an attempt to balance individualism (an individual's status as an autonomous human being) with paternalistic instincts, courts have affirmed the autonomy interests by adopting the general rule of the doctrine of informed consent (Malcolm, 1986). They have accommodated the paternalistic interests by coming up with four judicially developed exceptions to the informed consent doctrine (King, 1986). These are (1) emergency, (2) incompetence of the patient, (3) waiver, and (4) therapeutic privilege.

The legal doctrine of informed consent is consistent with the provision of good clinical care by all mental health professionals (Simon, 1992). It is important to emphasize that consent is an interactive process (Rozovsky, 1990; Stone, 1990). Many mental health professionals think of informed consent as a form to be signed (i.e., a static, one-time event). Informed consent is more than reading and signing a form. It is the beginning of a process, a starting point, an opportunity to ask questions and to gain knowledge that is explained in terms the patient can understand. Both parties must be active participants. A document cannot replace this important process. The emphasis is on communication, not the form (Wallace, 1990).

Significantly, Simon (1987) underscores that informed consent is not a solitary event that occurs only at the beginning of treatment. Rather, it is a continual process throughout therapy. In a related vein, Gutheil (1984) notes that informed consent is more than a legal formality. Indeed, it can become a focal point for establishing the therapeutic alliance. Informed consent thus becomes a powerful clinical tool; it allows the patient's helplessness to be supplanted by a degree of control, as the patient becomes a participant with the therapist in the treatment process (Simon, 1987).

In work with suicidal patients, both competent patients and their families should be given as much information as possible, to allow them to collaborate as active partners in each facet of the risk–benefit plan (Bongar, 1991). A patient must be properly informed of the nature and purpose of the proposed treatment, the risks and anticipated benefits, a cautious prognostic assessment, available alternative procedures (including risks and benefits), and the expected outcome with and without treatment (Simon, 1992). This open communication and ongoing dialogue protect the patient's right to self-determination.

Simon (1987) notes that "the therapeutic use of informed consent enlists the patient in an active alliance that discourages simplistic blaming, and reduces the alienation towards the clinician that often produces malpractice claims" (p. 126). Similarly, Gutheil and Appelbaum (1991) state that in the real world, the determination of malpractice often rests on the malignant synergy of "a bad outcome from whatever cause, in concert with 'bad feelings' in the plaintiffs" (p. 173), including betrayal, guilt, rage, grief, surprise, and a sense of being left alone with a bad outcome (psychological abandonment). Not only can an open discussion of the risks and benefits facilitate cooperation and increase available sources of vital information; such an open sharing of the risks with a patient and family can lessen the family's experience of shock and surprise, should the patient actually commit suicide. A family is less likely to launch litigation against a practitioner if good relations have been achieved.

Become Informed about Specific Risk Factors for Suicidal Patients

In order to exercise good clinical judgment, one needs to know what the literature and experts say about the epidemiology, risk factors, and management of the suicidal patient. It is important to stay current with developments in the field, and to be conversant with the law of the jurisdiction (Monahan, 1993).

A practitioner who has not had a great deal of experience managing suicidal patients should decide *a priori* how he or she will manage a crisis situation. Practitioners who see suicidal patients should have knowledge of community resources and access to the full armamentarium of resources for voluntary and involuntary hospital admissions, emergency backup, and crisis centers (Bongar, 1991).

Obtain Risk Assessment Data

A clinician needs to perform a thorough clinical assessment of elevated risk.[1] The data should be recorded in a careful, professional manner. The clinician needs to take a thorough patient history that provides indicators of the likelihood of suicide risk, based on diagnostic information and risk factors for suicide. It needs to include specific, forensically significant questions about depression and suicidal thoughts and feelings. The initial evaluation is not the exclusive opportunity to secure risk assessment data. At whatever time in the treatment a clinician gets indications that risk is present, he or she needs to be very thorough in exploring that risk, both currently and historically. VandeCreek and Knapp (1983) suggest that suicidal potential be evaluated several times during treatment, including at the time of hospital admission, at the time of transfer to less restrictive wards, before home visits, and before discharge.

We recognize that there are settings where rapid decisions must be made or where a brief screening device is needed. Nonetheless, for each patient seen as part of a mental health professional's practice, there must be an initial evaluation of suicide risk. The clinician should ask the patient directly about feelings of sadness and hopelessness and if thoughts of suicide come to mind. If the answer is "yes," then the clinician must ask follow-up questions to explore suicidal thoughts. If the patient admits self-destructive thoughts, the clinician needs to perform a very thorough evaluation of suicide risk. If, on the other hand, the patient denies suicidal thoughts and there is no reason to distrust that answer, an extensive suicide assessment need not be conducted. In assessing suicide potential, the clinician first needs to ask some direct, basic questions. If the clinician discovers anything that indicates elevated risk, he or she needs to do a thorough evaluation. If there appears to be a great deal of risk, the clinician should administer a suicide risk assessment tool and consider consultation. It is basically a three-step process: (1) identifying whether there is any risk at all; (2) identifying how much risk there is; and (3) if there is high risk, finding ways to protect oneself against future retrospective inquiries about one's practice (assessment instruments and professional consultations).

---

[1]For a review of systematic approaches to detect risk factors, see Bongar (1991) and Simon (1988).

Secure Past Treatment Records

Mental health professionals should make reasonable efforts to obtain patients' previous treatment records and to consult with past therapists. Previous therapists should be asked specific risk management questions, and treatment summaries should be requested. The absence of efforts to obtain prior medical and psychotherapy records is one of the signs of inadequate clinical care (Bongar, 1991). Several court cases have found mental health professionals liable for malpractice for failure to obtain prior treatment records (see *Bell v. New York City Health and Hospitals Corporation*, 1982; *Psychiatric Institute v. Allen*, 1986).

If a patient refuses to give a clinician permission to get past treatment records, it is an indicator of a high-risk situation (e.g., the patient has borderline personality disorder or another Axis II disorder, or is a victim of physical or sexual abuse). Unless there are very good reasons for the patient's refusal, a clinician should consider not treating a patient who is unwilling to give him or her permission to secure past treatment records.

Diagnostic Impression

It is important for mental health professionals to master the diagnostic system contained in the latest version of the *Diagnostic and Statistical Manual of Mental Disorders* (DSM) of the American Psychiatric Association and use it appropriately. No matter how skillfully a clinician handles a potential malpractice situation, if he or she is unfamiliar with the DSM diagnostic system or if the patient's diagnosis is incompatible with the clinical facts, the potential for an unfavorable legal result is high. Underdiagnosing to protect a patient from inappropriate stigmatization or other potential problems is an inadvisable psychological risk management practice.

Determine Competence to Treat Suicidal Patients

All mental health care providers are limited to varying degrees as to their specific areas of professional competence (Welch, 1989). Thus, practitioners must understand their own technical proficiencies and emotional tolerance levels for the demands of treating suicidal patients (Bongar, 1991). If a clinician decides against treating suicidal patients, he or she should develop a list of colleagues to whom these individuals can be referred. Clinicians who feel they have the adequate education, training, and competence to treat high-risk patients should consider limiting the number that they have in treatment at any one time.

Therapists who work in outpatient settings need to be certain that they can provide adequate service to suicidal patients. They need to have backup arrangements with a local hospital in case a patient requires hospitalization. Coverage must be available during evening hours and weekends (VandeCreek et al., 1987). When a therapist is on vacation or unavailable for some other reason, and a patient has an acute episode, there is a risk that the therapist's unavailability will be construed as patient abandonment (Stromberg et al., 1988). Accordingly, therapists should arrange proper coverage for their "off hours" and should inform patients how to obtain emergency or supportive care during their absences.

Documentation

One of the most important risk management techniques is good record keeping. Inadequate documentation can cripple a defendant's case, even if a therapist has acted in a professionally sound manner (VandeCreek & Knapp, 1989). In a legal sense, "if it isn't written down, it didn't happen" (Gutheil, 1980). Thus, if a clinician fails to record an action in his or her records, there is a good chance the jury will assume that the clinician failed to carry out the assessment or treatment completely, regardless of how convincing the clinician is as a witness. Thorough assessments of risk and competence, extensive histories, well-organized treatment plans, good records, and regular consultations all contribute to an impression of an excellent professional practice. This will also decrease any problems a clinician may have with a future utilization reviewer, and will protect the clinician against being made to look unprofessional if called to testify in court.

A model risk-benefit progress note would include the following: (1) an assessment of suicide risk; (2) the information alerting the clinician to that risk; (3) which high-risk factors were present in that situation and in the patient's background; (4) what low-risk factors were present; (5) what questions were asked and what answers were supplied; and (6) how this information (the patient's history and the clinician's professional judgment) led to the actions taken and rejected. This analysis should include specific pros and cons of each action from a clinical and legal perspective. Records that show a careful evaluation of benefits and risks of treatment often diminish the likelihood of a successful lawsuit (VandeCreek et al., 1987).

It is especially important for clinicians to document and articulate what steps they decided not to take and why these were not taken—that is, to show their thinking processes. Gutheil (1980) refers to this process as "thinking out loud" for the record, and cites an example of the decision not to hospitalize a suicidal patient. In such a case, informed record keeping would include "thinking out loud for the record" as to the dangers that the patient may be exposed to and the "careful articulation of the pros and cons, including known risks and disadvantages and the reasons for overriding them" (Gutheil, 1980, p. 482). For example, a clinician might document his or her thinking process as follows:

> "I considered hospitalizing the patient, but rejected it for several reasons. The patient did not meet the commitment criteria and did not want to enter the hospital. He had never tried suicide before. I was concerned that, given his declining self-esteem, if I hospitalized him at this point I would be making it much more likely that he would kill himself. So, even though I knew there was an elevated risk of not hospitalizing this patient, I determined that it was outweighed by the clinical risks of hospitalizing him."

In many respects, mental health practitioners "who make bad decisions but whose reasoning [is clearly articulated]" come out more favorably than practitioners "who have made reasonable decisions but whose poor documentation leaves them vulnerable" (Gutheil, 1984, p. 3).

A thorough case record also documents all consultations, interactions, and professional judgments (Halleck, 1980). Finally, it includes the patient's formal informed consent for treatment, including documentation of confidentiality considerations.

Documentation should be as contemporaneous as possible, but this should not prevent the inclusion of details at a later time that were neglected in the heat of the moment. However, tampering with or inserting new material tending to support the reasonableness of the decisions that the clinician has made can destroy any chances of winning a case (Monahan, 1993).

Obtain Consultation

Mental health professionals should routinely obtain consultations from professional colleagues who have expertise in dealing with suicidal patients. They also should obtain consultation and supervision on (or should refer) cases that are outside their education, training, or experience, as well as cases in which they are unsure of the best avenue for treatment (Bongar, 1991). Consultants should be retained professionally and given sufficient information to provide reasonable advice. Their advice should be carefully recorded in the practitioner's records. From a risk management perspective, consultation will be more forensically effective if it is formal. That is, the clinician and consultant should both provide notes for the written record, and both should formally acknowledge that a consultant relationship is in effect (Bongar, 1991). Importantly, in a malpractice case, the standard of care will be determined through expert testimony. When a clinician's own judgment is buttressed by the judgments of two or more senior colleagues, it is far easier to demonstrate that the clinician behaved appropriately, even when the result was unfortunate. Thus, consultation can provide legal evidence for the reasonableness of selected diagnostic and treatment plans (VandeCreek et al., 1987).

Clinicians should be knowledgeable about the effects of psychotropic medications and should make appropriate referrals for a medication evaluation if they are not physicians themselves (Bongar, 1991).

Provide Notice to Insurance Carrier

Most malpractice insurance policies require a practitioner to provide written notice to the company whenever he or she learns of anything "which might be expected to be the basis of a suit or claim" under the policy. Some attorneys and commentators suggest that if a patient makes a serious suicide attempt or commits suicide, the practitioner's insurance carrier should be contacted in a timely fashion. Other commentators state that an incident that could lead to a suit's being filed is not a sufficient incident to invoke the responsibility to report on the policy. Because there are many uncertain situations, and because the notice to the carrier must be carefully drafted to preserve the insured's rights, mental health professionals should consult with legal counsel before responding (Stromberg et al., 1988).

LEGAL ISSUES AND RISK MANAGEMENT IN A MANAGED CARE ENVIRONMENT

If there is an unfortunate clinical result in a managed care situation, two parties could bear some responsibility: the provider (clinician) and the managed care company. The difficulty for courts and providers has revolved around dealing with this dual potential. Patients have started bringing lawsuits against health plans and utilization review companies for adverse medical outcomes (Frankel, 1994). Courts have attempted to deal directly with the interaction between cost containment programs and traditional medical practice, but they are still not sure how these cost-conscious managed care entities fit into the traditional malpractice scenario (Frankel, 1994). Courts may be willing to extend liability to managed care companies, but they have refused to adjust the practitioners' duty of care to reflect practice in the current mental health environment.

In this section, we first discuss how courts assign liability. Second, we examine potential liability for managed care companies. Third, we outline potential provider liability issues and risk management strategies. Finally, we discuss the effect of malpractice suits and disciplinary sanctions on participation in managed care, and briefly outline the disciplinary complaint process.

How Courts Assign Liability

Hypothetical Case

The salient issues that confront courts and providers working in a managed care setting are illustrated by the following hypothetical case (Appelbaum, 1993). A depressed, suicidal patient is hospitalized for 2 months by an outpatient therapist. In the clinician's view, long-term therapy is indicated to keep the patient stable, even though the patient's acute symptoms of depression have resolved. There is still adequate coverage under the patient's insurance plan, but the patient lacks personal resources to pay for further care. An employee of the managed care entity overseeing the treatment determines that further treatment is not medically necessary. This determination is based on a record review and a telephone discussion with the clinician. No public sector resources are available for patients of this sort, due to recent cutbacks in state funding.

This scenario raises several questions (Appelbaum, 1993). Should the clinician continue treatment of the patient without compensation? Should the clinician simply terminate the patient's care, despite the belief that further treatment is indicated to prevent a relapse? If so, who is responsible if the patient again becomes suicidal and injures himself or herself?

Interaction between Medical Malpractice Doctrine and Cost Containment Programs

Medical malpractice doctrine holds physicians and mental health practitioners to a certain standard of care. The actions and interventions that the law requires are set without regard to cost (Frankel, 1994). Within this conceptual framework, clinicians have sole authority to define appropriate health care outcomes for society, and are obligated to do so without reference to patient or system resources (Frankel, 1994). Efforts to reduce the cost of medical care have forced professionals to alter their practices. Whereas malpractice law dictates that physicians ignore the cost of services provided, cost containment programs ask practitioners to ration care according to some notion of cost-effectiveness (Frankel, 1994).

The following three cases illustrate the clash between the new cost containment programs and medical malpractice doctrine. In each instance, the court had to decide the extent to which the insurer's cost containment mechanism could be liable for a treating physician's alleged malpractice (Frankel, 1994).

In *Wickline v. State* (1986), Lois Wickline was hospitalized for vascular surgery and had several postoperative complications. The treating surgeon requested an extended stay of 8 additional days for his patient. The Medi-Cal reviewers would only approve a 4-day extension of hospital care. Mrs. Wickline suffered severe complications following her premature release. She was readmitted to the emergency room 9 days after discharge, but by this point her leg had to be amputated. The patient sued Medi-Cal, alleging that it had been negligent in reviewing her need for further care. A jury agreed with Mrs. Wickline, but the California Court of Appeal reversed the decision. The Court of Appeal limited its attention to the actual decision to discharge the patient. The court found that responsibility for the discharge order rested solely with the treating physician, and Medi-Cal was not a party to that decision. The court also held that Medi-Cal never had a chance to review the treating doctor's concerns about his patient's discharge, because he never appealed the adverse decision:

> The physician who complies without protest with the limitations imposed by a third-party payor, when his medical judgment dictates otherwise, cannot avoid his ultimate responsibility for his patient's care. He cannot point to the health care payor as the liability scapegoat when the consequences of his own determinative medical decision goes sour. (*Wickline v. State*, 1986, p. 671)

The *Wickline* case was the first time a court attempted to partition responsibility for adverse medical outcomes in the new managed care practice setting. Because the court only focused on the decision to discharge, it failed to appreciate the role that the practice context played in structuring that decision (Frankel, 1994). Significantly, the court did not attempt to adjust the treating physician's duty of care to compensate for the provision of services within a cost containment program. In fact, some commentators noted that the court actually expanded the duty of care of practitioners operating in managed care environments by imposing new legal obligations—namely, "to navigate for their patients through the payor's minefield of cost and utilization controls" (Frankel, 1994, p. 1307).

In *Wilson v. Blue Cross of Southern California* (1990), a patient was hospitalized for major depression, drug dependence and anorexia. His treating physician determined that the patient required 3 to 4 weeks of hospitalization, but the managed care company cut off coverage after 10 days. The patient was discharged and committed suicide a few weeks later. The California Court of Appeal held that third-party payors are not immune from lawsuits in regard to utilization review activities. The court then remanded the case for trial, at which point the utilization review company settled with the Wilsons for an undisclosed amount. *Wilson* corrected some of the deficiencies in *Wickline* mentioned above: The court recognized the connection between utilization review decisions and medical outcomes, and the court did not make the third-party payor's liability contingent upon the treating physician's failure to challenge the utilization review company's decision (Frankel, 1994). But the *Wilson* court avoided defining the payor's legal duty of care.

In *Corcoran v. United HealthCare* (1992), Florence Corcoran was a long-time employee of South Central Bell Telephone Company and a member of the company's self-insured health plan. She became pregnant in early 1989. This was Mrs. Corcoran's second pregnancy, and several medical problems made this pregnancy, like the first one, high-risk. Her obstetrician recommended that she have complete bed rest during the final months of pregnancy. As in the first pregnancy, he recommended that Mrs. Corcoran be hospitalized so that the condition of the fetus could be monitored 24 hours a day. Although the health plan had paid for similar end-of-term monitoring for the first pregnancy, it now refused. United HealthCare, Bell's utilization review firm, denied certification for inpatient stay and instead authorized 10 hours per day of home nursing care. During the time when the home health nurse was not on duty, the fetus went into distress and died.

Corcoran and her husband brought a lawsuit against United Health-Care for wrongful death and medical malpractice. Because the health plan was a self-funded employee benefit plan governed by the Employee Retirement Income Security Act (ERISA), the defendants removed the action to federal court. The district court granted the defendants' summary judgment motion on the grounds that ERISA preempted the plaintiffs' tort claims made under state law. In the court's view, the only matter in dispute was the defendant's adjudication of benefits under the plan. Although the court recognized that United HealthCare did make medical decisions and give medical advice, the plaintiffs were not allowed to proceed to trial on a malpractice theory. The court agreed with United HealthCare that the ultimate purpose of its medical decisions was to adjudicate claims for benefits. Thus, the court concluded that ERISA preempted the Corcorans' lawsuit.

Liability for Managed Care Companies

Corporate Negligence Theory

Pursuant to the doctrine of corporate negligence, hospitals, clinics, and other facilities providing health care have a duty to select appropriate providers (Appelbaum, 1993). Corporate liability first emerged in the malpractice context in cases involving hospitals that had failed to properly check the credentials and qualifications of physicians to whom they had accorded admitting privileges (Abraham & Weiler, 1994). In other cases, hospitals had failed to monitor the subsequent quality of care provided by the physicians, or had failed to suspend or revoke admitting privileges where necessary (Abraham & Weiler, 1994). Corporate negligence in this context consists of the breach of a duty owed by a hospital directly to the patient "[to ensure] that its medical staff is qualified for the privileges granted and . . . to evaluate the care provided" (O'Neal, 1991, citing *Johnson v. Misericordia Community Hospital*, 1981, p. 165).

Courts have shown a willingness to extend corporate negligence theory to managed care entities (O'Neal, 1991). Thus, unreasonable actions by managed care companies in reviewing credentials and monitoring ongoing performance of clinicians leave these entities open to liability (Appelbaum, 1993). One of the sources of "corporate negligence" for a managed care company is "negligent credentialing." That is, if a managed care panel knows (or should know) that a professional presents a risk to the public, but accepts this professional nevertheless, it can be held liable for this person's future misconduct. (The effect of "negligent credentialing" on participation in managed care is discussed in a later section.)

Although the *Wickline* (1986) decision declined to impose liability on Medi-Cal, the California court held open the possibility of imposing liability for improper review and extending the theory of corporate negligence to insurers whose cost containment systems interfere with the physician-patient relationship (O'Neal, 1991). The *Wilson* (1990) opinion suggests that even if the clinician might share responsibility, the managed care provider cannot escape liability for a negligent decision (Appelbaum, 1993). Although the law in this area is in an early state of development, *Wickline* and *Wilson*, along with other reported cases in which managed care entities have been ordered to pay or have negotiated settlements for negligent review, make it clear that managed care companies will be held to reasonable standards of behavior (Appelbaum, 1993).[2] The standards (i.e., legal duty of care), however, have yet to be clearly defined.

ERISA Preemption

Although courts may be willing to extend liability to managed care companies under various legal theories (*respondeat superior,* ostensible agency, corporate negligence), ERISA raises an additional barrier, as suggested above in the discussion of the *Corcoran* (1992) case. Health insurance plans provided as part of an employee benefit package are regulated by the federal government under the ERISA. ERISA was enacted by Congress in 1974 to bring uniformity to the state laws governing private pension and benefit plans. ERISA also contains an explicit preemption clause, which provides that ERISA supersedes all state laws that apply to employee benefit plans. ERISA preempts almost all state laws affecting such plans, including claims of negligence that might ordinarily be filed in state court. Instead, such claims must be filed in federal court, and recovery is limited to payment of withheld benefits, excluding both compensation for harms suffered and punitive damages (Appelbaum, 1993). This makes it unprofitable to pursue many cases, which means that they are unlikely to be filed.

Managed care companies typically claim that they do not control treatment, but simply manage the benefit for the third-party payer. In a recent case challenging how managed care companies conduct their business (*New Jersey Psychological Ass'n v. MCC Behavioral Care, Inc.,* 1997), the U.S. District Court explicitly stated that managed care companies "exist to provide health care to the public." The decision also "signals that the court may consider scaling back managed care companies' ability to ignore providers' professional judgment" (Sleek, 1997, p. 22).

Most managed care companies provide management services to self-insured companies. This means that they are covered by ERISA, which in turn means that they cannot be sued for malpractice. As one considers the potential duties of managed care entities, the impact of ERISA must be kept in mind (Appelbaum, 1993).

Provider Liability and Risk Management Strategies

Maintaining Quality of Care

Although it is important to know that a managed care company may be held liable, this is of little comfort to the provider. Case law indicates that in the best-case scenario, the plaintiff will sue both the provider and the managed care company. In the worst-case scenario, the plaintiff is not going to be able to sue the managed care company, so he or she is going to sue the provider.

In *Wickline, Wilson,* and *Corcoran,* the courts have said that they are going to look at both parties (provider and managed care company) and determine which one is negligent. This approach puts providers in a difficult situation. It is almost always going to be true that a provider will be at least partly negligent, because it was the provider who made the decision not to provide the treatment. The managed care company could also be negligent in cutting off reimbursement. Importantly, the courts have made it quite clear that providers cannot rely on reimbursement in order to determine whether or not to give treatment. Clinicians must give treatment if it is needed, regardless of whether or not reimbursement is available.

In short, according to reported case law, it may be possible to hold both parties liable for an adverse medical outcome, but part of the liability is going to fall on the clinician anyway. From a risk management perspective, a provider's best course of action is to operate as if the managed care company is not involved at all. That is, decision making has to proceed without regard to the managed care company's potential liability. Importantly, mental health professionals must not let themselves be put in the position of choosing between patients' need for good-quality care and the economic and administrative requirements of the health plan (Simon, 1992).

Informed Consent: Disclosing the Effects
of Managed Care on Treatment

A practitioner must be aware of plan requirements that may interfere with the provision of good-quality clinical care and the traditional therapist–

patient relationship (Simon, 1992). The entry of managed care into clinical practice creates additional obligations on mental health professionals to discuss issues thoroughly with patients before embarking on treatment.

At the outset, clinicians should describe and discuss insurance reimbursement terms. Prospective patients should be told that in order to set realistic treatment goals, it is important to evaluate what resources are available to pay for treatment. A clinician might say this to a patient:

> If you have a health benefits policy, it usually provides some coverage for mental health treatment. I will provide you with whatever assistance I can in facilitating your receipt of the benefits to which you are entitled, including filling out forms as appropriate. However, you, and not your insurance company, are responsible for full payment of the fee we have agreed to. Therefore, it is very important that you find out exactly what mental health services your insurance policy covers.

Patients should be told to carefully read the section in their insurance coverage booklet that describes mental health services. If they have questions, they should call their plan and inquire. Practitioners should be willing to provide whatever information they can, to assist patients in deciphering the information received from the carrier, and (if necessary to resolve confusion) to call the carrier on the patients' behalf.

Mental health professionals should also discuss the benefits and limitations of short-term therapies, which managed care entities favor. Patients should be informed that payment for therapy may be terminated before treatment goals are reached (Appelbaum, 1993). Practitioners should explain how the escalation in the cost of health care has resulted in an increasing level of complexity in insurance benefits, which sometimes makes it difficult to determine exactly how much mental health coverage is available. A clinician could say the following to a patient:

> Managed health care plans often require advance authorization before they will provide reimbursement for mental health services. These plans are often oriented toward a short-term treatment approach. Short-term therapy is designed to resolve specific problems that are interfering with one's usual level of functioning. It may be necessary to seek additional approval after a certain number of sessions. In my experience, although quite a lot can be accomplished in short-term therapy, many patients feel that more sessions are necessary after insurance benefits are no longer available.

Importantly, when further coverage is denied, clinicians need to explain possible treatment options (Appelbaum, 1993). If coverage is denied, patients may elect to pay for care out of pocket. Patients may proceed with therapy during the appeals process, but they run the risk of being held responsible for charges accrued (Appelbaum, 1993). Another option is referral to alternative health care providers who may be less expensive.

In addition, clinicians should inform patients about all confidentiality considerations, including the possible release of sensitive treatment information to managed care reviewers as a condition of reimbursement. Specifically, patients should be told that most insurance agreements require patients to authorize their therapists to provide a clinical diagnosis, and sometimes additional clinical information such as a treatment plan or summary, or (in rare cases) a copy of the entire record. This information will become part of the insurance company files, and in all probability) some of it will be computerized. Clinicians should emphasize that all insurance companies claim to keep such information confidential, but once it is in their hands, clinicians have no control over what the companies do with it. In some cases, insurance companies may share the information with a national medical information data bank.

The best protection for both practitioner and patient is to discuss issues regarding the nature of benefits available, limits of coverage, and confidentiality at the outset of therapy. There should be an ongoing dialogue as the relationship and treatment plan evolves.

Abandonment and Managed Care

What are a clinician's duties after payment has been denied? In the view of most commentators, when mental health professionals believe an emergency exists—for example, in the hypothetical case presented by Appelbaum (1993) and discussed earlier, if the patient has been actively suicidal—there is an obligation to continue treatment until the crisis is resolved or until an alternative provider of care is found (Appelbaum, 1993; Simon, 1992). Patients in crisis should never be terminated.

A mental health professional always retains the option of continuing to care for a patient without payment or at a reduced rate. However, this is not an attractive option from the practitioner's perspective (Appelbaum, 1993). When insurance benefits expire and patients cannot or will not assume responsibility for the costs of care, clinicians' obligations are limited to referral or appropriate termination. Providers can, in fact, terminate treatment for a number of good reasons, as long as there are alternative places where the patients can get treatment. The issue for a provider when a managed care company cuts off coverage is really no different from the issue when indemnity insurance runs out. The clinician still has a patient with clinical needs. Because the patient cannot afford to pay, the mental health professional has to make a clinical decision about what to do.

Termination may require from one to several sessions, depending on factors such as the patient's diagnosis, the length of time therapy has gone on, and the nature of the therapy (Appelbaum, 1993). Thorough, professional notes on the treatment should be kept, including the reasoning behind a decision to terminate a patient and the alternatives considered. Practitioners can reduce their liability to malpractice allegations by showing that they have made sound, thoughtful treatment decisions. In any situation where a clinician is considering terminating a patient who has the remotest possibility of suicide, and that person's reimbursement has been cut off by a managed care company, the clinician should not make this decision alone. He or she must seek consultation with colleagues, because it is a very high-risk decision.

Duty to Appeal Adverse Decisions

When a patient has been denied payment for care that a mental health professional believes is indicated, the practitioner may have an obligation to contest, on the patient's behalf, the decision of the managed care entity (Appelbaum, 1993). This duty stems from *Wickline* (1986), discussed above. The *Wickline* court did say that in that particular case, the fact that the physician did not appeal was negligent. The court did not say that failure to appeal is automatically negligent. From a risk management perspective, some commentators suggest that at least an initial appeal of adverse decisions be undertaken when a mental health professional believes that the treatment in question is necessary for a patient's well-being (Appelbaum, 1993).

Effect of Disciplinary Complaints and Malpractice Suits on Participation in Managed Care

As previously mentioned, the application of corporate negligence theory to managed care explains why disciplinary complaints and malpractice suits pose significant risks for providers. For those practitioners who feel that managed care participation is important to their future practices, disciplinary complaints and malpractice suits are anathema. As noted above, one of the sources of "corporate negligence" for a managed care company is "negligent credentialing." That is, if a managed care panel accepts a professional who is known (or should have been known) to present a risk to the public, the panel can be held liable for that person's future misconduct. Significantly, if a clinician has a settled or lost malpractice action or some kind of disciplinary sanction, in essence this means that the clinician cannot work in managed care. Since there are many more applicants for managed care panels than positions, managed care panels can exclude providers who have been disciplined or who have settled or lost malpractice actions. Thus, any disciplinary sanction or malpractice claim puts most providers on a permanent blacklist.

In fact, an increasing level of professional risk has been created by the confluence of the growth of managed care and the increase in the number of disciplinary complaints against mental health professionals. The incidence of consumer complaints to licensing boards and ethics committees has increased dramatically, making disciplinary complaints an even greater problem than malpractice suits. If a clinician is found to have violated the ethical principles of his or her profession and receives a sanction from a professional board, there is a good chance that he or she will be permanently barred from managed care participation.

Professional disciplinary boards, unlike courts of law, are less bound by due process concerns and evidentiary restrictions in prosecuting and sanctioning providers who they feel are violating professional standards. In these disciplinary actions, unlike malpractice actions, a board needs only to prove that the standard of care was breached or an ethical principle was violated. There is no need to prove damages or to demonstrate that the damage was related to the breach of the standard of care. In fact, a disciplinary body has the freedom to sanction a health care provider for conduct that had nothing to do with the complaint.

In light of the increasing number of complaints being filed against mental health professionals, we mention some techniques that can benefit practitioners in defending themselves.[3] If a practitioner receives notice that a complaint has been filed, he or she should immediately consult with an attorney who has experience with the mental health field and the disciplinary process. This is true even if the practitioner believes that the complaint is "frivolous," "false," or "retaliatory." A practitioner who chooses to deal

---

[3]For a discussion of the disciplinary complaint process, see Stromberg et al. (1988) and Harris (1993).

with a complaint by himself or herself in order to save money is taking an enormous risk.

A great deal of care should be exercised in preparing a written response to the complaint, since this is the practitioner's first opportunity to demonstrate his or her professional competence. After the board considers the written response, it will usually ask the practitioner to attend an informal hearing. This informal hearing is often the most crucial element in determining the outcome of the proceeding. Accordingly, the practitioner should be thoroughly prepared substantively, tactically, and emotionally for the hearing. It is often helpful to have several practice sessions to become comfortable verbalizing the themes from the written response. It is very important for the practitioner's attorney to attend the informal hearing. Clinicians have noted that it is supportive to have an advocate present who understands the procedure. Because the procedure is anxiety-provoking, even the best-prepared practitioner may require prompting about some of the salient points. The attorney can also raise some points independently, ask clarifying questions, and make legal points and substantive arguments.

If the board believes that there has been a violation of the law or of its regulations, it may either refer the matter for a formal administrative hearing to revoke or suspend a license, or it may seek to negotiate a mutually acceptable solution called a "consent agreement." Consent agreements typically require the acknowledgment of a violation. Because a consent agreement is a public document, such an admission can have adverse consequences. Under most state laws, a consent order is considered to be equivalent to a formal finding and order of the board. Therefore, the practitioner should study carefully what it says; what implications it carries; and what collateral consequences it is likely to have for hospital privileges, provider selection, insurance, malpractice, and other matters (Stromberg et al., 1988).

CONCLUSION

Allegations of malpractice are startling realities in modern psychiatric and psychological practice. In the current litigious climate, it would be naive for mental health professionals who treat high-risk patients not to consider appropriate clinical and legal management issues (Bongar, 1991). In fact, Simon (1988) contends that it would be not merely naive but foolhardy to ignore risk management techniques in the course of treating such patients. The risk management guidelines discussed above, if used effectively, will significantly minimize the risk of being found negligent in a malpractice action. They are also designed to help clinicians defend themselves against complaints filed with professional ethics committees, licensing boards, and other bodies by which they may be held responsible. Ideally, these procedures will allow clinicians to identify potential problem areas, to decide on appropriate clinical and legal responses, to consult with other professionals to confirm their conclusions, and to record this process in a manner demonstrating professional competence.

REFERENCES

Abille v. United States, 482 F. Supp. 703 (N.D. Cal. 1980).

Abraham, K. S., & Weiler, P. C. (1994). Enterprise medical liability and the evolution of the American health care system. *Harvard Law Review, 108*, 381–436.

Appelbaum, P. S. (1993). Legal liability and managed care. *American Psychologist, 48*, 251–257.

Bell v. New York City Health and Hospitals Corporation, 90 A.D.2d 270, 456 N.Y.S.2d 787 (1982).

Bellah v. Greenson, 81 Cal. App. 3d 614, 146 Cal. Rptr. 535 (1978).

Berman, A. L., & Jobes, D. A. (1991). *Adolescent suicide: Assessment and intervention.* Washington, DC: American Psychological Association.

Bongar, B., & Greaney, S. A. (1994). Essential clinical and legal issues when working with the suicidal patient. *Death Studies, 18*, 529–548.

Bongar, B. (1991). *The suicidal patient: Clinical and legal standards of care.* Washington, DC: American Psychological Association.

Canterbury v. Spence, 464 F.2d 772 (D.C. Cir. 1972).

Chemtob, C. M., Hamada, R. S., Bauer, G. B., Kinney, B., & Torigoe, R. Y. (1988). Patient suicide: Frequency and impact on psychiatrists. *American Journal of Psychiatry, 145*, 224–228.

Chemtob, C. M., Hamada, R. S., Bauer, G. B., Torigoe, R. Y., & Kinney, B. (1988). Patient suicide: Frequency and impact on psychologists. *Professional Psychology: Research and Practice, 19*, 416–420.

Conner, M. A. (Ed.). (1994). *Clinicians and the law: A legal handbook for therapists and counselors.* Providence, RI: Manisses Communications Group.

Corcoran v. United HealthCare Inc., 965 F.2d 1321 (5th Cir. 1992), *cert. denied*, 113 S. Ct. 812 (1993).

Dillmann v. Hellman, 283 So.2d 388 (Fla. Dist. Ct. App. 1973).

Dinnerstein v. State, 486 F.2d 34 (2nd Cir. 1973).

Frankel, J. J. (1994). Medical malpractice law and health care cost containment: Lessons for reformers from the clash of cultures. *Yale Law Journal, 103*, 1297–1331.

Fremouw, W. J., de Perczel, M., & Ellis, T. E. (1990). *Suicide risk: Assessment and response guidelines.* New York: Pergamon Press.

Furrow, B. R. (1980). *Malpractice in psychotherapy.* Lexington, MA: Lexington Books.

Gutheil, T. G. (1980). Paranoia and progress notes: A guide to forensically informed psychiatric recordkeeping. *Hospital and Community Psychiatry, 31,* 479–482.

Gutheil, T. G. (1984). Malpractice liability in suicide. *Legal Aspects of Psychiatric Practice, 1,* 1–4.

Gutheil, T. G. (1992). Suicide and suit: Liability after self-destruction. In D. Jacobs (Ed.), *Suicide and clinical practice* (pp. 147–167). Washington, DC: American Psychiatric Press.

Gutheil, T. G., & Appelbaum, P. S. (1991). *Clinical handbook of psychiatry and the law* (2nd ed.). Baltimore: Williams & Wilkins.

Halleck, S. (1980). *Law in the practice of psychiatry.* New York: Plenum Press.

Harris, E. (1993). Articles on risk management, managed care and professional disciplinary process. *The Massachusetts Psychologist, 1* (2, 3, 4), 5.

Hess, A. K. (1985). The psychologist as expert witness. *The Clinical Psychologist,* 75–78.

Hunt v. Bradshaw, 242 N.C. 517, 88 S.E.2d 766 (1955).

Jobes, D. A., & Berman, A. S. (1993). Suicide and malpractice liability: Assessing and revising policies, procedures, and practice in outpatient settings. *Professional Psychology: Research and Practice, 24,* 91–99.

Johnson v. Misericordia Community Hospital, 90 Wis. 2d 708, 301 N.W.2d 156 (1981).

King, J. H. (1986). *The law of medical malpractice in a nutshell.* St. Paul, MN: West.

Malcolm, J. D. (1986). Treatment choices and informed consent in psychiatry: Implications of the *Osheroff* case for the profession. *Journal of Psychiatry and Law, 14,* 9–107.

Meier v. Ross General Hospital, 69 Cal. 2d 420, 445 P.2d 519, 71 Cal. Rptr. 903 (1968).

Monahan, J. (1993). Limiting therapist exposure to Tarasoff liability. *American Psychologist, 48,* 242–250.

Nemiah, J. C. (1982). Foreword. In E. L. Bassuk, S. C. Schoonover, & A. D. Gill (Eds.), *Lifelines: Clinical perspectives on suicide.* New York: Plenum Press.

New Jersey Psychological Ass'n v. MCC Behavioral Care, Inc., No. 96-3080 (D.N.J. Sept. 15, 1997).

O'Neal, R. (1991). Safe harbor for health care cost containment. *Stanford Law Review, 43,* 399–443.

Paradies v. Benedictine Hospital, 77 A.D.2d 757, 431 N.Y.S.2d 175 (1980).

Pope, K. (1989). Malpractice suits, licensing, disciplinary actions, and ethics cases: Frequencies, causes, and costs. *Independent Practitioner, 9,* 17–23.

Pound, R. (1978). *An introduction to the philosophy of law.* New Haven, CT: Yale University Press.

Prosser, W. L. (1971). *Handbook of the law of torts* (4th ed.). St. Paul, MN: West.

Psychiatric Institute v. James Allen, 509 A.2d 614 (D.C. 1986).

Rachlin, S. (1984). Double jeopardy: Suicide and malpractice. *General Hospital Psychiatry, 6,* 302–307.

Robertson, J. D. (1988). *Psychiatric malpractice: Liability of mental health professionals.* New York: Wiley.

Ross v. Central Louisiana State Hospital, 392 So.2d 698 (La. App. 1980).

Rozovsky, F. (1990). *Consent to treatment: A practical guide* (2nd ed.). Boston: Little, Brown.

Schein, H. M. (1976). Obstacles in the education of psychiatric residents. *Omega, 7,* 75–82.

Simon, R. I. (1987). *Clinical psychiatry and the law.* Washington, DC: American Psychiatric Press.

Simon, R. I. (1988). *Concise guide to clinical psychiatry and the law.* Washington, DC: American Psychiatric Press.

Simon, R. I. (1992). *Psychiatry and law for clinicians.* Washington, DC: American Psychiatric Press.

Sleek, S. (1997, November). [Interview with Russ Newman, PhD, JD.] *APA Monitor,* p. 22.

Stone, A. A. (1990). Law, science, and psychiatric malpractice: A response to Klerman's indictment of psychoanalytic psychiatry. *American Journal of Psychiatry, 147,* 419–427.

Stromberg, C. D., Haggarty, D. J., Leibenluft, R. F., McMillan, M. H., Mishkin, B., Rubin, B. L., & Trilling, H. R. (1988). *The psychologist's legal handbook.* Washington, DC: Council for the National Register of Health Care Providers in Psychology.

Tarasoff v. Board of Regents of the University of California, 131 Cal. Rptr. 14, 551 P.2d 334 (1976).

Topel v. Long Island Jewish Medical Center, 55 N.Y.2d 682, 431 N.E.2d 293, 446 N.Y.S.2d 932 (1981).

VandeCreek, L., & Knapp, S. (1983). Malpractice risks with suicidal patients. *Psychotherapy: Theory, Research, and Practice, 20,* 274–280.

VandeCreek, L., & Knapp, S. (1989). *Tarasoff and beyond: Legal and clinical considerations in the treatment of life-endangering patients.* Sarasota, FL: Professional Resource Exchange.

VandeCreek, L., Knapp, S., & Herzog, C. (1987). Malpractice risks in the treatment of dangerous patients. *Psychotherapy: Theory, Research, and Practice, 24,* 145–153.

VandeCreek, L., & Young, J. (1989). Malpractice risks with suicidal patients. *Psychotherapy Bulletin, 24*(3), 18–21.

Wallace, T. E. (1990). The doctrine of informed consent [Review of *Consent to treatment: A practical guide* (2nd ed.)]. *Journal of Legal Medicine, 12,* 249–255.

Welch, B. (1989, October). A collaborative model proposed. *APA Monitor,* p. 28.

Wickline v. State, 192 Cal. App.3d 1630, 239 Cal. Rptr. 810 (1986).

Wilson v. Blue Cross of Southern California, 222 Cal. App.3d 660, 271 Cal. Rptr. 876 (1990).

Wilson v. State, 14 A.D.2d 976, 221 N.Y.S.2d 354 (1961).

APPENDIX 7.1. Checklist for Clinicians: Risk Management Procedures to Minimize Liability

Issues	"To do" list
Know legal and ethical responsibilities	• Develop confidentiality policies • Inform patients of confidentiality limits at onset of therapy • Use informed consent therapeutically—ongoing dialogue with patients throughout therapy
Become informed about suicide risk factors and develop resources	• Stay current with developments in the field • Know community resources, referral sources, hospitalization procedures

Obtain risk assessment data (e.g., demographics, suicidal thoughts and feelings, plan)	• Evaluate suicidal risk:
	  Is there any suicidal risk?
	  Identify how much risk
	  If high risk of suicide: Professional consultation and formal suicide risk assessment

Secure past treatment records	• Make reasonable attempt to procure past medical and psychotherapy records
Assure clinical competence	• Master DSM-IV and use it appropriately • Determine competence to treat suicidal patients
Provide adequate documentation	• Maintain thorough, detailed, risk–benefit progress notes • Articulate steps taken and steps not taken—show the thinking process
Obtain consultation	• Consult professional colleagues who have expertise in handling suicidal patients • Establish formal consultation arrangements and record consultant's course of action
Obtain adequate malpractice insurance and have access to an attorney	• The more insurance coverage, the better • Retain an attorney—someone knowledgeable about malpractice liability for mental health professionals

APPENDIX 7.2. Guidelines for Providers: Liability Issues and Risk Management Strategies in a Managed Care Environment

Issues	"To do" list
Maintaining quality of care	• Operate as if managed care entity is not going to be held liable • Do not compromise the patient's quality of care
Informed consent	• Discuss with patients the effects of managed care on treatment—benefits and limitations of short-term therapy, confidentiality considerations, nature of benefits available, limits of coverage
Duty after denial of payment: Abandonment issues	• Patients in crisis should never be terminated • Continue to treat at reduced rate, refer, or terminate in appropriate manner • Clearly document decision to terminate • If considering terminating potentially suicidal patient, seek consultation
Duty to appeal adverse decisions	• Undertake an initial appeal when the treatment in question is believed to be necessary for patient's well-being

Postscript: Commentary on Chapters 1, 3, and 4

ROBERT E. LITMAN

As a postscript to the series on "Standards of Care" (reprinted as Chapters 1, 3, and 4, this volume), I wish to add a correction and a comment.

Correction: Litman and Farberow surveyed suicides in Los Angeles in the 1960s and found that 1 % of the suicides occurred in hospitals (Litman, 1982). The statement in paragraph one of Chapter 3 "that 1% of patients being treated in general medical–surgical and/or psychiatric hospitals committed suicide during their hospital treatment" is a terribly inaccurate misquotation.

Comment: Dr. Silverman succeeded in his effort to provide standards of "good clinical practice" (see Chapter 4), but in my opinion he lost sight of the original concept of "minimal standards." His proposed "remedies" for "alleged failures" embody ideal performance, as different from minimal standards as the grade A+ is from the grade C–.

REFERENCE

Litman, R. E. (1982). Hospital suicides: Lawsuits and standards. *Suicide and Life-Threatening Behavior, 12*(4), 212–220.

Postscript: Reply to Robert E. Litman

MORTON M. SILVERMAN

As senior author of one of the three recent papers exploring the application of standards of care to suicidal patients in outpatient and inpatient settings (reprinted as Chapters 1, 3, and 4, this volume), Dr. Litman's letter provides me the opportunity to further clarify the intent of this work. One of the explicit goals of formulating these papers was to attempt the integration of clinical and legal issues in a peer-reviewed journal read by those who are most affected by working with suicidal patients. By so doing, we had hoped to generate a dialogue that would advance our understanding of the legal criteria often used to assess the clinical care provided to suicidal patients. To that end, we welcome other comments and critiques of the papers.

Another goal was to formulate some general principles and guidelines to assist clinicians, hospital staff, and hospital administrators in the daily decision-making process and daily execution of reasonable and prudent clinical care for suicidal individuals. The challenge was to integrate existing case law and legal concepts of the minimal standards of care with clinical risk management and clinical judgment as it pertains to the assessment, management, and treatment of patients who exhibit suicidal behaviors.

Whenever one attempts to codify a set of clinical activities to be applied to a specific clinical condition in a specific clinical setting, one runs the risk of being criticized for overemphasizing certain actions believed by some to be unwarranted, and/or omitting other actions deemed by some to be "essential." One always is reminded of those clinical situations when certain actions or "standards of care" either do not apply or are not appropriate to a particular set of circumstances. This is why we often cited clinical judgment, clinical experience, the establishment of a therapeutic alliance, and documentation of omissions as being important components of the clinical care of suicidal patients.

The final papers represented the consensus agreement of the coauthors after multiple drafts and correspondence. The process of reaching consensus for each paper took many months. The fact that there are multiple authors from different disciplines suggests that these standards of care defy "cookbook" formulas. Our published "standards of care" represented neither the "ideal" (hopefully those taught in academic training sites to clinical students-in-training) nor the absolute "minimum" that would constitute cursory clinical care for very ill suicidal patients requiring outpatient or inpatient evaluation and treatment. Rather, the guidelines presented were ones that the coauthors felt are reasonable to consider or implement in work with most suicidal patients based on their own clinical work and forensic experience.

These proposed standards of care are not a guarantee of successful outcomes or achievable in every situation. No one can be so prescient to assume that absolute adherence to these proposed standards are foolproof when working with very ill patients. Working with suicidal patients entails known and sometimes unforeseen risks. Adhering to a set of standards of care is but one means of reducing some of that risk, while providing some guidelines for managing the remainder of the risks.

In the final analysis, I accept full responsibility for the paper of which I was senior author (see Chapter 4), and for the standards proposed. In my forensic consultations, I use these standards as "benchmarks" by which I assess the performance of clinicians, hospital staff, and hospital administrators. Sometimes they can be applied neatly, and sometimes not. Sometimes they are appropriate to the particular circumstances of the case, and sometimes not. Nevertheless, for me, they are a starting point. In my own clinical work, I attempt to adhere to these standards. I would hope that anyone assessing or treating a suicidal individual would attempt to do likewise.

Index